THE FAILURE OF CHILD SUPPORT

Gendered Systems of Inaccessibility, Inaction and Irresponsibility

Kay Cook

First published in Great Britain in 2022 by

Policy Press, an imprint of
Bristol University Press
University of Bristol
1–9 Old Park Hill
Bristol
BS2 8BB
UK
t: +44 (0)117 954 5940
e: bup-info@bristol.ac.uk

Details of international sales and distribution partners are available at
policy.bristoluniversitypress.co.uk

British Library Cataloguing in Publication Data
A catalogue record for this book is available from the British Library

ISBN 978-1-4473-4886-3 hardcover
ISBN 978-1-4473-4888-7 ePub
ISBN 978-1-4473-4887-0 ePdf

Cover design: Nicky Boroweic
Front cover image: Valenty/AdobeStock

Bristol University Press and Policy Press use environmentally responsible print partners.

Printed and bound in Great Britain by CPI Group (UK) Ltd, Croydon, CR0 4YY

FSC
www.fsc.org
MIX
Paper from responsible sources
FSC® C013604

For Mark, Mabel, Isaac and Oscar

Contents

List of abbreviations		vi
Acknowledgements		vii
1	Introduction	1
2	Child support and gendered governance practice	14
3	Child support regimes and relevance	35
4	Sites of child support failure	49
5	Divergent views of success and failure	75
6	The interests served by failure	89
7	Rendering gendered social problems technical	112
8	The gendered offer of personal solutions	128
9	Conclusion	151
References		160
Index		176

List of abbreviations

CSA	Child Support Agency
CSRA	Child Support Recovery Act
DWP	Department of Work and Pensions
KPI	key performance indicator
OECD	Organisation for Economic Co-operation and Development
TANF	Temporary Aid for Needy Families
UBI	Universal Basic Income
UNCRC	United Nations Convention on the Rights of the Child

Acknowledgements

This research was supported by an Australian Research Council (ARC) Future Fellowship 2017–20 (FT160100115). Thanks to each of the anonymous reviewers, and the ARC College members who recommended it for funding. I owe a great deal of thanks to Dr Natalie Jovanovski and Dr Lara Corr for prodding me into action to finally get started on this book. I probably wouldn't have – and couldn't have – done it without your encouragement and support. During the course of writing, I lost two fabulous research assistants, Georgia Keam and Zoë Goodall, who were each awarded a PhD scholarship to begin what will surely be their stellar research careers. All the best for your research, and thanks to you both for your assistance with mine. Your attention to detail, immaculate research and editing skills and ability to keeping me on task were greatly appreciated.

1

Introduction

This book aims to contribute to feminist policy research by examining child support as gendered governance practice. It provides an empirical example of the gender of governance by conceptualising child support not merely as law or policy implemented by states, but as a programme used to manage and discipline 'unruly' and 'problematic' populations. The population governed by child support, however, is not comprised of separated fathers who, across contexts, are consistently unreliable or unwilling payers. But, rather, the population governed by child support is comprised of separated mothers, who are hopeful child support recipients. The purpose of the book is to outline how child support systems are structured – often in increasingly technical and personalised ways – that render them ineffective and simultaneously position women as responsible for these systemic failures. As such, this book – rather than providing a descriptive account of how much money child support provides – serves as a provocation for how child support could be reimagined, resisted and contested.

The contention that motivates this analysis is that child support policy and law across countries – and their interactions with state support – hold with them fundamental and gendered assumptions about the 'appropriate' roles of mothers and fathers post-separation. As such, the analysis pursued here is a radically different approach to typical child support scholarship, which has set about conducting the necessary work of describing the nature, process and effects of law and policy in this relatively new scholarly domain. In such traditional accounts, the intention is to describe and refine policy and legal settings to improve practice and produce 'better' outcomes. In contrast, my intention is to critique the nature, process and effects of child support law and policy in order to theorise why, when, how and for whom child support policy works, or does not work. The assumption underpinning this book is that the answers to these questions sit within state-organised relations of power that serve and reflect social hierarchies, predominantly on the basis of gender. Reflecting on a range of child support systems internationally, I suggest that systems typically do not work as intended, as they are often inaccessible, fail to produce meaningful outcomes, or ignore or implicitly condone fathers' non-compliance. Yet, these same systems often render women responsible for the failure of fathers to make payments, the failure of system administration and the failure of child support policy. Understanding these processes as gendered governance practice is what this book seeks to achieve. While individual women's agency is not explored in detail, the concepts identified here set out how mothers and women's advocates can act to improve, resist or contest hegemonic child support systems at local, national and international levels. As such, while this book provides a largely systemic account, the purpose is to provide women with room for increased agency within the tight personal, administrative, legal and policy spaces where child support is practised and governed.

While child support is a relatively obscure area of policy or family research compared to other topics – such as welfare benefit analyses or comparisons of the gender distribution of care time in families – child support is significant to many of the world's children and their resident mothers. For example, across the OECD (2019c), on average 17.2 per cent of children live with a single parent. Despite the introduction of child support laws and policies that seek to redistribute funds from an earning to a caring parent post-separation, child support has largely failed to institutionalise this behaviour en masse. Rather, despite the introduction of modern child support systems as 'feminist interventions', and the subsequent de-gendering of some countries' child support policies, child support remains deeply gendered, as does the poverty that it seeks to ameliorate. Echoing Risman's (2004, p. 436) general cultural critique, 'we have often found that despite changes in gender socialization and gender neutrality on the institutional dimension, gender stratification remains'. To interrogate these processes, and again following Risman (2004), this book examines child support as the enactment of gender as a social structure.

Child support as a concept provides insight into a range of important social and political issues. For example, the state-prescribed transfer of private cash payments from one parent to another throws into question the role of the state in private financial transactions. The prescription of private payments implicates the state in the financial management of the (post-separation) family, a sphere of life where the state otherwise has little oversight. Because of this involvement in private familial financial affairs, and perhaps to legitimise the state's role, many countries have entwined child support with welfare benefit eligibility criteria and payment calculations. As Garfinkel et al (1998, p. 14) described not long after the introduction of child support policy in the US:

> One mechanism that has protected children from the economic consequences of the loss of a father is the private child support system, which is regulated by state law. Another mechanism is the public assistance – or welfare system – which provides cash support to poor children who live apart from their fathers and which may pursue private child support on behalf of the child.

Notwithstanding the state's interest in payments, child support is rarely included in academic welfare benefit analyses. This is despite the fact that child support can have a significant impact on whether single-mother-headed families live above or below the poverty line (Hakovirta, 2011; OECD, 2011; Skinner and Main, 2013; Skinner et al, 2017a, 2017b).

In this book, I examine how the nature, process and effects of child support place gendered expectations on women, which they must enact at institutional and interpersonal levels in order to facilitate payments. Yet, at the same time, the way that child support systems operate (whether legal or administrative), means that payments are often unlikely to eventuate, despite women's efforts. However, in looking across countries to illustrate these processes, this book does not claim to offer a definitive account of child support law and policy operations in specific countries, nor to identify or quantify the impact of particular policy settings or changes. The legal, policy and administrative knowledge required to understand the history and complexities of child support within a single country is a voluminous task, and often requires scholars working in a diverse range of fields. Indeed, attempts at mapping and explaining a single tranche of policy change within one country have proven to be onerous (for an account of the gender of child support policymaking and practice in Australia, for example, see Cook and Natalier, 2013, 2014, 2016; Natalier, 2017; Natalier, 2018; Cook, 2020). As such, the contextual specificity required to understand and account for within-country change cannot be done justice in this book. Instead, I seek to describe the broad contours of policy similarities and differences between countries and locate these within gendered interpersonal and institutional contexts, which I describe as 'symbolic policy analysis'. The purpose is to analyse the symbolic practices of child support in order to problematise child support as a gendered social structure, rather than identify particular policy or administrative settings for incremental reform.

In many countries, as the following chapters illuminate, seeking child support is mandatory for benefit recipients. As such, low-income families are the focus of this book. For low-income separated mothers, the mandatory nature of seeking payments marks child support out as one of the earliest forms of welfare conditionality, where compulsory requirements to seek child support as a condition of benefit eligibility were introduced across countries as early as the 1980s. This was well before the 'game-changing' imposition of conditional welfare requirements that occurred in Canada, the US and Australia between the mid-1990s and 2000s (Gorlick and Brethour, 1998; Seccombe et al, 1998; Lens, 2002; Summerfield et al, 2010; Brady and Cook, 2015). Child support in liberal welfare states thus also marks a move away from socialised protection based on moral principles, to introduce mandatory behavioural requirements – in this case, for benefit recipients to seek individualised transfers from the family, albeit from their ex-partner.

In this book, while the child support systems of liberal welfare states feature prominently, examples from Asian, South American, continental European, Middle Eastern and African systems are used as counterpoints to tease out child support's universal, as opposed to context-specific, failures.

Through child support, states make deliberate interventions into the relationships that individual benefit recipients have with their ex-partners. Rather than delving into welfare history, however, the point that I argue here is that these interventions are made in ways most likely to benefit the state. As Crowley (2003, p. 29) argued with respect to new conditions introduced into the US child support system with the passing of the Personal Responsibility and Work Opportunity Reconciliation Act 1996, 'these conditions made certain that the child support system was pursuing its "single focus: welfare cost recovery"'. However, in both the US and elsewhere, child support as a measure of welfare conditionality does not act as a barrier to prevent separated mothers from entering the welfare benefit system. Rather, child support serves the purpose of reducing welfare expenditure by limiting benefit outlays. For example, in the US, Temporary Aid to Needy Families payments are reduced by 25 per cent for failing to cooperate with child support (Battle, 2019). In Australia, Family Tax Benefit cash payments are paid only at the base rate if child support is not sought (Department of Human Services, 2019). Child support's interactions with the welfare state thus throw into relief the extent to which the state regards women's dependence as located most appropriately on the state, the family or the market. While these debates have occurred with respect to women's compulsory enrolment in 'active labour market programmes', the governance of gender as enacted by child support has yet to be thoroughly examined.

Previous welfare state analyses of women's dependence – many focused on separated mothers – have neglected or downplayed the significance of child support. However, across countries post-separation child support compels the continuation of the male-breadwinner role, irrespective of the breakdown of the nuclear family and also often despite the loosening of rigid gender roles within families (Eydal and Friðriksdóttir, 2012; Cook and Skinner, 2019). While other areas of policy have moved on from rigid gender roles, child support in many countries has not. Surprisingly, the Nordic countries provide some of the most antiquated gender regimes with respect to child support. For example, in Iceland and Finland separated fathers must often continue to pay child support, irrespective of the extent to which they share children's care equally with their ex-partner (Eydal and Friðriksdóttir, 2012; Hakovirta et al, 2020). Just as the position of gender within welfare state interactions warranted investigation at the turn of the last century, so too does the position of gender in child support policy now. Researchers have begun this task, finding what child support policy reform reveals about the possibility of gender equality in parenting and earning (Cook and Skinner, 2019), and how the practice of child support constructs and reinforces the gendered roles of 'good' mothers and fathers (Natalier and Hewitt, 2014; Cozzolino and Williams, 2017; Battle, 2018, 2019; Keil and Elizabeth, 2019; Goodall and Cook, 2020). What this book adds to these accounts is an analysis of the state's role in managing post-separation finances through a reliance on gendered patterns of interaction and the institutional child support contexts that frame them.

Finally, and following on from the discussion of welfare states and gendered identities, researchers have demonstrated that child support has expressive, symbolic and material dimensions (Natalier, 2012; Battle, 2018, 2019; Skinner, 2013; Goodall and Cook, 2020). Child support gives affect as well as effect to the transfer of payments across households. Payments or their withholding can be used to express love, anger, resentment and care (Natalier and Hewitt, 2010; Skinner, 2013). These emotions reflect and reinforce social norms tied up with gender roles and responsibilities, as well as gendered notions of good mothering and fathering, entitlement, gift relations and power. Given the emotional context in which child support exists, the mandatory seeking of child support may place women in danger (Patrick et al, 2007, 2008; Natalier, 2018; Douglas and Nagesh, 2019). In some countries, child support can offer aggrieved fathers a highly effective means of maintaining economic control and perpetuating abuse post-separation.

Given that mandating separated mothers to seek child support can be problematic, some countries have introduced 'work-arounds' to bypass the child support system, such as exemptions for women whose ex-partners are violent or guaranteed payments to mothers when child support payments are withheld (for a summary of countries with guaranteed payments see Skinner et al, 2007; Hakovirta, 2011; OECD, 2011). Such measures, and the assumptions on which they rest, warrant critical attention. The analysis pursued throughout this book will discern what states expect of separated mothers and fathers, which actions are recognised, rewarded or ignored, and which actions are conceived of as the required, reasonable or (in)appropriate behaviour of each parent. Before moving on to examine these issues in detail, however, it is important to first set out how child support is understood.

Defining child support

Child support, known also as child maintenance, is a term that is difficult to define. As the OECD (2011, p. 225) notes, at a systemic level

> Child-support systems can have a number of different aims, including: i) increasing the income of children living in sole-parent families, with direct positive consequences for child poverty and indirect positive consequences for other child outcomes; ii) reducing the fiscal burden on taxpayers from having to support resident parents and their children;

iii) ensuring that non-resident parents take financial responsibility for their children; iv) promoting gender equality in family income (given women are more likely to be resident parents); and v) promoting shared parental care of children.

These aims can entail contradictions and can serve competing interests between the state, child support payers and child support payees. They pit the interests of states to reduce welfare expenditures against those of child support payers who are expected to instead take up this 'responsibility'. Income shares models for calculating child support can place the goal of sharing care, sharing income and increasing children's income in opposition. At the same time, gender equality aims can entrench non-resident fathers' breadwinning role despite concurrent efforts in some countries to eliminate the gender contract that prescribes such behaviour. Australian research has found that it is fathers' forced continuation of the breadwinning role post-separation that underpins their resentment of the mandatory child support system (Cook and Skinner, 2019). As such, it is no wonder that child support is often highly contested while, simultaneously, often highly ineffective.

At an individual level, child support can be defined as money paid by a minority-time non-resident parent to a majority-time resident parent for the purpose of supporting children following relationship breakdown. However, this definition also problematises the very nature of child support. First, child support is often not paid. Rates of child support receipt by sole-parent families in the 2000s were reported as being consistently low (Skinner et al, 2007; Hakovirta, 2011; OECD, 2011). Several countries were reported as having receipt rates below 30 per cent, including Estonia, France, Ireland, Italy, Spain and the UK. Most countries surveyed had receipt rates of between 30 and 50 per cent, including Australia, Belgium, Canada, Finland, Germany, Greece, Hungary, the Netherlands, Poland, Slovenia and the US. As such, in almost all of the countries assessed, child support was received less than half of the time. This was even the case in countries that were reported to have 'advanced maintenance' (or guaranteed payment) schemes, such as Estonia, Belgium, France, Hungary, Slovenia and Spain. Clearly, there are significant policy and administrative failures. Despite the failure of advanced maintenance in these countries, all of the best-performing countries, namely Austria, Denmark, Finland, Norway, Sweden and Switzerland, provided such guaranteed payments (OECD, 2011). However, here, receipt rates may be artificial. For example, Sweden's reported compliance rate of 100 per cent in 2005 (Hakovirta, 2011; OECD, 2011) included all payments paid by the government. This figure does not represent the number of non-resident parents who are contributing towards their children's upkeep. Across all countries included in these studies, it was only when the government paid child support on the non-resident parent's behalf that more than half of lone parents received payments. These poor and largely stagnating compliance rates have been bemoaned by a small number of academics but have received relatively little policy or administrative attention. The US experience runs counter to this policy apathy, as national funding provided to individual states is tied to compliance (for overviews of recent interventions see Cancian et al, 2019; Hahn et al, 2019). However, at a broader level, the failure of child support to deliver on its promise to low-income mothers and their children – by not actually ensuring payments – is what motivates this book.

Second, to return to what child support 'is', or rather 'is not', child support may be paid by someone other than the minority-time non-resident parent. In countries that operate an income shares formula, which seeks to determine child support on the relative proportion of each parent's income (for examples see Skinner et al, 2007), it is the income disparity between parents, as well as the proportion of care that each parent provides, that determines how much is paid and by whom (for empirical analyses of mothers paying child support, including majority time parents, see Fehlberg et al, 2010; Vnuk, 2010). Here, payments can be made by a higher-income majority-time resident parent to a lower-income minority-time non-resident parent. Alternatively, child support may be paid by the state in place of the non-resident parent, as described previously. The Nordic countries, as well as several Central European countries, provide guaranteed or advanced payments in instances of non-compliance or low non-resident parental income (Bradshaw and Finch, 2002; Skinner et al, 2007; OECD, 2011; Jeans, 2014).

Finally, child support may not be paid to a resident parent. In New Zealand, for example, the state withholds all child support money paid up to the full value of the main benefit when a payee receives welfare payments (Fletcher, 2016). Other jurisdictions, such as some states within the US, withhold a portion of child support, while Australia provides all child support money paid, but reduces cash Family Tax Benefits by 50 cents for every dollar of child support above a threshold (Skinner et al, 2017b). Also in Australia, when parents collect payments privately, the child support does not even need to be received, just expected, for benefits to be reduced (Department of Social Services, 2020). As such, these 'clawback mechanisms' (Skinner et al, 2017b) expose the ways that states use child support to reduce welfare outlays that would otherwise be spent supporting children in separated-parent households.

What is not included in the definition of child support provided previously is a reference to the gender position of parents. Most countries have moved to gender-neutral terminology to describe 'parents', 'payers and recipients', 'majority- and minority-time carers' and other descriptors of income and care time. However, this does not mean that gender is not central. At the same time, some researchers – and more specifically, anonymous grant and manuscript reviewers that I and others have encountered – have taken issue with the use of gender pronouns and gendered claims in child support research, claiming that gender is irrelevant to child support and merely represents the demographic category of each parent in their position as payer and recipient. However, I argue that this gender-blindness is complicit in – and plays an organising role in – the permanence of the gender-unequal outcomes that child support produces (Cook and Skinner, 2019). Subsequently, the role and consequences of gender are central to this book, which – inspired by the seminal work of Lisa Brush (2003) – illustrates both the gender of child support governance and the governance of gender through child support. These operate at what Risman (2004) describes as the three structural levels of gender, namely institutions, interactions and identity.

What is also absent from the definition of child support is how payments are administered. As I will describe in more detail in Chapter 3, in some countries, child support processes are governed by social policies, whereas in other countries, these processes are overseen by the courts. Elsewhere, a combination of legal and administrative processes is used, and sometimes parents can choose between these two, often discrete, systems. To transform these complexities into a manageable form, I refer to both laws and social policies as 'policies' for the remainder of this book. My intention is not to examine policy- or law-making processes, but rather examine how these tools of state governance are enacted and experienced and what social norms and hierarchies they symbolically legitimise. What is typically most important is the state's expectation rather than the entity – be it legal or bureaucratic – that administers this.

In many countries, parents can also make arrangements privately, which may or may not need to be registered with official systems. Some countries allow payments to be transferred privately, outside the purview of the state, whereas others require payments to be made through state systems to ensure appropriate benefit interactions. Given welfare benefit interactions, parents' 'choices' are usually contingent on mothers' class position and engagement with their country's benefit system, illustrating intersectional advantages and disadvantages of class, race and disability status that are not well recognised in policy or research.

Across countries, irrespective of legal or administrative enactment, more could be done to ensure eligible children are covered by child support programmes and that payments are enforced. The mechanisms used to determine and distribute payments instead implicate child support as a tool in state governance practices, including when payments are and are not made, and when they do or do not reduce the recipient parents' benefit incomes. Across countries, different means achieve similarly gendered strategic ends, socially and politically. I argue that the implicit ends achieved through the enactment of child support law and policy, across countries, include the maintenance of separated mothers as financially dependent and impoverished while separated fathers are rendered increasingly financially autonomous, often free to choose how and whether to engage with their non-resident family and with the child support system (Municio, 2013). This is, of course, not an explicit aim of child support law or policy. However, it is the 'unintended' effect of laws, policies and procedures that reference and reflect the extant gendered social order. As such, what is required is a critique of the supposed purpose of child support policy, to offer a new perspective and a pathway to future reform.

The purpose of child support

Sifting through the multitude of aims described by the OECD (2011) and working backwards from the policy solution to identify its implicit social problem (Bacchi, 2009), the transfer of child support payments from one parent to another can be seen as providing children in single-parent households with more income by drawing on the resources of both parents. In some countries, and for some children, child support serves this purpose, but in many countries, when welfare benefit interactions are taken into account, child support does little to increase children's financial well-being or reduce their poverty (Hakovirta, 2011; OECD, 2011; Skinner et al, 2017b). However, all such analyses can only calculate poverty reduction effects when payments are received. This is a highly problematic caveat and one that is – conveniently – glossed over by many countries, including in the OECD statistics.

In Australia, when received, child support reduces child poverty by 21 per cent (Skinner et al, 2017). This is a similar rate of poverty reduction to those found in other liberal welfare states (Hanewall and Lopoo, 2008; Hakovirta, 2011; OECD, 2011; Skinner and Main, 2013). Yet, one quarter of eligible Australian children do not receive payments in full, on time or at all (Qu et al, 2014), a figure which is again mirrored internationally (Hakovirta, 2011; OECD, 2011). Unpaid liabilities in Australia were recently reported to exceed AU$1.64 billion, of which fathers owe AU$1.54 billion (Stewart, 2019). In addition, current compliance statistics exclude a further, unknown number of mothers who do not seek payments (Cook et al, 2015b), or do not report or pursue payment arrears (McKenzie and Cook, 2015). Most strikingly, however, these debts cover only those parents who transfer payments through the state's system; more than half of parents transfer payments privately, and these payments are knowingly and erroneously assumed to be 100 per cent compliant (House of Representatives Standing Committee on Social Policy and Legal Affairs, 2015). While Australia's long history of 'fudged' compliance figures (Alexander, 1995; Cook, 2020) provides a stark example of the power of governments to define child support reality, Sweden's purported 100 per cent compliance rate (OECD, 2011) provides a similar example. In Sweden, child support 'success' has relied on the inclusion of guaranteed payments, known as 'maintenance support' payments, paid by the state to the mother when non-resident ex-partners are non-compliant (Fernqvist and Sépulchre, 2021). Parents could also opt to collect solely from the state rather than their ex-partners. In a reform introduced in 2016, Sweden moved to a preferred system of private payments whereby true compliance is obscured. In both cases, the stylised accounts of compliance put forward by governments serve a purpose, as child support compliance rates 'do' things.

In Australia, treating private child support payments as 100 per cent compliant allows governments to reduce women's Family Tax Benefits by 50 cents for each dollar of child support 'received', irrespective of whether this money is ever received at all. In Sweden, reports of full compliance under the pre-2016 guaranteed system meant that separated mothers and their children received the income that they were entitled to, albeit from the government in the form of guaranteed maintenance rather than the non-resident parent in the form of child support. Externally, child support was seen as 'working'; internal to the government, the cost of the guaranteed system may have precipitated the government's move to private arrangements. In addition to 'doing' these things in Australia and Sweden (both prior to and following the 2016 reform), child support compliance rates also 'do not do' things. In both cases, the nature and extent of child support non-compliance is obscured and non-resident parents who do not pay are downplayed as actors in their children's financial welfare. The need for the state to intervene to improve child support compliance is lessened. Indeed, both countries have been positioned as leaders with respect to the effectiveness of their child support regimes.

Exposing and unpicking the interests served by child support policy enactment and inaction is a pressing concern, as child support provides a precise lens into social norms and expectations faced by mothers who live outside the bounds of the nuclear family model. Despite poor compliance rates and difficulties in calculating and transferring payments, child support is becoming increasingly significant to governments as children's needs grow in the face of rising parental separation and non-marital births. The dissolution of the traditional gendered division of earning in western nuclear families, yet the enduring gender of caring labour, marks out child support as a particularly gendered ideological battleground. As Skevik (2006, p. 182) notes, 'attitudes, or the legitimacy of the norms expressed in child support systems, may be crucial for the systems' success, and such norms may vary widely from the policy-making elite to the fathers who are actually obliged to pay'.

In this book, I take Skevik's (2006) assertion further, asking what the norms expressed in child support seek to achieve, how these norms are institutionalised and operationalised in child support systems, and the implications of these norms for gender relations. This analysis locates child support within gendered processes of social reproduction, where women's subordination is entrenched at individual, interactional and institutional levels (Risman, 2004). To examine these processes, I take up the interpretivist turn in policy analysis by foregrounding meaning and representation rather than solely policy-related or legal characteristics and rules. Other texts that have provided a comparative account of child support regimes have done so by developing typologies (Skinner et al, 2007), describing each country individually to provide a compilation of legal and policy examples (Beaumont et al, 2014; Walker, 2015) or comparing a small number of countries on a range of conceptual points (Rush, 2015). The various typologies of child support internationally that such analyses produce are described in Chapter 3. However, rather than fitting the failures of child support into these existing typologies, I take a different approach. The ideas presented here align most closely with Rush's (2015) comparison of US and Nordic fatherhood policies, where policies and legal settings are articulated and compared on symbolic grounds. However, while child support is the focus of this text, my approach provides insights that extend beyond a single policy context, as child support provides the case study through which larger social processes, gender relations and governing practices can be viewed. Unlike Rush, the international scope of this text provides a global framework for understanding the governance of single-mother-headed households. The inclusion of data from Asian, African and South American countries, in particular, expands the conceptual gaze beyond the usual North American and European contexts and speaks to new ways of understanding and intervening in seemingly intractable social problems.

Outline of the book

To pursue the tensions in child support policy set out previously, and identify the role that inaccessibility, inaction and irresponsibility play in the failure of child support, the remainder of the book proceeds as follows. The following chapter describes the conceptual lenses that will be applied to the study of contemporary child support arrangements across contexts. This framework draws on a range of sociological, anthropological and interpretive policy analyses that have examined the way that social 'problems' are managed at varying levels of analysis. This chapter is constructed in two parts. First, a scalar conceptual framework sets out how 'what child support is' can be understood, drawing on such diverse theories as Brush's (2003) concepts of the gender of governance and the governance of gender, Risman's (2004) conceptualisation of gender as a social structure, Smith's (1999) gender of institutions, MacKinnon's (1989) critique of the gender of the state, Bacchi's (1999) analysis of the gender of policymaking, and Graycar and Morgan's (2002) explication of the gender of law. Together, these diverse and multi-level theories allow an analysis of the symbolic work that child support does, or does not do, from a gendered perspective. The use of a range of theories, with varying ontological, epistemological and conceptual positions, is used to problematise child support, rather than offer a definitive explanatory framework. Conceptual boundary-spanning rather than orthodoxy is preferred to deliver new insights and assemblages.

The second half of Chapter 2 sets out the tools useful to the analysis of governmental processes, allowing the critique of why child support policies have developed as they have, and how these have been justified and established in ways that buttress the extant social order through system inaccessibility, state inaction and a lack of responsibility. Here, Jamrozik and Nocella's (1998) account of the conversion of social problems into technical and personal problems is instructional, and is complemented by Li's (2007) rich anthropological work on the history of the governance of 'development' in Indonesia. Bacchi's (2009, 2012) later work adds further insights regarding how assumed and unspoken policy problems can be retrospectively identified from the solutions created to address them. But, further, I explore how the causes of social problems can be foregrounded or backgrounded in order to locate responsibility for the problem with the state or others. This is what Stone's (1989) work on 'causal stories' illustrates. The theories presented in this section align, to some extent, with Risman's (2004) three dimensions of gendered social structure, namely the individual, interactional and institutional levels. The purpose is not to examine women's agency within each level, as such an analysis cannot be done justice here, but rather to examine how these structural dimensions shape the opportunities for women's agency as mothers, advocates, administrators, legal professionals and policymakers. As such, while child support law and policy are operationalised in a range of settings, women as would-be child support recipients are bound in each of these domains by gendered systems of social stratification that reproduce their social and economic subordination. As child support claimants, women engage in interactions as gendered, and maternal, beings.

Chapter 3 then moves to provide a broad history of child support law and policy across countries, to foreground the subsequent analysis. The subsequent chapters draw on a range of policy documents, research studies and interviews with 18 key informants from 16 countries to describe and critique the points in the process where women fall out of the 'leaky pipeline' of child support payments (Chapter 4). This chapter provides the empirical basis for the subsequent analytical chapters that examine how child support problems can be 'seen' and understood (Chapter 5), the interests served by these sites of failure, and the role of masculine interests and the men's rights movement in shaping child support policy reform (Chapter 6). The following two chapters then draw on Jamrozik and Nocella's (1998) account of the residualist conversion of social problems into technical and personal problems to examine how the gender order that underpins child support is maintained. Specifically, Chapter 7 examines the technical management of child support as a neoliberal 'improvement' practice, while Chapter 8 focuses on individualising processes that reinforce the gender of child support through reliance on interpersonal interaction. The book concludes by consolidating the insights developed throughout the analysis by charting the demise of child support as a feminist intervention and resituating it as a gendered governance practice that operates by making child support inaccessible, failing to act to deliver child support outcomes and condoning or ignoring fathers' lack of responsibility.

Despite the complexities of child support law, policy and administration, understanding child support on a conceptual and international level is important in its own right. Observing and identifying patterns and meanings that exist across child support systems offers new insights into how child support is done, is not done or could be undone. These critiques are necessary for imagining ways that child support could be done better. The first half of the Conclusion draws together the examples of how child support relies on and perpetuates gendered systems of inaccessibility, inaction and irresponsibility to condone and ignore fathers' failure to provide material support for their children. The second half of the Conclusion sets out how child support could be reimagined in new ways that align with feminist ideals and provide space for women's agency. Connell's (2019) account of the 'good university' and Ahmed's (2017) principles for 'living a feminist life' underpin a rethinking of the purpose and implementation of child support policy in advanced and developing systems to better respond to the gender inequities that child support so inadequately addresses, yet so often exacerbates and obscures. However, imagining child support as a renewed feminist intervention is not a romantic exercise conducted in the absence of critique. Rather, following the characteristics of the romantic movement as described by Dinçer (2010, p. 219), romanticism involves a rebellion against rational objectivity, a foregrounding of emotion and intuition, and 'freedom from formalism, tradition, and conformity'. These characteristics share many features of the critique of governance and bureaucracy pursued here. However, there is an important footnote to this. Like the romantic tradition, the focus here is dual, on both the 'light romantic', feminist vision of child support and the 'dark romantic' focus on problems or decay. By focusing on the darkness of child support as it currently stands, it is possible to imagine and conceive of the light – a feminist vision that overcomes the problems of inaccessibility, inaction and irresponsibility to foreground autonomy, agency and dignity for all.

2

Child support and gendered governance practice

This chapter, and indeed this book, takes as its starting point the assumption that child support policies – and administrative systems that attend to and enact court-based decision-making – were introduced as means to address social problems that were not well-managed by previously existing arrangements. Typically, early child support systems were exclusively court-based or individualistic in nature, whereby social norms and conventions, rather than an external decision-making body, determined what was to be provided to children following parental separation (Wyss, 2001). While many such systems still exist, over time 'improvements' (Li, 2007) were deemed necessary in some states whereby existing systems – or their lack thereof – were found to be inadequate for managing the social problems experienced by children in single-mother-headed families and by the states that governed them.

As this chapter sets out, 'improvements' to the management of support for separated families hold with them assumptions about the nature of the problem to be solved, the best solution to address the problem, and the nature of the population affected. These are the symbolic assumptions that this book seeks to tease out, for the purpose of identifying what the problems, solutions and population assumptions say about the roles of mothers, fathers, institutions and the state post-separation; and to assess whether these assumptions still hold in the face of changing work, gender, family and internationalising norms that have and are changing the nature of post-separation families and the societies in which they exist. However, I do not take the position that the development of child support policy and administrative techniques – or lack thereof – has occurred as a strictly rational response to an evident problem, as would be pursued by mainstream policy analysts. Rather, I take an interpretivist approach (Yanow, 2000) wherein I see child support law, administration and policy development as political choices to manage problems that have come to the fore within a constellation of social and political influences. Here, I do not use 'political' to illustrate the formal, parliamentary system, but rather I use the term in the Foucauldian sense, to represent the contestation and enactment of power in diffuse and opaque ways (Foucault, 1980). I also do not refer exclusively to the division between politicians and the voting public as a division between those who have power and those who do not, as power is held and wielded in contextually mediated situations within institutional and interpersonal interactions in ways that reflect the underlying social, and in this case gender, order. My assertion is that the gendered acts, omissions and effects of child support are not the coincidental, unintended or random effects of 'rational' policy, but are the intelligible, constructed and normatively justifiable consequences of existing, gendered, power relations. This book seeks to examine why and how the acts, omissions and effects of child support exist and what they symbolise. It provides a critical reading of child support as an intervention that serves to pursue the 'goals and interests of the dominant social structure' (Jamrozik and Nocella, 1998, p. 174). This purpose acknowledges a gendered notion of governance (MacKinnon, 1989), whereby who is heard, who is in control of the system, how the system is applied, and what is considered a public or a private matter is deeply gendered, and reinforces and reflects the gendered social order.

By examining the activity or lack thereof within child support programmes, I seek to identify the practices through which boundary work is achieved, rendering some issues as non-political and thus entrenching the permanence of these conditions and their effects. The theoretical framework employed in this book for tackling these aforementioned essential yet largely neglected issues comprises institutional, administrative and interpersonal levels.

At an institutional level, child support is understood as governance practice (Li, 2007) that is particularly gendered in nature. Insights from Bacchi's (1999, 2009) problem representation approach and Stone's (1989) work on causal stories provide a framework for understanding how child support can be identified or ignored as a social problem requiring intervention and improvement, thus illustrating how child support comes to be symbolic of wider issues. Here, child support draws upon a 'masculinist worldview' (Nicholas and Agius, 2018) to develop and implement child support laws and policies that frame individual, administrative and institutional concerns from the position of men's knowledge, claims and interests – to the detriment of women. As a result, despite child support reform, resultant 'benefits' have typically not accrued to women and their children, while at the same time there have been financial and social benefits conferred to fathers. Concurrently, in countries that have not reformed their child support systems despite barriers to access and a lack of action the primacy of men's interests continues to dominate. Women in these countries again often fail to reap the benefits of child support systems that were purportedly set up to assist them. In addition to gender, these failures typically confer along the lines of intersectional social disadvantages, such as income, race, disability and rurality.

I examine how separated mothers are rendered responsible for child support's success, despite women not being afforded meaningful agency within child support systems, while fathers' failure to engage or contribute is systemically condoned or ignored. Smith's (1987, 2001) work on the gender of institutional practice and Graycar and Morgan's (2002) analysis of the hidden gender of law then provide a language through which gendered practices can be described and understood. My focus on administrative practices centres upon the rendering technical of child support through the introduction and refinement of formulae, compliance frameworks and increasingly onerous administration that apply to mothers but are rarely applied to fathers. Here, Jamrozik and Nocella's (1998) work is pivotal, alongside the conceptual insights of Li (2007). Together, these frames assist in examining the ways in which child support institutions collapse or differentiate the economic and the social, and how institutions allocate responsibility in gendered ways. The focus is on how governance structures privilege or compel women's economically 'responsible' activity in some domains, and how these align with or contradict women's child support requirements and concerns. These frames conceptualise child support requirements as a form of women's labour – work that has yet to be understood as governed by systems of sociotechnical devices, such as laws, forms, service rules and bureaucratic requirements.

At an administrative level, the meanings that women assign to child support are experienced in the context of the systems through which child support is managed. Here, research focuses on women's everyday service encounters (Liegghio and Caragata, 2016; Natalier, 2017) that empower or disempower separated mothers, including the ways that gender, race/ethnicity and class infuse such interactions to reinforce structural disadvantages. Across contexts, Law and Urry's (2004) description of the productive value of survey categories can be extended to describe administrative data practices and processes that confine women's experiences to existing response options, such as which box to check on a form or which button to press in response to a phone script. As research shows, these processes shape women's opportunities to give expression to their child support claims (Cook, 2021a).

At an interpersonal level, child support money is understood as a means by which people define, express and manage identities, relationships and the transactions appropriate to these (Zelizer, 1994). In the context of child support, people invest money with social and cultural significance other than merely its use value, so that it becomes both an instrumental as well as an expressive tool (Natalier and Hewitt, 2010; Skinner, 2013). This conceptualisation will be used to explore the ways in which the social meanings of child support money shape its pursuance or avoidance. Following on from the administrative, I contend that the interpersonal management of child support follows a process of residualisation (Jamrozik and Nocella, 1998; Li, 2007) that renders social problems technical and then further residualises these into private concerns, enacted through interpersonal interaction and the gendered dynamics that these interactions entail (Risman, 2004). Through these processes, women are rendered responsible for not accessing an inaccessible system, or for not facilitating or ensuring state child support action. Fathers' failure to engage or comply is rendered invisible, as women's engagement with technical systems obscures the state's focus on child support payment outcomes.

There are various levels of governance that are implicated in the gendered process of child support inaction, ranging from the ideological to the personal. In the following empirical chapters, I work through these levels to reveal how child support is managed, and how some countries have moved the management of child support through these levels. Typically, child support is moved from being a sociocultural problem to being a technical or even private concern. The purpose here is to examine the symbolic reframing of child support and its management to examine the implications for, and governance of, women. To support the empirical analysis that takes place in Chapters 4 to 8, the current chapter sets out the levels at which child support exists. While it is not actively managed at all of the levels outlined previously, each is implicated in how states configure their child support arrangements. Some countries, particularly Nordic countries, seek to intervene in the cultural conditions that see single-mother-headed families experiencing significantly higher rates of poverty than others, through such means as guaranteed payments. But this does not mean that individual relationships and interactions do not feature in their child support settings.

By contrast, other countries such as the UK have rendered child support a personal problem, through individual claimants pursuing child support privately from their ex-partners, with minimal state involvement unless administrative fees are paid. However, despite this individualised approach, the UK system references technical formulae and wider sociocultural norms regarding the legitimacy of this approach. Across these examples, and across countries, I argue that the management of child support fits within an overarching, symbolic logic of gendered governance.

Describing these frameworks allows for child support to be understood as a gendered governance practice that operates across state, policy, institutional, legal, administrative and interpersonal contexts. Across all sites, child support may have one purpose (to transfer funds to support children in separated-parent households); but at the same time child support has a parallel purpose – achieved through its enactment – of disciplining single and separated mothers to conform to the dominant social order. As such, the purpose of this chapter, and indeed this book, is more than describing the gender of various levels of state practice. By mapping the contours, similarities and differences of the symbolic logics of gendered governance, the framework described here can identify how child support is configured in ways that preserve masculine interests, irrespective of the level at which interventions are made or who is made responsible for conducting the work of child support. There is permanence in the problems that child support purports to resolve, namely the poverty of households in which children from separated families live – households that are predominantly headed by women. This gendered permanence exists in the expectations placed on men and women who enter child support systems, by prioritising masculinist world views while simultaneously being blind to feminist concerns. The gendered outcomes of child support systems almost universally place women at risk of financial, legal, physical and/or emotional harm, often irrespective of whether child support is actually paid or received. More insidiously, the risk of harm to women can be compelled by states who require women to engage in often unhelpful child support processes. These harms can be simultaneously legitimised by men's rights discourses that positions women as acting in ways that are contrary to their culturally assigned gender roles of passivity, docility, being subordinate to men's financial autonomy and authority, and as facilitators of men's social and emotional needs, including fathers' relationships with children.

In the following sections, I begin by describing how states are conceptualised as responding to social problems, and how these processes are inherently gendered. Across the subsequent chapters, the level of analysis and the mechanisms of gendered governance become increasingly narrow, beginning with a gendered sociocultural worldview of the state and ending with the gender of interpersonal relationships. The points to be taken across these conceptual layers and chapters are how they intersect, are mutually reinforcing, symbolise social priorities and interests, and require significant intervention to challenge the status quo on behalf of women – but often do not allow women's efforts, evidence or claims to be included in implementation or reform processes. These processes, from the construction of child support systems to their technical enactment, and ultimately their return to privatised states of affairs, reinforce the permanence of women's subordinate social position. The impenetrability of child support systems to the concerns, experiences and needs of separated mothers – and indeed, systems' ability to exacerbate risks and even cause harm – marks separated mothers out as a particularly subordinated group. According to state practices, this group requires active management, which renders women responsible for enacting the child support system, albeit in ways that are often unlikely to succeed. As a result of the failure of state programmes, of unresponsive systems and of non-compliant fathers, separated mothers' disadvantaged social position is maintained – although through the enactment of child support as a governance tool, women themselves are more able to be positioned as responsible for this failure.

The state's role in governing gender

To identify and analyse the problems, solutions and assumptions that have resulted in child support law, policy and administrative developments (or lack thereof), a conceptual framework is required that can interrogate the distribution of benefits and the impositions that programmatic child support developments and non-developments have created. This focus relies on a framework that foregrounds power and its operation at a range of 'levels', namely sociocultural, political, institutional, administrative and interpersonal. Each of these interlocking sites of power are evident in child support. To examine these programmatic developments and non-developments, and the ways in which they 'do nothing' (Ahmed, 2006) in the face of interpersonal, administrative or structural inequity, or 'intervene' (Jamrozik and Nocella, 1998; Li, 2007) in ways that reinforce the existing social order, a scalar conceptual framework is required to explain the inertia or trajectory of child support system development as gendered governance practice. An analysis of the symbolic elements of child support involves an elaboration and articulation of theories of power relevant to the levels at which child support law and policy operates.

To prise apart and examine the gendered configurations, mechanisms and symbolic effects of child support, I rely on conceptualisations that centre power in their analyses of law and policy arrangements. Most typically, these theories begin from a gendered perspective, but often draw in other forms of intersectional power differentials along the lines of class and race (Crenshaw, 1991). A gendered perspective is essential to the analysis of child support, as child support as a concept and as a practice is fundamentally gendered. As was set out previously, child support policies were introduced in liberal welfare states at a time when the male-breadwinner model was dominant, while legal systems have buttressed male interests for far longer. Child support payments are typically made by a male, non-resident or minority-time parent and paid to a female, resident or majority-time parent. While some academics claim that the gendered nature of these arrangements is irrelevant, I argue that the gendered nature of payers and recipients, and the finances (and thus power) available to each party is fundamental to the design, operation and conduct of child support law and policy. Indeed, it is because child support is gendered that its failures are so easily able to be ignored; thus entrenching the problems these systems purportedly set out to resolve.

As Brush (2003, p. 18) notes, visible changes, such as the introduction of child support systems in this case, can mask the permanence of invisible structures, such as the gendered distribution of labour and extant social relations. So, when introducing radical changes, such as a child support system, what was achieved for women and what was masked as permanent? I contend, as Bacchi (1999) claims with regard to the extension of the welfare state to women, that this was not designed to achieve 'women's equality', but rather the reverse, entrench women's traditional roles. When women have complained about the unmet promises following the introduction of child support systems (Alexander, 1995; Hancock, 1998), the state has typically 'nodded along' (Ahmed, 2006), but has done little of substance to address women's concerns. As a result, rather than enabling or empowering women as heads of households, child support systems have rendered separated mothers responsible for the failures of fathers, systems and states, thus locating the source of child support failure with women themselves. To begin to unpick these connections, I turn to provide an account of gender, power and governance that underpins this analysis.

Governance and power

Theorists have long grappled with the nature and enactment of power, most typically carried out through, or underpinned by, physical force or sanctions than can be legally meted out by those in positions of authority. However, while the state can legitimately act with authority to exert power over its citizens, through such measures as the penal system, fines and other explicit measures, the most relevant theorisation of power to the current analysis is provided by Foucault. While traditional conceptions of power set out 'power over', as exemplified by the state's ability to control populations under the spectre of penalty, Foucault (1980) was concerned primarily with 'power to' control the conduct of others. While the operation of power in 'power over' models is explicit – if you do not comply you will be sanctioned – in Foucauldian conceptions of power, these relations are obscured. These obfuscations benefit some and disenfranchise others in ways that may not be visible, transparent or immediately understood.

In my analysis of child support policy, both conceptions of power – power over and power to – are important, and both contribute to explanations of what child support 'does' and why. Formal laws, policies and regulations set out what is expected of parents who separate with respect to their responsibilities to children. In some jurisdictions, there are explicit penalties for non-compliance – for both mothers and fathers, as intended child support recipients and payers. For example, in Australia recipient parents are compelled to seek child support or their indexed family benefit payments are reduced to the minimum amount (Cook, 2013). In the US, payers can be incarcerated for child support non-compliance (Cozzolino and Williams, 2017; Cozzolino, 2018), although the severity of the US's approach has been tempered somewhat since the Flexibility, Efficiency, and Modernization in Child Support Programs final ruling, which came into effect in January 2017. On the one hand, explicit child support law and policy measures demonstrate the power of the state over its citizens, whereby the rules are set regarding when and to what extent non-compliance confers sanctions. But, on the other hand, these same measures illustrate the soft power of the state, whereby mothers and fathers are disciplined into acting how they 'should' behave as responsible citizens. For many parents, these disciplining forces set out when separated parents should seek or provide financial resources within the family before calling on the state.

The exercise of disciplinary power works best when those being disciplined feel that they are making choices in their own interest, and of their own free will, where interest may include such motivations as financial or relational gain, or the avoidance of penalties. Brush (2003, pp. 30–1) suggests that rather than quibbling over which kind of power is superior within state practice, including gendered aspects of power, it is 'best to treat it as an empirical question [as to] whether and when money, force, cunning, technology, or love triumphs'. Child support provides a core empirical example to examine these competing gender-laden power dynamics in practice, as the enactment of child support systems across countries entails a variety of incentives and power structures. For example, legal and policy levers may include such mechanisms as imprisonment (force), liabilities, benefit reductions and fines (money), asset and income investigations and evasion (cunning), bureaucratic rules and procedures (technology), or the prioritisation of private relations (love). The configuration of these settings is telling of how states operate, the extent to which they reflect masculinist (Nicholas and Agius, 2018) or feminist interests (MacKinnon, 1989) and the degree to which these render permanent the extant gender order.

But the disciplinary forces that Brush identifies do not apply equally to all citizens. For example, some Australian recipients can be exempt from seeking child support. Some American and New Zealand fathers can be freed from their child support debts, or have their payments restructured. These arrangements can have gendered, classed and even racialised dimensions, which align with societal interests and normative assumptions about 'good citizenship' therein. In Australia, victims of domestic violence can be exempt from seeking child support, but this process is not well advertised and entails victims 'proving' their circumstances to a welfare services bureaucrat and social worker (Department of Social Services, 2020). Successful applicants may have to re-apply for this exemption, which may or may not be granted each time. The intensive evidentiary requirements and need for periodic reassessment contain within them implicit assumptions that child support recipients would make up claims of violence, if they could get away with it, in order to avoid seeking child support. Extensive proof of violence is thus needed to separate out those who are deserving of full family benefits without seeking support from their ex-partner. Indeed, the specific terminology regarding 'making up' claims of domestic violence was used by controversial MP and Deputy-Chair of the 2019–21 Joint Select Committee on Australia's

Family Law System inquiry, Pauline Hanson (2016). The mainstream uptake up such terminology – while offensive and dismissive to domestic violence survivors – illustrates the symbolic importance of who gets to define child support issues and oversee their subsequent management. Returning to Australian domestic violence victims, if an exemption application is successful, violent ex-partners are freed from the imposition of paying child support, and are thus financially rewarded. The disciplining forces these practices have are important. Men's violence is implicitly condoned and rewarded by the Australian child support system, where no scrutiny or disciplinary measures are applied. Women's experiences of violence are implicitly regarded with suspicion and must be continually monitored to ensure that they are not cheating the state out of money to which they are not entitled. The unanswered questions that these state logics throw up are 'why', 'for what purpose' and 'to whose benefit'?

Despite providing particular examples of policy or legal settings, such as the previous Australian example of domestic violence provisions, this book seeks to move beyond the particular to examine the symbolic and recursive logics of child support as a global, disciplining practice. This analysis moves beyond detailed technical or economic cross-country policy analysis, as has been conducted previously (Skinner et al, 2007; Beaumont et al, 2014; Walker, 2015; Skinner et al, 2017b) to step back and examine the normative logics on which expectations of what child support 'ought' to do are built. While researchers have set out the policy measures and explicit rules that determine child support payments and procedures across countries (see, for example, Skinner et al, 2007; Beaumont et al, 2014; Walker, 2015), what I am most interested in are the implicit rules, assumptions and symbolic effects that these policies have. Why is it that it is 'easier' for women to live in poverty than seek child support from a violent ex-partner or engage in burdensome state systems? What are these systems 'doing', 'to who' and 'why'?

The questions that I pose are not unique to my home country of Australia. As is outlined in the substantive chapters of this book, these problems are experienced worldwide, where child support systems, on paper, transfer money from a non-resident parent to a resident parent, but rarely with universal effect (cf. Hakovirta, 2011; OECD, 2011). Rather, these systems are typically either inaccessible, ineffective or ambivalent to the problems they create. When these systems are effective, it is typically not because they are collecting and transferring payments, but rather are 'working around' a lack-of-payment reality. So, why are we 'doing' child support? Who is it for? Who is being disciplined within child support arrangements and who is being freed up? As the following chapters set out, the answers to these questions often have gendered, classed and sometimes racialised dimensions that speak more to where power lies in society: typically in the hands of the wealthy, often the White, and almost always men. Here, cunning – often described as masculine autonomy, discretion or manipulation – wins. But men's cunning can also be buttressed by technology, as state administrative technologies cannot keep up with changing financial, work, family and care patterns. Women often bear the financial penalties as a result.

Understanding the process of institutional and administrative failure

Given the power and governance structures outlined in the previous sections, a framework is required for understanding how social problems are pushed down from institutional to administrative to personal levels. Brush's (2003) analysis of the gender of governance and the governance of gender provides a framework through which to examine the exercise of power at the level of policy and government. While ontologically and epistemologically divergent, her findings combine well with the work of Bacchi (2009), Stone (1989) and others (Smith, 1987; Jamrozik and Nocella, 1998; Smith, 2001; Risman, 2004; Ahmed, 2006, 2007) to foreground how social problems are identified and understood, who controls the rules of these programmes and the ways of knowing and being that inform them. These processes share features of Nicholas and Agius's (2018) articulation of the persistence of masculinism. They cite the work of Brittan (1989, p. 4) to define masculinism as 'the ideology that justifies and naturalizes male domination. As such, it is the ideology of patriarchy'. Nicholas and Agius (2018, p. 4) invoke the concept of masculinism to explain the co-option and rejection of feminism in ways that 'reshap[e] modes of hierarchy, protection and ordering', identifying three processes through which this occurs: individualising, protectionism and strategic efficacy.

Drawing together the work of Brush (2003) and Nicholas and Agius (2018) frames child support as a tool to reinforce the gender order, often in spite of – or, as I would argue, as a result of – interventions designed to promote feminist ideals. However, what Brush's (2003) work does not provide is an empirical examination of the contours and limits of her useful theoretical treatise. Here, Li's (2007, p. 7) work on the translation of 'the will to improve into explicit programs' provides an empirical account of three governmental practices that dovetail neatly into the other, often gendered, theories of power and governance that are central to this book.

Li identifies two improvement practices that have relevance to an analysis of child support law and policy enactment. A major process of improvement is that of rendering technical, which involves: boundary work between those who are positioned as being able to identify problems and their solutions, and those who are subject to them; and the simultaneous rendering of issues as non-political, given the technical remit of the identified problems and their solutions. The 'improvements' that states introduce to address social problems, however, can often have the opposite effect to what is being claimed. In such instances, as the following chapters will show is often the case in child support policy 'improvement', those purported to receive the benefits of reform are often subject to additional burdens, surveillance and control. At the same time, the inaction of ex-partners, the system and the state are ignored or rendered invisible.

Li's work on governing practices of improvement also identifies practices of problematisation, whereby power is implicated in which problems come to be seen as 'governable' and how their solutions are identified. Jamrozik and Nocella's (1998) work on the sociology of social problems covers similar conceptual terrain to Li's (2007, p. 8) practice of improvement, which she described as 'antipolitics', defined as, 'the design of programs as a deliberate measure to contain a challenge to the status quo'. Antipolitics, in turn, shares many features of Ahmed's (2006) description of 'nonperformatives', Nicholas and Agius's (2018) description of 'doing nothing' and Brush's (2003, p. 18) uptake of Bourdieu's (2001, p. 106) work to contend that 'visible changes can also "mask the permanence of … invisible structures" that reproduce masculine domination.' Taken together, these frameworks offer significant opportunity to critique the symbolic importance of the impotence of child support systems worldwide.

To summarise, the primary works on which my analytical framework is built include Bacchi's (1999, 2009) work on the framing of policy problems and their solutions, Stone's (1989) account of the political management of policy problems through the use of causal stories and, most importantly, Jamrozik and Nocella's (1998) sociological account of the residualisation of social problems into technical and personal concerns. Each of these theorists, working from different disciplinary perspectives, share a Foucauldian understanding of power as diffuse and able to be enacted in: 1) the definition of problems, 2) the technical apparatus used to address them and 3) what is left out of these definitions, problems and solutions. Across all accounts, the authors share the position that action or inaction is taken in ways that buttress the existing social order and align with the interests of dominant groups, while making these problems and their solutions seem palatable to affected populations and their wider political constituents.

Technologies of gendered governance

Given international efforts by some states to govern child support in increasingly technical ways, albeit to limited effect, I argue that child support represents an instance of antipolitics, or in legal settings, of 'antilaw'. Here, technologies of governance are deployed to seemingly 'improve' child support, while simultaneously deflecting attention away from measures that would materially improve women and children's circumstances. In some instances, antipolitics frames problems in ways that impose further technologies of surveillance or responsibility on poor women, often in the name of 'improvements'. These processes guide the construction of child support as an issue to be managed through increasingly technical means.

There has been a small body of research over recent decades which has sought to understand and theorise the socially constructed nature of contemporary policy problems and state responses to them (Stone, 1989; Jamrozik and Nocella, 1998; Bacchi, 1999, 2009). Aside from Bacchi (1999, 2009), these works to do not foreground gender as an explanatory force in how states manage social problems in legal, administrative and policy domains. Rather, these works foreground state interests and power, but locate this power as enacted within interaction and institutions. However, what draws these works together is that they each take an interpretivist approach to policy analysis that can be used to describe and critique the implementation and roll-out of child support policy internationally.

Rather than viewing policy formation in terms of responses to particular social problems, Bacchi (1999, p. 48) argues that policy constitutes a discursive process through which both problems and solutions are constructed. Moreover, policy issues are often constructed in ways that 'mystify' power relations and emphasise individual responsibility, thus drawing attention away from structures and institutions and the state's responsibility for solutions. The ways that policy issues are represented have effects 'that limit the impact of reform gestures' and 'subvert' their progressive intent (Bacchi, 1999, p. 48). Stone (1989) offers a similar explanation in her theorisation of 'causal stories' where she argues that issues don't have inherent properties that make them more or less likely to be seen as problems. Rather, she argues that 'political actors deliberately portray them in ways calculated to gain support for their side' (Stone, 1989, p. 282). This work is done by portraying issues so that they fit with various causal ideas. In policy, Stone (1989) argues, there is always a choice over which causal factors to address, with different choices assigning the responsibility to different actors. She argues that a common strategy in policy debates is to push the responsibility for the policy problem onto someone or something else, through stories of 'inadvertent cause'. Inadvertence can be constructed as a result of irresponsible personal behaviour and as a result victim blaming is common. The idea is that if only people would change their action then the problem would cease to exist. For example, in child support debates, it is often suggested that if mothers gave fathers more access to children, or worked privately to request and receive payments, fathers would be more likely to pay (Fernqvist and Sépulchre, 2021).

Stone suggests that, in policy debates, causal stories are 'fought for, defended and sustained' in a 'tug of war between political actors asserting competing causal theories' (Stone, 1989, p. 295). Some causal stories become dominant beliefs and 'guiding assumptions' for policymakers, particularly when proponents of the causal stories have ready access to media and hold prominent positions, and if their causal theory 'accords with widespread and deeply held cultural values' or responds to the particular cultural 'mood' (Stone, 1989, p. 294). Success or failure of a causal story is often reliant on or constrained by law and science – as powerful social institutions, they can legitimate the claims being made about causation. Moreover, because causal stories can be used as a form of social control, by maintaining existing patterns of power and dominance, struggles over causal definitions of social problems are thus 'contests over basic structures of social organisation' (Stone, 1989, p. 296). In policy, Stone (1989) argues, there is always a choice over which causal factors to address; different choices assign the responsibility to different actors. I suggest similarly that causal factors shape what researchers choose to address in their studies, which then locate responsibility and construct the 'problem' of child support in different ways. The issues researchers choose to focus on highlight assumptions about the 'desirable' or 'normative' nature of mothers, fathers, poverty, payments and states.

To deepen the analysis of normative assumptions, state interests and their management, Jamrozik and Nocella (1998, p. 5) provide a framework for understanding and describing the conversion of social problems into technical and private problems, in ways that 'emerge logically from societally pursued dominant values, interests and corresponding goals'. Like Bacchi (2009) and Stone (1989), their focus is on how policies, programmes and interventions manage social problems and package them into socially acceptable forms that reinforce rather than challenge the existing social order. Jamrozik and Nocella's framework (1998, p. 5) provides an analysis of the 'so called pathological conditions that are commonly referred to as social problems – such as poverty, unemployment, family dislocation and so on'. As Jamrozik and Nocella note, the solutions to such problems can be found in changing structural arrangements, but these would not be welcomed by society's dominant interests. For example, addressing poverty would require a fundamental redistribution of income that would be unpalatable to society's financial and political elite who benefit from the status quo. For them, social problems are instead best managed in a way that reinforces the legitimacy of the existing power structure. As should be evident, child support touches each of the social problems listed previously, as identified by Jamrozik and Nocella. However, it does not 'solve' any of these problems, but rather manages them. In doing so, I contend that child support stands in for a solution and deflects attention away from the need to do anything further.

With respect to the social conditions that existed prior to calls for child support policy, the poverty of lone parents (predominantly lone mothers) was a result of rapidly escalating divorce and separation that occurred in the 1970s. Women's independence could be seen as a challenge to the existing patriarchal structure, while their poverty perpetuated the extant gender order. As Jamrozik and Nocella (1998, p. 6) describe, 'every silver lining creates a cloud'. However, the growing incidence of women's and children's poverty brought the issues to the fore. According to the theories of Jamrozik and Nocella (1998) and Stone (1989), once a social problem comes to societal and political attention, it must be dealt with in ways that preserve the social order, but provide assurance that the problem is being managed. For Jamrozik and Nocella (1998), this is achieved by converting the political problem from a social issue into a technical problem that can be dealt with by administrative and technical experts, such as the bureaucracy. Here, the problem is depoliticised, while solutions can be found in ever more expansive and rigorous administrative settings and programme operation. I argue that the development and implementation of child support formulae and their attendant administrative regimes provide an example of where the problem still exists, but has been reframed and thus depoliticised.

However, despite depoliticisation, technical problems can still provide a source of concern for governments who are ultimately held responsible for their functioning and success. As Jamrozik and Nocella (1998) note, technical measures that challenge the social order will also be met with resistance and ongoing efforts to reframe the problem and its solutions. Ultimately, to move responsibility away from government, the aim is to reframe the technical problems encountered as being a result of the incompatible personal attributes of programme participants. An example they cite is blaming the unemployed for their unemployment, due to lack of motivation, skills or enthusiastic attitudes. Because of this reframing, the solutions to unemployment lie not in structural adjustments to the economy and labour market, or in technical solutions such as job-matching or subsidised wages, but in the skills and attitudes of the unemployed. Ideally, as in this example, the problem at hand can be residualised into a private problem, whereby the individual attributes of programme participants come to be understood as the locus of responsibility. Such problems lie outside the control of the state, absolving governments of responsibility for their solutions. I argue that this is the process through which child support policy has also evolved, particularly in the UK, Sweden and Australia, where the state-operated system is positioned as a last resort for families who do not have the personal wherewithal to carry on outside of the state's supervision. My purpose here is to analyse such policy developments within their gendered socio-political context.

According to Jamrozik and Nocella (1998), the conversion of a problem into a personal issue serves primarily to reinforce the social order along classed, gendered and racial lines. For example, they note that for a problem to be noticed within a class society, it must be noticed by the dominant and ruling class. As child support can be regarded as primarily a classed and gendered issue, the problems that these laws, policies and procedures seek to address must be recognised by both the ruling class and gender within our patriarchal society. I argue that while child support was championed (and condemned) as a feminist intervention (for examples of each perspective see Edwards et al, 2001 and Morgan, 1995; Edwards, 2019, respectively), it was unable to deliver upon the feminist policy ideals of autonomy, agency and dignity for all. Rather, research reveals that despite the relatively low likelihood of receiving payments, women have been co-opted into conducting the work of government and saving money for government. This work is conducted in the slim hope of providing a material benefit to their children, contingent upon their successful management of often fraught post-separation relationships. At the same time, men's rights groups have vehemently opposed child support, and have sought significant technical amendments to buttress their financial autonomy and authority over money beyond the couple unit. As a result, child support governance has been narrowed into a personal issue, to be governed through the gendered logics of interaction.

The governance of gender within interaction

Each of the governance practices described previously can be regarded as operating in the public arena, at a level that Risman (2004) and Smith (2001) would describe as institutional. However, as outlined earlier, child support simultaneously operates at an interpersonal and very private level (Risman, 2004). The public/private dichotomy that pervades child support is a mechanism through which the permanence of the gender order is structured. As outlined earlier, Jamrozik and Nocella's (1998) insights are useful for considering child support as state governance practice to discipline unruly women's personal inclination for irresponsibility and the state's need to manage this problem within the public sphere. Compulsory child support programmes often seek to develop welfare recipient mothers into more 'responsible' citizens (Treloar and Funk, 2008) by reducing their burden on the welfare budget. At the same time, a relative lack of state involvement in the collection, transfer and enforcement of payments relegates the public issue of single parenthood and child poverty into a private trouble (Mills, 1959), reinforcing gender hierarchies in their wake. The solutions – as the following chapters demonstrate for both 'public' and 'private' collection systems – are for women to conduct more emotion work, to be more 'deserving' of child support payments by facilitating fathers' access to and relationships with children, demonstrating a responsible use of funds, and keeping the peace (Bradshaw et al, 1999; Khunou, 2006; Natalier and Hewitt, 2010; Goodall and Cook, 2020). As Natalier and Hewitt's (2010) research demonstrates, building on Bradshaw et al's (1999) work with fathers, mothers must position themselves as worthy recipients of the gift of child support (for a further elaboration of gift relations see Zelizer, 1996). Similarly, my recent work with Goodall identifies the social norms that women, as child support recipients, transgress. These include maternal norms of good mothering, which women purportedly transgress by spending child support payments in ways that supported their lifestyle rather than on child-centric goods; patriarchal norms that centre fathers as the arbiters of appropriate spending in families, enacted post-separation as fathers determining child support payment terms and amounts; and – to a lesser extent – familial norms, which re-partnered mothers transgress by continuing to seek child support money from their ex-partner when a new, resident breadwinner is available to take on this responsibility (Goodall and Cook, 2020).

Through these social processes, child support's status as children's entitlement is erased and fathers' conduct is lauded when payments are voluntarily provided. At the same time, non-compliance is rendered invisible when payments are not forthcoming. The permanence that results from such relations, as this book seeks to make explicit, is the gendered social order whereby women must defer to men's financial authority and autonomy (Natalier and Hewitt, 2010), while being held responsible for failures at state, institutional and interpersonal levels. For mothers, their relative poverty vis-à-vis the post-separation incomes of fathers (de Vaus et al, 2017; Fletcher et al, 2020) is entrenched. Institutionally, the lack or winding back of systems means that child support non-compliance is often administratively invisible. These data gaps obscure the need for programmatic reform (Cook et al, 2015a), again entrenching women's disadvantage as their financial and social vulnerabilities are unacknowledged and unable to be countered. At a state level, politicians are able to remain unaware of the problems with child support as these are too complicated or too obtuse. The causes of women and children's poverty remain the consequences of the behaviour of the poor, or too complex to solve with simple, technical fixes. Taken together, the unspoken work of child support is achieved: to render poor women responsible for their social and financial predicament whereby they must 'work harder' within dysfunctional systems, often without reward, to demonstrate that they are 'responsible' and have done everything they could for their children. Within the neoliberal logic of child support, when mothers walk away from such systems due to barriers to access, poor likelihood of success or harms they may experience, they must accept the financial consequences of their decisions; they, after all, chose to be poor.

Rendering women's concerns invisible

Given the rise of relationship breakdown in societies since second wave feminism and the introduction of no-fault divorce laws in a range of countries, child support has become an increasingly significant issue for the families involved. Child support is a particular concern for the resident parents of eligible children in countries where payments are compelled in order to receive benefits, and such payments interact with state welfare. At times, and especially in countries where child support involves welfare benefit interactions, child support has also become a significant political issue, particularly for separated fathers. However, in most countries, when child support is not at the forefront of the political agenda, child support is 'out of sight and out of mind'. As such, despite it impacting on a sizable portion of any nation's population, child support receives very little research consideration.

Child support's problems are bound to its organisation. It spans law and social policy, often with complex interactions between the two, making it difficult to describe and more difficult for non-specialists to include in wider social policy analyses. For example, child support is almost never included in studies of lone parent poverty and welfare benefit expenditure, despite the fact that studies explicitly designed to test its contribution have shown that child support can significantly reduce child poverty (Hakovirta, 2011; OECD, 2011; Skinner et al, 2017a, 2017b; Hakovirta et al, 2019). But these poverty reduction effects also often involve complex interactions between welfare benefit payments and child support cash transfers, which are difficult to disentangle.

While child support as a topic is marginalised within the social sciences, legal scholars have also struggled with the relevance of child support, given that it often sits outside of legal processes, in administrative realms. It fits most typically within the discipline of family law, another somewhat marginalised sub-discipline within the legal profession, as it focuses on the more 'trivial', feminised, personal domains. In sum, child support is typically put either in the 'too hard' or 'irrelevant' baskets by welfare policy researchers, despite the role that child support can play in reducing child poverty. It is at best a niche issue, which adds little to the cross-national, 'big data'-based, more 'masculinised' studies of welfare states, benefit payments and poverty status. The social science child support scholarship that has been conducted typically measures and models the predictors of orders and payments, the effectiveness and impact of various policy settings, and the outcomes for payers and payees, with far less scholarship – almost none – foregrounding the experiences of children within these processes. A much smaller body of social science research has taken a qualitative approach, examining how payments are organised, why parents make the decisions they do and how policy and legal settings are experienced (Natalier and Hewitt, 2010, 2014; Cook, McKenzie and Natalier, 2015; Cozzolino and Williams, 2017; Keil and Elizabeth, 2017; Battle, 2018, 2019; Natalier, 2018; Douglas and Nagesh, 2019; Keil and Elizabeth, 2019). These studies sit at the intersection of interpretive policy studies – which is a somewhat marginalised discipline within political sciences – and qualitative sociology, another often subordinated, 'soft' and 'feminised' methodology. It is on these studies that my analysis builds, drawing on governance theory to explain parents' experiences across contexts and along class, gender and sometimes racial lines, identifying the power structures inherent in existing knowledge and policy logics.

Within the qualitative, interpretivist tradition, I ask what is child support, what is it for, and is it achieving what it purports to? However, rather than providing a descriptive account of the legal and policy contexts across countries, as others have done, I take a socio-political approach. To apply this to the rudimentary questions previously outlined, I first take child support as a tool of government – and thus a governmental technique. Second, I review a wide range of child support systems cross-nationally to examine what these governmental tools claim to be achieving. However, rather than taking these assertions on face value, or using key informants' accounts to map out the technical specificities of each country's programme, my purpose is to examine child support processes as governmental techniques, existing within relations of gendered power. Here, child support offers a lens into the social relations within countries, as child support makes explicit – and often even prices – the appropriate caregiving and breadwinning roles of parents following separation. But, child support research has done less well at understanding whether payers view these as gifts, children's entitlements or compensation for mothers' caring labour (Eekelaar, 1991a; Zelizer, 1998; Natalier and Hewitt, 2010). Finally, my socio-political approach to these questions examines how the 'rubber hits the road' in terms of the gendered effects and symbolic consequences of child support law and policy. I aim to make explicit the extent to which child support's effects match, or are contrary to, the purported aims of child support policies – often described as achieving a mix of reducing child poverty, reducing welfare expenditure or increasing parental responsibility. The result of this analysis is that, across systems, women are positioned as responsible for enacting child support, but are not provided with tools for ensuring their success as systems are often inaccessible, fail to result in action or apportion responsibility to mothers while absolving fathers of theirs. The likelihood of success depends instead on women's conformity to gendered hierarchies and standards of behaviour: deferring to fathers' and states' authority, while performing the roles of what constitutes a good separated mother and a good, financially independent citizen.

I examine how child support policy has sought to manage the social 'problems' that the law or policy originally sought to solve. I argue that child support, in a range of countries, has been 'residualised' into a technical issue – where more refined formulae for calculating child support liabilities and compliance mechanisms have been posed as the solution – and further, as a personal issue, where parents are encouraged to resolve their financial arrangements and transfers privately. Liberal welfare state trends, in particular, see reforms that decouple child support from state policy regimes through the privatisation of child support agreements and payments. However, at the same time, and within the same countries, there is often the simultaneous strengthening of the state as it pursues its own financial interests. This occurs through the mandating of child support agreements for low-income separated parents and increasing the value of transfers so as to reduce welfare state expenditure. These reforms have the unintended – or perhaps intended – consequence of entrenching gender inequities, a consequence which is anathema to the original purpose of child support in particular, and redistributive liberal welfare states in general. Following Risman (2004), the purpose of the feminist project conducted in this book is to identify processes that explain the failures of child support and, in doing so, discover sites for change.

Gaining access to and insights into governance practices

In order to examine child support law and policy making and their enactment on a conceptual scale, I take an 'asymmetrical' comparative approach for the purpose of critique, rather than linear causal explanation (Krause, 2016). This lies in contrast to Li's (2007) detailed anthropological account of governmental practices enacted within a discrete geographic context, as I seek to examine what I consider to be global processes, rather than describe their localised enactment. The purpose of this book is to make the case that child support is a technology of governance and, as such, one that works in the interests of the status quo with respect to the gender and social order. Within this remit, I use international child support law, policy and procedural settings to mark out the taken-for-granted logics of child support, how improvements have occurred, and how reforms are justified.

Gaining access to such insights requires the input of child support experts who can speak not only to the history of child support in each country, but also the technical specificity of the system's workings and its politics of reform. Given the legal, policy, practical and personal complexity of child support, the expertise required to understand its history, functioning and logics across an array of settings is diffuse. No one person is sufficiently knowledgeable of child support as it is conceived, implemented and experienced. Indeed, Jamrozik and Nocella's (1998) framework for evaluating organisational performance tells us that policymakers, programme administrators, front-line service providers and clients will each have different accounts of how child support is understood and experienced. Advocates and researchers too will enter the field from different perspectives and at different levels, be they political, organisational, operational or experiential. As such, following descriptions of the enactment of governmentality as diffuse, so too are the data that can inform understandings of governmental practice.

Given the operational complexity of child support and the technical differences in systems across countries, as will be touched on in the following chapter, the purpose of this analysis is not to set out the technical details of each system or develop an overarching typology. Indeed, other researchers conducting comparative research have identified the impossibility of this task (Skinner and Hakovirta, 2020). The aim here is not to conduct a comparative analysis of child support outcomes or design features, as has been conducted previously (Corden, 1999; Skinner et al, 2007; Hakovirta, 2011; OECD, 2011; Skinner et al, 2012). Rather, this study is located within the qualitative tradition, but differs from interpretive policy analyses of expert informants' insights into policy frameworks and principles by providing a conceptual analysis of child support's symbolic dimensions.

Examining child support as a gendered governance practice relies on an understanding of its context, history and interests. However, the analysis pursued in this book is not focused on administrative, technical details of child support implementation in each country. Rather, the focus here is on the big picture of interests and their expression through the technical features of child support policy across countries. All accounts of child support policy, particularly at this international scale, will necessarily be incomplete and partial. I hope that given these omissions, this book will prompt further research into the institutional practices and outcomes within countries, or even within states or local administrative regions. What this book does provide, however, is a framework for locating and understanding the interests served by child support archetypes and reflecting upon these in light of gendered theories of governance and how gender is socially structured and enacted through institutions and interactions. This task necessarily requires an understanding of the context of child support, although it is acknowledged that this context can never be complete.

While the data presented here describe the particulars of specific countries, the analysis is abstracted beyond the particulars of any given country. While it is not possible to reconcile all of the divergent child support policy principles, procedures and outcomes described by informants into a singular universal account of child support policy, it is possible to locate informants' interpretations within a framework that explains the function of child support as gendered governance practice. As such, informants' accounts do not feature heavily in the analysis, as they are necessarily grounded in the technical particulars of their own context. Where direct excerpts do feature, they provide an illustration of how political and social processes play out on the ground, yet in ways that are familiar across contexts when viewed through the lenses of gender and governance.

Eighteen informants provided information on the child support systems in operation across 16 countries, with interviews conducted between March 2017 and March 2019. While previous international child support research has focused almost exclusively on English-speaking, European and OECD nations, I sought to include a much wider array of nations and regimes so as to tease out the universal failures of child support, irrespective of system design and its purported sophistication. As such, informants span the 'usual suspect' English-speaking countries of the UK, the US (at national and state levels), New Zealand and Canada, where informants were comprised of academics, government administrators and legal professionals engaged in the child support process. Another 'leading' child support country, Australia, is represented by my own and others' research, and the volume of government documentation that exists for this ever-changing and much-debated topic. From continental Europe, informants provided data on the Nordic systems of Sweden and Norway, where guaranteed payments were, or are, a defining feature, respectively, and the court-based regimes of Germany, Portugal and Malta. Again, the European informants span the spectrum of professions engaged with child support, including academia, the law, social services and administrators. Finally, expanding the remit and thus the research gaze across the Global South (Connell, 2007; Dados and Connell, 2012) – including Asia, Africa and the Middle East – informants were also sourced from countries not often included in comparative child support research. Countries include new and emerging voices in the international child support debate, with informants providing insight into the administrative enforcement regime of South Korea, the legal systems in operation in Israel and Japan, and the colonially informed legal systems existing in Nigeria, Hong Kong and Peru. Finally, Malaysia and Nigeria provide examples of Shariah customary law regimes, although in Malaysia, both Shariah and common law systems exist. Interview participants in these countries were academics, advocates and legal professionals. Together, the data provided by the informants evidence the processes of residualisation described by Jamrozik and Nocella (1998) and Li (2007) in other contexts. The following chapters serve to describe these processes and illustrate how child support failures are not noticed, or are understood as intractable. The effect across cases is the maintenance of gender privilege and the benefits of this privilege that accrue to the state and individual fathers as a result.

3

Child support regimes and relevance

This chapter consolidates previous child support research that has developed typologies of legal or policy forms (Skinner et al, 2007; Beaumont et al, 2014; Walker, 2015). It adds a critical social science perspective by examining the social problems that child support law and policy purportedly seek to resolve, marking out for whom this is a problem, and where solutions to this problem purportedly lie. The purpose is to outline how child support has been categorised and conceptualised in previous research, but moves beyond these descriptive, administrative accounts, to examine how it intersects with changing normative paradigms, namely evolving work and income assumptions, the continuation and discontinuation of the gender contract, and increasing diversity in family forms.

What the three variables used in child support determinations – namely income, care-time and family forms – foreground is either the 'blindness' of systems to these issues, or the complexity of data required to sufficiently address variations to these within child support orders. Some countries do not seek to respond to these changes, operating a one-time 'set and forget' model that ignores changing circumstances rather than dealing with them effectively. However, for other countries these issues are not limited to the setting of a child support order. Over the life of a child support order, there can be enormous complexity built into the system if it seeks to respond to changing income, care-time and family patterns. For all systems, whether they recognise or ignore the inequities created by changing income, care-time and family forms, the bad news is that social trends are making these issues increasingly relevant and increasingly variable. This variability exacerbates the data needs and procedural demands existing within child support systems that respond to these changes, and exacerbates the inequities caused by ignoring them.

Types of child support internationally

Historically, child support has existed in some form well before administrative systems were introduced. Court-compelled financial support for children whose father had left the family unit has existed in some contexts for centuries. For example, in many countries, legal notions of family responsibility governed the payment of monies across households in instances of abandoned wives (Simmonds, 2016). Early court-based systems reference children's rights and fathers' moral obligations to children (Chambers, 1982; Waller and Plotnick, 2001; Cuesta and Meyer, 2014). In these early systems, child support was taken up as a means of enacting children's right to share in their parents' resources. Such sentiment has since imbued both court-based and administrative regimes (Waller and Plotnick, 2001; Rissanen and Aaltonen, 2019), which assume that children sharing in their fathers' finances will reduce child poverty. As Skevik (2006, p. 182) says with respect to the Norwegian system, 'for economists and social policy analysts, child support is one tool in the struggle against child poverty'.

The rationale that child support policies would reduce child poverty by providing separated mothers with more income has underpinned the introduction of child support policies internationally (Mokgoro, 2003; Keil and Elizabeth, 2017). In many countries, court-based systems were coming under pressure following the introduction of no-fault divorce laws, beginning in the late 1960s and 1970s. The subsequent rise in the number of single-mother-headed households meant that cumbersome, inaccessible and personally expensive court-based systems were no longer effective in meeting children's needs. Similarly, welfare states – particularly liberal states – were under pressure to support the growing number of single-mother-headed families. While poverty reduction was central to state benefit provision, child support offered a means of reducing state outlays at the same time. Here, administrative systems to award and/or enforce child support are encouraged as the most effective systems, as they replace often costly and cumbersome court-based systems to deliver uniform outcomes based on underlying child support policy. But significant efforts have been made by nations to learn from the policy efforts of others, in the pursuit of best practice policy and implementation. As such, there has been the significant rationalisation of post-separation financial management across countries, where the financial obligations of separated parents are receiving increasing state attention.

A body of research has sought to categorise the array of child support laws and policies that exist across countries, organising these into typologies of legal, administrative and hybrid systems. This work was most comprehensively set out by Skinner et al (2007) in their report for the UK Department of Work and Pensions (DWP). The authors of the DWP report note that child support systems internationally are influenced by 'history, culture and socio-political institutions and there is a deal of similarity and difference in the considered role of the state in the lives of the family' (Skinner et al, 2007, p. 29). The remainder of their report on child support systems, however, concerns itself with the administrative organisation of child support, including such topics as whether payments are determined primarily by a court, agency or a combination of both; the degree to which private agreements are possible within these structures; and the degree of standardisation and discretion possible within child support related decision-making, including whether responsibility for decision-making is devolved to states or other administrative units within particular countries.

Across jurisdictions, a wide variety of child support models operate. The 14 countries included in Skinner et al's (2007) analysis consist of Western European nations including Belgium, Denmark, Finland, France, Germany, the Netherlands, Norway and Sweden, and countries from the Anglosphere, such as Australia, Canada (Ontario), the US, the UK and New Zealand. While Skinner et al mark an important step in categorising the features of some of the world's most advanced child support systems, the difficulties faced in collecting data from key informants excluded less advanced systems, such as those existing in the Global South. Their research has noted that Belgium, Austria, Canada, Germany, Sweden and France have primarily court-based systems for the determination and enforcement of child support. South American, African and most Asian nations provide further examples of this type. Bureaucratic agencies are largely responsible for determining and administering child support in Australia, Denmark, New Zealand, Norway and the UK. In other countries, such as Finland, the Netherlands and the US, an amalgamation of courts and agencies are responsible for the various child support decision-making and enforcement functions. South Korea is a further addition to Skinner et al's typology, having recently introduced an administrative child support regime to enforce court-based determinations.

Children's right to financial support from their parents has also been enshrined in the United Nations Convention on the Rights of the Child (United Nations 1989, hereafter UNCRC), where Article 27.4 states, 'States Parties shall take all appropriate measures to secure the recovery of maintenance for the child from the parents or other persons having financial responsibility for the child, both within the State Party and from abroad.' However, the extent to which countries take up this responsibility, and how parents' financial responsibility is conceived of by states, varies considerably. In western liberal democracies such as the UK, the US and Australia, significant rhetorical and legislative attention has been given to mandating payments by fathers, consistent with Article 27.4 that foregrounds individual parental responsibility. In these countries, often meagre welfare benefits for single parents are set with the assumption that mandated child support payments are received – and indeed, the receipt of child support often reduces the value of government benefit payments (Skinner et al, 2017). However, the responsibility for monitoring and reporting non-compliance with child support orders in these countries can lie with recipients, who in some cases must manage payment reporting to the state to ensure their correct benefit entitlements. Unpaid child support liabilities are not compensated for by the state, and the pursuance of arrears is positioned increasingly as the responsibility of recipients. In contrast, Nordic and Central European states can provide guaranteed child support payments in the event of non- or under-payment (OECD, 2011). In these cases, child support arrears are compensated for by the state, which then recoups payments from fathers. As such, compliance in countries with guaranteed payments is increasingly framed as the responsibility of the state.

However, systems such as those operating in the Caribbean (Wyss, 2001), Africa (Armstrong, 1992; Mokgoro, 2003; Khunou, 2006), Asia (Nor et al, 2018, 2019, 2020; Chung and Kim, 2019), the Pacific (Keil and Elizabeth, 2017, 2019) and Latin America (Cuesta and Meyer, 2014; Cuesta et al, 2018) provide useful insight into the gender norms and assumptions about the appropriate conduct of the state, mothers and fathers, and the financial support available to parents who occupy these roles. For example, in what stands as a socio-legal critique of Jamaica's child support system, Wyss (2001, p. 421) explains:

> Deep-seated notions of what types of conduct are 'appropriate' and of what types of outcomes are 'legitimate' … help regulate child support behaviour. The desire (or compulsion) to live up to social ideals of masculinity and femininity may motivate fathers' and mothers' child support behaviours, even when these ideals dictate actions that conflict with individual economic self-interest.

Returning to Skinner et al's claims regarding the socio-political and cultural basis of child support, the norms identified by Wyss apply far beyond the shores of Jamaica. Gender roles and the conduct appropriate to them provide the fundamental basis for child support across contexts (Natalier and Hewitt, 2014). Irrespective of – and often in spite of – child support formulae and their application, parents' conduct is deeply tied to what is positioned as appropriate and legitimate. As Wyss (2001, p. 421) goes on to explain, 'Jamaican parents make purposeful choices about supporting children within structures of constraint that include social norms and endogenous preferences, in addition to assets and formal rules'. While Wyss attributes parents' behaviour to purposeful choices within structures of constraint, I attribute more emphasis to the role of the state, which provides a guiding hand for how fathers and mothers should and are expected to behave – constraining their choices to the point of non-choice (Cook, 2021a). While child support may be legally available, it is not always pursued, or it is given up on because its enactment or enforcement is too difficult (Herd and Moynihan, 2018; Cook, 2021b).

The importance of child support to the state

As touched on in Chapter 1, I assert that child support has moved away from socialised protection to introduce individualised protection provided by the family. Whereas welfare states had previously intervened to provide protection for those without an adequate income (see Luzkow, 2016 for a history of the rollback of the wage-earners welfare state in the US), child support broke with traditions of socialised protection to place the onus back upon the family, albeit on separated family members where transfers were made from a non-resident breadwinner to a resident caregiver.

However, separated parents in liberal welfare regimes are not directed to seek support from their extended family, such as exists in 'familial' welfare regimes where the assumption is that the 'ties that bind' place moral and reciprocal obligations on extended family members to support their own (see Zelizer, 1994 for accounts of the expressive and moral dimensions of financial transfers within families). Rather, child support policy directs separated parents to seek support from a specific individual, namely the family's former breadwinner. Problematically, financially vulnerable mothers are directed to seek support from an individual who may hold little allegiance to them, personally, on behalf of their children. The assumption is that fathers' moral obligations to children will override parental differences, but research suggests that tensions and disagreement over fathers' responsibilities to their ex-partner continue to simmer just below the surface (Natalier and Hewitt, 2010; Municio, 2013; Natalier and Hewitt, 2014; Cook and Skinner, 2020). To maintain this problematic and tenuous, yet compulsory, relationship, states may intervene to compel the behaviour of one or more parties, or may turn a blind eye to the personal issues inherent in child support. How states respond, to which issues, and why, reveal the priorities of states, as well as norms and expectations for how children's care is provided and funded within society.

Positioning child support as a function of the welfare state also allows for an examination of deservingness. As Luzkow (2016) suggests, and as is described further in Chapter 6, the establishment of a successful welfare state is dependent upon the inclusion (and benefitting) of the middle classes, which he describes as 'levelling up'. While Luzkow does not examine gender within his analysis, the middle classes that he describes are male breadwinners and, by association, their dependant wives and children within the household that they support. Child support, however, is antithetical to this model of welfare state success, in that payments made beyond the household by separated fathers from the middle classes result in breadwinners' individualised 'levelling down'. As a result, middle class separated fathers in liberal welfare regimes have often been affronted by child support – and have been its most staunch opponents (Garfinkel et al, 1998; Kaye and Tolmie, 1998; Boyd, 2004; Cook and Skinner, 2019, 2020).

Luzkow (2016) identifies that the key feature of successful welfare state transfers is trust. I contend that in problematic cases, such trust is fundamentally absent from child support, thus undermining the programme's social acceptability. As Luzkow (2016) describes, to socialise welfare benefits and collect taxes to pay for them, there needs to be a shared understanding and trust. In the individualised realm of child support, however, fathers' trust over how mothers spend 'their' money is a key battleground (Khunou, 2006; Natalier and Hewitt, 2014; Cozzolino and Williams, 2017; Goodall and Cook, 2020). To compel child support payments within this context requires increasingly more complex and technical solutions to manage fathers' concerns and enforce payments. The increasingly individualised and technical nature of child support thus diverges further away from the socialised benefits and nature of a welfare state that Luzkow describes. Rather, the introduction of child support has re-individualised welfare state support for separated mothers. This has reasserted men's financial autonomy and authority over separated mothers' finances, which has in turn made way for incremental reforms that render child support increasingly technical. In the most extreme cases, under the guise of 'helping parents', child support has been rendered entirely personal. This can result in decoupling child support from welfare, as in the UK, or can leave women's welfare benefit determinations beholden to men's financial discretion, as in Australia. How these tensions have been managed by states – including states avoiding managing these issues – is an example of gendered governance practice.

In the US, as Case et al (2003, p. 171) noted almost two decades ago, 'child support has become an increasingly important policy instrument for reducing economic insecurity among single mothers and their children'. However, more recently, Cuesta and Meyer (2018) note that the purpose of child support in the US (as well as in Colombia) is not explicitly focused on reducing child poverty. Rather, they argue that for resident parents receiving public assistance, for whom seeking child support is mandatory, 'the focus is generally on recovering public costs' (Cuesta and Meyer, 2018, p. 144). Indeed, at the time that child support guidelines were being drawn up in the US (for an overview see Elrod, 1990), Hunter (1983, p. 15) remarked that 'indeed it was a reaction to the increasing costs of AFDC [Aid to Families with Dependent Children] and the desire to cut back expenses, rather than social alarm over the plight of mothers raising children with insufficient support amounts, that led to most of the current attention to issues of child support enforcement'.

The history of the child support system in the US reveals how the interests of the government were prioritised over the interests of poor women and their children. Similarly, while Australia's child support policy was originally introduced as a child poverty reduction measure, this aim was subsequently removed from the scheme in favour of a welfare state expenditure reduction measure. However, while some may argue that fathers' interests were relegated to below those of mothers and children, compliance rates and commentary during the early era of child support tell another story. Across countries, fathers have often been able to evade their responsibilities to children, particularly if they are able to minimise their taxable incomes. In the US, for example, the severe penalty of incarceration for non-compliance is reserved almost exclusively for impoverished men of colour (Cozzolino and Williams, 2017), while middle class men may operate outside of punitive state surveillance.

Changing gender roles and the gender of child support

Across countries, regimes and systems, child support is inherently tied to gender roles and how the costs of children can be covered when the primary breadwinner is absent from the household. As Goonesekere (2006, p. 361) notes: 'Maintenance legislation that is intended to promote accountability and the fulfillment of a male head of household's obligation to provide for a spouse and children thus often fails to achieve this objective. However, it reinforces gender-biased legal values on male and female familial responsibility.' While many countries have moved towards a partial dissolution of gender roles that has seen women's access to income grow, women typically remain the primary carer. Upon separation, mothers either need to access affordable childcare to allow them to work or reduce their employment to allow them to care. Thus, the child support literature has repeatedly acknowledged the gender relations and inequities that underpin the need for child support law and policy.

> [South African] men have more than their share of financial resources, including greater access to jobs, education, land, and so on. Therefore, if the maintenance of children is left in the hands of women alone, the children will suffer simply because they have less access to wealth. (Armstrong, 1992, p. 220)

> It is not for the child support system to 'fix' gender inequality, as these structural issues run much deeper than the Band-Aid solution provided by distributing income from a breadwinner to a caregiver post-separation. However, until Australian policies can more meaningfully grapple with the gendered distribution of earning and caring responsibilities in society, child support will remain a flashpoint for challenging seemingly 'unfair' gender relations that are impossible to resolve using this policy instrument. (Cook and Skinner, 2019, p. 184)

When parents separate, it is most typically, and indeed overwhelmingly, the mother who assumes the majority of care, reflecting the deeply gendered distribution of work and care that occurs in most families prior to separation. The distribution of care-time has shifted slowly over recent decades, but it is still very far from equal. Even if mothers and fathers assumed equal time with children post-separation, my recent work with Christine Skinner (Cook and Skinner, 2019) outlines why child support would still need to be transferred to ensure that children shared equitably in their parents' incomes. Due to their caregiving responsibilities, mothers face significant opportunity costs that reduce their ability to earn. In addition, the gendered structure of work and care prior to separation serves to fragment and erode women's labour market attachment, making it more difficult for separated mothers to piece together a living wage from employment alone. Finally, in all OECD countries, women experience a gendered pay gap (OECD, 2020) where, within the industries they tend to work in, and even within the same industries as men, women typically receive less income than their male counterparts. As a result, single-mother-headed families are one of the most disadvantaged family types, internationally. In some respects, crises such as the COVID-19 pandemic have further entrenched these gendered positions, with women undertaking additional care work and foregoing employment at much higher rates than men (Craig, 2020; Workplace Gender Equality Agency, 2020; Collins et al, 2021). However, emerging research from the UK, for example, shows that COVID-19 furloughs have also offered the opportunity for fathers to renegotiate their caring roles (Tarrant et al, 2020).

In addition to the changing expectations placed on carers to secure their own income, care-time and family forms are also becoming more fluid as social roles and structures dissolve. The complexity and diversity of families has implications for the successful technical management of child support. With changing expectations regarding how care is funded, separated mothers are now expected to enter the paid labour market. However, women's increasing labour market activity in turn complicates child support. The distribution of parental labour across households no longer neatly reflects the male breadwinner/female caregiver gender division on which the child support system was originally built and sought to reproduce. In addition, as work evolves into increasingly deregulated, deindustrialised and de-unionised forms (Standing, 2011), the stable, reliable and predictable income on which child support calculations are based also begins to erode. Crises such as COVID-19 expose the precarious nature of child support calculations and payments. Given the nature of existing child support formulae, falling wages and insecure incomes will result in one of two outcomes: either lowered child support obligations that may or may not be compensated for by increased state benefits; or constant child support obligations that are less able (and thus less likely) to be paid. As Chapter 7 describes, increasing the technical precision of child support calculations allows for 'real-time' responses to income fluctuations, but such technical complexity has gendered and material effects.

Mirroring women's entry into the labour market and men's entry into the home, care across households is also far more complex than the previous male breadwinner/female caregiver segregation of these roles and children's care within them. With non-standard, gig economy, sub-contracted and increasingly precarious work intensifying, care could more easily be – and in some cases needs to be – shared across households. But such unpredictable work schedules also complicate and render unworkable the child support formulae that are based on predictable and enduring care patterns to determine how much money needs to be exchanged to compensate for the opportunity costs of care. This is a fundamental problem of monetising care. Increasing complexity in family relationships that have followed parental decoupling and recoupling add another moving part. What is of relevance for child support, however, is that welfare states have been unable to keep pace with the rapid configurations in work, care and families, as they have been unable to imagine what policies are required to protect vulnerable citizens in these futures. Both prior to and in response to the COVID-19 crisis, a Universal Basic Income (UBI) has been floated as the panacea. However, while a UBI foregrounds the valuation and recognition of socially reproductive care-work as child support intended, and could mitigate child poverty, it cannot deliver reductions to welfare state expenditure and is silent on enforcing parental responsibility. As such, it cannot deliver the panacea that policymakers so desperately desire.

While a UBI is a solution to a different policy problem, solutions to child support problems have also been identified and implemented worldwide. These solutions are rendered acceptable and thus made possible by jettisoning one or even two of the aims of child support outlined by the OECD (2011). The aims that have been most easily jettisoned are those that align least with the state's neoliberal interests: namely recognising and valuing socially reproductive labour in ways that promote gender equality in income and care work; redistributing money to reduce child poverty; and enforcing (non-resident) parental responsibility. Viewed through this lens, policy development in child support becomes understandable as an intervention to reduce welfare expenditure at the expense of resolving the gender inequities that necessitated the system in the first place. Such policy interventions are legitimised by converting social problems, which require systems-scale solutions such as financial redistribution and gender equity, into technical problems to be managed by more complex formulae, or personal problems to be managed privately. In this way, the original social problems that child support sought to resolve, most notably single mother and child poverty, are rendered invisible, or worse – as will be explored with respect to the UK, which effectively dismantled its child support system in favour of private transfers – are actively used to defend policy changes that achieve the opposite.

Considering the complexity of income, care-time and family forms

Across the various child support systems existing in legal, administrative or hybrid regimes (Skinner et al, 2007), numerous features of family and economic life are taken into consideration. In order to determine the share of the non-resident parent's income that children in such systems are entitled to, an assessment of income is required, typically for the non-resident parent. In some systems, the income of the recipient parent is also required, so as to determine an equitable proportion of funds to be provided by each party. As I will elaborate on later, systems that rely only on the non-resident parent's income adhere closely to a male-breadwinner model of family relations. Here, men are assumed to be the income earners and women the carers. This gendered model of the division of household labour does not deviate following the breakdown of the gender contract upon separation.

Countries that include both parents' incomes – which were later modifications to original child support formulae – take a fundamentally different approach to gender relations, positioning both parents as possible earners and carers. However, the cultural norms prevailing in these countries often have not moved as fast as child support policy reform. For example, Australia, New Zealand, the UK and the US, where such 'income shares' models dominate (Skinner et al, 2017), are far from gender-equal. Nordic countries are far more gender-equal, but some Nordic countries, such as Iceland and Finland, do not consider both parents' incomes in the determination of child support (Eydal and Friðriksdóttir, 2012; Hakovirta et al, 2020). What child support says about parents' 'appropriate' gender roles post-separation, and what child support is recognising with respect to what parents 'ought to' do, is a central feature of this book.

By responding to parents' respective share of income, and thus capacity to pay, 'income shares' systems need to be perpetually responsive to changes in parents' earnings. In an era of the 'gig economy' (Friedman, 2014), where wages are unpredictable, the male wage-earner model on which child support is predicated becomes difficult to manage. How income fluctuations are managed within child support systems can reveal what 'problems' the technical workings of a child support system seek to resolve (Bacchi, 2009). Systems that respond in real time to fluctuations in earnings can be seen as attentive to the problem of payer capacity. However, by addressing the problem of capacity to pay, the problem of children's need at any given time is diminished. Here, interactions with the benefit system become paramount, as they can either make up for a shortfall in expected child support income within children's households, or they can be unconcerned. Unpacking how child support is configured, and why, can tell us a lot about where children in single-parent families are expected to source an income, and how realistic and adequate these sources are.

In addition to parents' relative share of income, some child support systems take into consideration the proportion of time that children spend with each parent. Here, payments can be scaled to reflect the distribution of time, and thus costs, borne by each parent. Again, there are inconsistencies and contradictions across countries. For example, Hakovirta et al (2020) compare Australia and Finland. Australia's deeply unequal societal distribution of care-time pre- and post-separation flies in the face of its recognition of care-time in the child support formula. By contrast, Finland has much more equal sharing of care, but does not recognise this within its child support determinations. Again, these findings illustrate what each country considers to be an appropriate valuation of the work associated with particular gender roles. They also illustrate the appropriateness of women's work and men's care through the recognition of their income and care-time in child support formulae. In this instance, however, it is the inclusion or omission of each parent's share of care that illustrates the extent to which paternal care is deemed appropriate and thus valued financially within child support calculations. The systems that do include the distribution of care as a consideration then require data on the distribution and take-up of care-time when making and administering child support orders.

Finally, in addition to the distribution of income and care-time between parents, some systems also take into consideration the other children that each parent is financially responsible for. These considerations may include whether additional children live in the parent's home as part of a new dual-parent family, or whether they live elsewhere, and as such to whom additional child support orders apply. Some systems, particularly those operating in some states of the US, simply add the value of each new child support order and require the non-resident parent to pay them all. As a result, in the US, fathers with multiple child support orders may face impossibly high child support payments. The failure to pay orders can result in imprisonment, which is a punishment that has been disproportionately applied to poor African American fathers (Lerman, 2010; Cozzolino and Williams, 2017; Cozzolino, 2018). Thus, as described by Cozzolino and Williams (2017), the governance of child support can be seen to have racial as well as classed and gendered dimensions.

In court-based jurisdictions, which operate in many US states, but also predominate internationally, it is not clear how additional dependants are taken into consideration in setting child support orders; these decisions are often at the judge's discretion and rely on payers providing sufficient evidence to support their claims. How to consider children born after the determination of a child support order is also unclear, but raises significant symbolic and empirical questions. In jurisdictions that do take into consideration all of the payer's dependants, child support orders can be scaled across households, so that each payee receives less, but the payer has the capacity to pay the total amount. Likewise, the addition of new children to the payer's household can also reduce the amount payable to previous children in non-resident households. While 'affordability' is being prioritised, what does the lesser amount say about the purpose of child support in recipient families? Administratively, across all systems that set liabilities with respect to the totality of the payers' dependants, decision-makers then require information on the number and residential arrangements of dependants, which may change over time as new children are born and if these new relationships dissolve.

In western liberal democracies, such as the UK, Australia and the US, the growth and increasing technical complexity of child support policies align with the rollback of redistributive welfare state programmes and ideologies. Child support now serves as a punitive mechanism for the governance of separated mothers while reducing state expenditure on them and their households. As family, financial and cultural norms rapidly reconfigure, child support is at the core of state responses to balance the competing aims of reducing child poverty, enforcing parental financial responsibility for children and reducing welfare state expenditure. Within this context, I argue that it is useful to regard changes to child support policy and administration as governance practices that compel or urge separated mothers in particular to undertake some behaviours and forego others. These governance practices entrench gender inequity through the erosion of transfers across households while at the same time requiring more from women in the management of their own inequity.

As outlined earlier, in many western countries, single parent welfare benefit recipients (who are overwhelmingly women) are compelled to seek child support as a condition of eligibility. Women are thus made responsible for seeking and managing payments, which serve to reduce welfare state expenditure and enforce fathers' financial responsibility for children. Yet, in some countries, child support orders are becoming less likely (Harris, 2015; Meyer et al, 2015). In the US, increases in shared care, the narrowing of parents' relative incomes, and greater freedom to choose whether to engage in state child support systems accounted for approximately half of the decline in child support orders in Wisconsin between 1996–98 and 2004–07 (Meyer et al, 2015). In Australia, qualitative research has reported that in the face of mandatory child support seeking, mothers are willing to accept fewer benefits than they are entitled to in order to avoid the harms that child support may expose them to (McKenzie and Cook, 2015), while US research in the 1990s found that more than half of women compelled to seek child support had withheld details of their child's father so as to avoid the child support system (Edin, 1995). Women may avoid payments for many reasons, often linked to the enforcement of familial ties and the individualisation of responsibility for managing payments. For example, establishing orders, seeking payments, or reporting non-compliance may lock women into unwanted relationships, place them at greater risk of violence, entail onerous administrative demands or renew custody disputes. Child support institutions, however, are often insensitive to such issues, which tend to disadvantage women and their children along class and sometimes racial lines. Existing scholarship provides little guidance for policy development in this area; women's reasons for child support avoidance are largely unacknowledged in research. As a result of such avoidance, the significant poverty reduction benefits that child support payments can provide are foregone.

Where child support law and policy has sought to intervene in gendered social relations, as I propose was the case when administrative child support schemes were first introduced to improve compliance – and save the state money – in liberal welfare states, they have faced significant backlash. In these countries, technical modifications have offered some recalibration of formulae to reinforce the extant gender order. At other times, such as in the UK, Sweden and in Australia's private collection model, child support systems have been significantly reduced, to return arrangements to a somewhat 'pre-child support system' state of affairs. Such systems ignore the existence of gendered interactions (Risman, 2004), positioning often poorer and more dependent resident mothers on equal footing with wealthier, independent, non-resident fathers from whom they seek payments. The underpinning neoliberal assumptions about each parent's autonomy, capacity and motivation are seriously flawed. However, countries that have moved towards private agreements hold such payments up as the gold standard of post-separation relations, where parents mutually agree to work in the children's best interests of their own accord (Fernqvist and Sépulchre, 2021). The UK has even gone so far as to effectively disband the Child Support Agency (CSA), requiring parents to pay fees if they wish to return to the skeleton system. While critiques of private payments have emerged, particularly for families with histories of payer control and abuse (Cook, 2013; Allbeson, 2017), the move towards private payments and arrangements, internationally, has continued. In this book, I locate these trends within a conceptual framework that makes them comprehensible and explainable from a gender perspective. The task is then to identify the consequences that the expansion of neoliberal assumptions about autonomy, capacity and motivation bring into socially embedded areas of life, such as child support.

The strong promotion of, and even compulsory move towards, private child support agreements by a number of states with 'high functioning' administrative and legal systems identifies the state's interest in shaping how child support policy is enacted and how such administration is gendered. What Skinner et al's (2007) typology adds to such an analysis is insight into the trends facing child support in some of the most advanced systems. In their concluding remarks the authors note that,

> In all countries parents could make private agreements and this may sometimes have been the preferred and promoted method with the formal system acting mainly as a back up should parents be unable to agree or where there is non-compliance. Parents' choice to make private agreements however varied, especially by their social benefit status. For example, in Australia, Canada (Ontario), the Netherlands, New Zealand, UK and the USA, if they were in receipt of social assistance this limited their freedom to choose a private agreement. (Skinner et al, 2007, p. 45)

While the benefits of private agreements across countries were noted as being more consensual, non-adversarial, relatively quick and inexpensive and tailored to family circumstances, the disadvantages of such systems were identified as follows:

> National informants noted that private arrangements in some countries had no legal standing – could be precarious unless ratified; they could also exacerbate any power imbalance between the parents with the weaker party potentially being pressured into an agreement that was not in their or their children's best interests. Additionally, they could produce inequitable outcomes where children in different families with similar circumstances/characteristics could receive differing amounts. (Skinner et al, 2007, p. 46)

Critical reflection on the gendered social processes that tie together these benefits and risks suggests that the benefits of private agreements may be achieved through gendered compromises. Here, women may acquiesce in order to avoid hostility, which may be taken by their ex-partners and the state as active and informed consent. Rather than principles of equity, the benefits of child support systems to the state, in terms of their reduced administrative costs and less money spent on enforcement, may be more influential in shaping the nature of child support regimes. It is these issues that I now turn to explore.

4

Sites of child support failure

In this chapter, I draw on the international child support literature, as well as key informant interviews, to define and illustrate the points at which child support 'fails'. I do so in order to provide an account of the common sites of dysfunction across systems, be they in advanced liberal welfare states, developing child support systems or social democratic welfare regimes. My focus on failure is not meant to be taken as proof that child support never works. On the contrary, there are many instances across countries where child support works well and lifts single-mother-headed families out of poverty. However, there is less to be learnt from a focus on success than there is from a focus on failure. My aim here is to examine when child support does not work and why. My contention is that while child support laws, policies and programmes vary widely, they all share one feature: they often do not work as a mechanism to transfer payments from a non-resident parent to a resident parent for the purpose of supporting children post-separation. Rather, child support systems often operate as a 'leaky pipeline' (Pell, 1996; Clark Blickenstaff, 2005) where separated mothers fall out of the system at some point, resulting in payments either not being made or received. At times, mothers are prevented from accessing systems. At other times, systems fail to act or fail to ensure that payments are transferred. The points of child support failure are then taken up in the subsequent chapters that examine how these failures come to be seen or remain unseen (Chapter 5) and why (Chapter 6), and how child support has been managed in increasingly technical (Chapter 7) and personalised (Chapter 8) ways.

Again, by focusing on the leaky pipeline of child support, I am not claiming that systems never work. Indeed, some countries have highly functional systems that determine, order and transfer payments. However, even within high-functioning systems, problems occur. My concern is that by foregrounding what works, what does *not* work and who child support does not work for is lost. The reality that a number of women make their way successfully through the child support system to actually receive payments obscures the reality of all those never made it in, or who fell out along the way. For a proportion – often less than half of the caseload, based on figures from the OECD (2011) and other sources (Hakovirta, 2011) – the system works, and these cases are held up by governments and studied by researchers as examples of system function. But the focus on the positive case denies the reality of the negative case – women who are excluded from government records and research datasets because they did not make it into the child support system or did not have any payments to record. As a result, child support systems rely on evidence of what is within their system as evidence of their system's functioning. At the same time, what is not within the system is not recorded and as such does not provide an account of system dysfunction. Japan provides a case in point. According to my key informant on the Japanese system, approximately half of couples with children do not include child support orders in their divorce proceedings. Standalone court proceedings to determine child support post hoc were also reported to be extremely rare. This left women without child support orders, and without a means of establishing a need for a new system.

> 'The divorce without agreeing on child support is the most problematic part, I think. Because if they agree – you know in Japan they are very compliant. I mean if they agree, yeah, many people will follow, will comply. So, I mean they have to agree when they divorce, and we have to encourage them. Maybe if we can change our system, at least when they have children they have to go to court. I mean, they have to have an agreement – I mean, without that agreement, they cannot divorce. Such a system would be advisable.' (Japan)

Without a critical focus on the problems with child support, improvements are unlikely – especially improvements that take note of women's concerns and seek to address them.

For some parents, the state intervenes to compel agreements or quarantine payments. For others, however, state child support systems are superfluous. The Norwegian state of affairs is illustrative here:

> 'I mean, people are dissatisfied with it [child support] because no one likes to pay. Yeah, [but these are the] cases we see. Like I said, about 50 per cent have an agreement and it works perfectly fine and we don't see them. The other 50 per cent have not been able to agree. So, they're going to be more of an issue, I guess. But I don't find it highly problematic. I think most parents … it's something that they have to pay when they separate. Yeah, they're okay with us deciding [the amount of child support to be paid].' (Norway)

For 50 per cent of families in Norway, they have agreed on payment terms privately and the state is not involved. From the state's perspective, these agreements 'work perfectly fine'. As I set out in this chapter, however, the fact that 50 per cent of families have made an agreement privately does not mean that child support is necessarily received. It may be the case in Norway that some of these families are just not complaining. Similarly, for the 50 per cent of families who needed the state to help them agree on payment terms, this does not mean that the agreement will be followed. What is of interest in this book is what happens when parents cannot or will not work in children's best interests. As '*no one* likes to pay', what happens when fathers – as the de-gendered payers in the Norwegian example – do not accept state processes, or seek to avoid their responsibilities? Where does this leave mothers? How can they find agency within the tight spaces afforded in their relationship with ex-partners and the state? In the context of guaranteed payments in Norway, how accurate are claims that 'it works perfectly fine'? As the following chapters examine in more detail, in such cases, what do states see as the problems of child support, what is done to address payment concerns, and how are the needs, experiences and interests of women included within child support system design? For now, however, attention turns to identifying the sites where child support rhetoric may not match reality, especially when viewed from the perspective of women.

The failures identified here are derived from both 'high-functioning' systems, depicted as existing within liberal welfare states and Nordic regimes, but also from less well-developed systems operating in Latin American, Asian, African and Middle Eastern contexts. However, the purpose is not to mark out less advanced systems as inferior or in need of reform. Indeed, the analysis pursued here and throughout the subsequent chapters identifies marked similarities in the failures, and structures of power, that exist in seemingly advanced and less well-developed systems. Indeed, it is the ubiquitous nature of child support failure across contexts, countries and systems described by interview participants that led to this analysis. Irrespective of purported intention, design or reform, there was no magic bullet – beyond fathers' willingness – to make child support work and ensure that mothers and their children received support. Within child support systems, irrespective of design, men's payment behaviour often lay just beyond state control.

The leaky pipeline of child support

Following the masculinist worldview that shapes law, policy, administration, science and research, often disguised in gender-neutral language, what is known and unknown about child support is similarly 'framed by political and social power' (Clark Blickenstaff, 2005, p. 383). This worldview affects what data child support administrators and governments collect, and how such data are interpreted. As Pell's (1996, p. 2843) analysis of the leaky pipeline of female academics described, 'constant repetition [of success] gives credibility to otherwise unsupported assertions'. Here, the data that are collected about child support systems buttress the status quo by allowing the repetition of concepts that serve the system, such as focusing on caseloads, order values and compliance targets. What is unknown is who does not enter the child support system, who is not reporting failures of the system and how the system is failing. Sweden's reports of 'full compliance' despite the state providing guaranteed payments in instances of non-compliance (OECD, 2011), and Australia's assertion that all privately collected payments are fully compliant (Ministerial Taskforce on Child Support, 2005), are illustrative of such repetitions and the erasure of failure. The argument pursued here is that while official statistics or taken-for-granted knowledge 'demonstrate' how well child support works, systems are often configured, or are reconfigured, in ways that promote or reinforce gendered hierarchies of masculine authority and autonomy, sometimes without making any substantive difference to the lives, agency and autonomy of separated mothers and their children who are the purported beneficiaries of the child support system.

While child support systems can often compel mothers' engagement, systems are regularly designed in ways that produce failure in all but the most amicable relationships or easy-to-collect payment cases. In other contexts, women's access to the child support system may be hampered from the outset as gender norms, structural barriers or interpersonal relationships prevent women from even entering the leaky pipe. The remainder of this chapter sets out a child support process, conceptualised as a pipeline running from system entry to payment receipt, and maps women's experiences onto this in order to identify where women may 'fall out' along the way. The child support process onto which academic research and interview data are mapped is largely artificial, as part of the problem is that many countries do not have one or several of the steps identified. The steps in the process are taken from Australia's highly complex, yet purportedly 'simple', eight-step system (Services Australia, 2020).

The failures, or places where women 'fall out' of the system, as outlined in this chapter, do three main things. They can: 1) resign separated mothers to not seeking child support, due to the lack of systems, the difficultly accessing these or the futility of the process; 2) compel separated mothers to seek child support but fail to consistently deliver on their efforts; or 3) assuage separated mothers' immediate financial needs through the provision of guaranteed payments, but in doing so normatively and effectively limit separated fathers' responsibilities to children following separation. These processes render child support systems inaccessible, inactive or irresponsible in ways that condone the failure to uphold children's right to financial support from both of their parents. To support these claims, in this chapter I examine the points at which women are deterred from entering or proceeding within the child support systems. The purposes of the following sections are to identify how child support systems work, but more fundamentally, to also identify when they do not work and why. The barriers to child support that women face are structural, technical and personal. The barriers focused on here are not intended to suggest that women have no agency in the child support process.

However, documenting women's experiences and action within the child support pipeline would require significant, additional data, and thus lie outside the remit of this book. As such, in the following sections, I focus on what each point in the process entails and how the structural, technical and personal barriers that women face align to produce the outcomes identified previously.

Barriers to entry

One of the most fundamental barriers to accessing the child support system is whether women know that the system exists. Interviews with key informants on non-mandatory systems revealed that child support was often not widely advertised or understood. For example, in Japan, most separating couples do not know that child support can be combined with divorce proceedings, as the family law informant explained:

> 'In Japan, the divorce can be made by agreement and so they don't go to court. I mean almost 90 per cent of the couples don't go to the court for divorce. So, they just can agree on divorce without determining anything about the child support. That is a very important part. So, without determining anything, and after some time, if a mother was to have child support, she has to contact the ex-husband and that's a difficult thing. … Recently there is a non-profit organisation which gives advice about the system and they encourage the mother to go to court to get child support. So that's – I mean more people will know how to get child support now. But still some people don't want to go to court to get child support.' (Japan)

In those countries without mandatory entry into child support as a result of welfare benefit receipt, it is entirely at women's discretion as to whether they enter the system or not. For example, in Peru, the academic informant notes:

> 'Fortunately, in Peru we're like – it's not related to your – to any – the welfare system, which I think is okay … because there might be some real cases in which the other person was so violent they don't want to keep contact with them. So, they have to – they should be – they should have the right to just decide they don't want to.' (Peru)

Even if women are not deterred from seeking child support by violent ex-partners, they are still subject to the leaky pipeline. Here, the adversarial and privatised nature of the system, irrespective of whether it is court-based or administrative, can see women exit without a child support order in place. However, rather than the type of system, I contend that it is the degree of compulsion that makes child support adversarial or not. When all parents are entered into the system, and entered into a uniform system (be it legal or administrative), then child support becomes a routine and normalised expectation placed on separating parents. For example, there are countries where all separated parents are entered into court or administrative processes as a matter of course, but these 'routinised' processes only apply to previously married parents:

> 'Child maintenance is a criterion for divorce to be granted in Malta. Another thing is that the court may also apply out of its own motion, even if the mother doesn't ask for maintenance.' (Malta)

> 'Well, in Portugal it's relatively simple … child maintenance in cases of divorce is mandatory by law … it doesn't even have to be one of the parents to start proceedings when there may be risk or an issue which may affect the child's well-being. In those cases, the institution that represents the children's welfare and the children's well-being is the public prosecution. It may be the public prosecutor of the area of residence of the child to start proceedings either for what we call parental responsibilities to be established and custody to be regulated in which child maintenance is included.' (Portugal)

For never-married mothers, the pathways into child support are more difficult, as Boyd et al (2015) have described in historical perspective. They describe the constraints that never-married mothers faced in such countries as the UK, US and Canada; however, similar barriers continue to exist across a range of countries. For never-married mothers, women either have to actively seek out child support, or – in a more limited number of settings – have child support imposed on them by welfare systems. The point to be taken in this chapter, however, is that when child support system processes are not standardised, and thus do not render child support as a 'normal' obligation imposed upon all non-resident parents to uphold their children's rights, then women's entry into the system is less likely.

In a context of ad hoc processes, the responsibility for pursuing payments rests upon women, who are typically the more vulnerable member of the ex-couple dyad. When multiple pathways to seeking child support exist, such as making private arrangements, going to court or seeking an administrative determination, women's entry into a 'formal system' can be read as one party – namely women – being 'difficult' and imposing conditions on the other. Such sentiment was found across contexts, again, irrespective of the formal organisational structure of the child support system. A Portuguese family lawyer provides an illustrative example of their system, despite child maintenance orders being previously described as mandatory in divorce cases:

> 'The problem is that child support is mandatory by law, unless you can agree [privately with your ex-partner]. When people get divorced or each go their own way, if they're separated, they can either agree and then that's fine. One [person] starts paying. Or they don't agree, and you have two options, either they don't agree and … you just don't want to be bothered or you need to apply to the courts. There's always this step of having to apply to the courts. What happens in practical terms is … usually children stay with their mother, this is when they're separated. Unfortunately, a lot of fathers don't pay child support because the mothers are – people are still a bit afraid of the courts and they don't like the courts and having to go to court and being involved in proceedings. They [women] just leave it and just pay for everything themselves … they can either go to the public prosecutor and make a complaint. The public prosecutor will issue proceedings. I think people, either because they don't know they have this right, they don't know that child maintenance is mandatory or just because they don't want to be involved with the courts, I don't know, out of fear, discomfort, whatever.' (Portugal)

As the aforementioned examples illustrate, the design of child support systems and processes may mean that women are prevented from accessing them. Even when court processes are entered, however, unless these are state-funded, they are likely to be prohibitive to the less wealthy party. This is almost always the encumbered, caregiving mother vis-à-vis the unencumbered, breadwinning father.

In some countries, such as Portugal and Malta, the state can initiate child support action on parents' behalf. However, in most countries, there is no compulsion to enter the child support system, illustrating the first point in the leaky pipeline of child support. While I am not suggesting that women should be *forced* to engage with child support, for many women, the fact that there is a child support system is often irrelevant. By contrast, in advanced welfare states, or at least in countries where child support has implications for welfare eligibility and payment amounts, entry into the child support system is often compulsory, as the following US state-level administrator describes. However, even when women were required to begin child support proceedings as part of their welfare benefit application, this does not mean that child support will easily follow.

> 'Sometimes the welfare department will refer cases over [to the child support agency] and they have to fill out a "screen" – that's terrible language – they call it the "absent parent screen". But they fill out the screen and they can't continue on in the [welfare] eligibility process

until they put an entry on there. So, they've become creative with doing things like "comma", "comma", "unknown", "unknown", just to type something in so it comes over. Then our staff have to begin detective work. The trickiest part at the beginning of opening the case – so the mom has no say in this – I mean, it comes over to us automatically. The trickiest part for us, and the most challenging part, is figuring out who the putative father is to track him down, to find out here he lives. Then, if we can do that, if we have enough information, then we can move the process along and actually serve him with a summons and complaint which lets him know that we plan to take him to court.' (US, state level)

However, such compulsory engagement in child support is waning. Several 'leading' liberal – and even Nordic – welfare states have limited women's ability to enter the very child support systems that were designed to support them while simultaneously reducing welfare expenditure. As a federal US administrator described:

'Our census data, which is collected through survey panels, and census forms, find a rise over the last ten years or so in the number of custodial parents who say they're not seeking an order for child support in the first place because the other parent can't pay, or he's paying informally, he or she – whatever – to the best of their ability. That number, that percentage of parents who say they're not seeking an order for those economic reasons has gone up in the last ten years according to census data. In addition, there continues to be a cooperation requirement that mandatory or compelled participation [to seek child support] in the public assistance programme. But the public [assistance programme] is TANF [Temporary Aid for Needy Families]. But TANF has gotten – TANF caseloads are very small now. The policy over the last – since 1996 – has systematically reduced the eligibility and attractiveness, if you will, of participating in the TANF programme. So that TANF caseload, that mandatory caseload, always was sort of the foundation of the child support programme when the child support programme was set up here in the US in 1975. But the large majority of families in the caseload were mandatory public assistance participants. Now it's just a sliver of participants. The child support caseload is going down pretty rapidly in lock-step with the decline in the public assistance caseload.' (US, federal level)

The (re)privatisation of the responsibility for children – and thus the state's role in child support in English-speaking countries – harkens back to the Poor Laws of 1576 and their subsequent amendments (Boyd et al, 2015). These laws sought to reduce the state's financial burden by locating responsibility elsewhere. However, while 'the family' was rendered responsible, mothers of illegitimate children were unable to apply to have fathers provide support. Amendments in 1834 allowed mothers of illegitimate children to seek support from fathers, but mothers did not receive any of the monies obtained (Boyd et al, 2015) – similar to the state's clawback of child support in modern schemes when a mother is in receipt of benefit payments. During the Poor Law era, the state took issue with mothers' marital status, supporting the withholding of child support money so as not to reward 'bad women' for their moral transgressions. Today's moral transgression that supports the state's withholding of child support money is mothers' financial dependence on the state. In both cases, 'bad women' are being disciplined. However, while keeping women in their place is one outcome, an overriding factor when determining child support obligations is ensuring that men are not unduly or unjustly burdened. As Boyd et al (2015, p. 67) noted with respect to early-20th-century Canadian child support history, 'no man should have an order for maintenance made against him unjustly, and the aim was not to afford a woman opportunities to blackmail a man'. These same undercurrents of mothers' untrustworthiness and fathers' right to autonomy continue.

Making child support application a condition of welfare eligibility in Australia, the US and Canada often forces separated mothers to commence child support action, irrespective of their wishes. The compulsory nature of child support also exposes governments' interests in cost-shifting the expense of supporting separated mothers away from the state and onto individual fathers. These relations and their disciplinary forces apply most readily to formerly nuclear families, excluding other forms of familial, economic and social relations, such as Indigenous Australian family relationships which Tam, Findlay and Cohen (2017) have described to disrupt colonial conventions, or separated Pacific Islander families described by Kiel and Elizabeth (2019), to name but a few. Atkin (1994, p. 632) similarly noted the colonial and westernised family norms underpinning the establishment of the New Zealand system in 1991, where a large Maori and Pacific Islander population exists:

> The Child Support Act of 1991 is similar to the Children, Young Persons and Their Families Act of 1989 in that it emphasizes the responsibilities of families to care for their children, in this case financially, but unlike the 1989 Act, the notion of family contained within the Child Support Act is not that of the whanau or wider family group, but of the nuclear family, with the obligations under the Act being imposed almost exclusively on biological or adoptive parents.

Returning to the barriers to child support entry that women experience, given the state's involvement in governing family forms, one of the first barriers they encounter is whether they are eligible to enter the system on the basis of their previous relationship status. When a father has not signed the child's birth certificate, establishing paternity is key to commencing the child support process (Armstrong, 1992; Hansen, 1999; Case et al, 2003; Goonesekere, 2006; Cuesta et al, 2018). In many countries, there are procedures for determining parentage depending on whether parents were married (and in some cases cohabiting) prior to separation. For never-married parents, or where paternity is disputed, genetic testing can be costly, and can in some cases prove prohibitive for single-mother-headed families in most need of financial support. Here, never-married mothers then face additional barriers to child support, particularly when fathers do not willingly participate and court orders are required. A US state-level informant described why paternal information may not be included on initial child support application information that is collected during welfare-eligibility assessments:

> 'It's not the applicant, it's the worker. What we know – and I used to – I ran the welfare department before I came here, many years ago. The eligibility workers do not feel – and I'm generalising here – but in answer to your question, they do not believe it is their responsibility to delve into personal information concerning conception of the child. … The other [reason for not collecting paternity information] is oftentimes quite frankly the mom has been threatened – I'm sure you've heard this before – has been threatened by the dad. "Don't get me hooked up with those people or with the government, so lie or tell them you don't know who the father is." Sometimes that's why we get the "comma, comma", it'll be "unknown, unknown" [in the form's response boxes asking for the father's first and last names].' (US, state level)

Hellum (2000) illustrates the gender of legal systems that prioritise – or inadvertently buttress through ineffective institutions – the autonomy and authority of separated fathers over the needs and rights of mothers and their children. In Peru, similar barriers were evident due to weak institutions, the result often being that separated mothers are unable to claim or enforce their child support entitlements.

> 'We have a hybrid process for – actually, they try first to motivate women to have a private agreement, but in case of court those – and, usually, those tend to work with couples that are divorcing or separating. I think when they were not a couple, a long-term couple, then they tend to go directly through to the court. I think it's more how it works. That's not a rule or anything. It's just that's how things work. Then they have to go to the court. They make a demand and they assign them – they

can do it without a lawyer, but it's still – in many cases – especially for low income women – it's very hard to know which is the procedure that they should follow. Because there are so many women who are making the demand, then it is very hard for the court to follow all the cases. … The main issue that we have is institutional. Our institutions are very weak, very – we don't have enough people to provide assistance to all the women who need it.' (Peru)

These legal barriers to child support exist even in systems with 'high-functioning' administrative systems, such as Australia (Victoria Legal Aid, 2020). In Australia, the government department that administers child support does not assist women in seeking proof of paternity, although women in receipt of government benefits are financially penalised if they fail to take reasonable child support action (Department of Social Services, 2020). While legal aid funding is available to some mothers, such funding is limited and demand is high. As a result, not all women may be able to pursue paternity testing, despite the onus being on women to 'prove that the other person is the biological, intended or adopted parent' (Victoria Legal Aid, 2020, p. 4). As such, access to child support varies according to women's conformity to patriarchal social expectations of marriage and reproduction that reference masculine privilege, alongside their classed, racial, cultural and sexual identities.

As Hellum (2000) described with respect to relationship status and child support in Africa – but which applies equally elsewhere – even at the very beginning of the child support process, women experience the gender of law (Graycar and Morgan, 2002). Hellum (2000, p. 643) states:

> A major problem is that by linking access to economic resources such as child maintenance and property to the institution of marriage, both customary and common law defines women's entitlements through male relationships. Women who don't conform to this patriarchal norm, such as single, cohabiting, and divorced mothers, are thus placed in a disadvantageous position.

For example, as Carlson (2009, p. 29) explains with respect to establishing orders when parents live in different countries:

> One of the major concerns of some countries was the cost of paternity establishment, which the U.S. delegation was told could be as much as \$3,000 in some countries. The U.S. delegation presented information about how the cost of testing both the child and the putative father had been reduced in the United States, through technology and economies of scale, to as little as \$150.

In the US, these paternity procedures apply largely to low-income families with high rates of multi-partner fertility. These classed and racialised processes require particular critical attention given the disproportionate impact on already disadvantaged groups, which has been well established for over two decades now:

> The racial politics of America's welfare system in which welfare is perceived primarily as a program for young African-American women, who are demonized as 'welfare queens,' are well-known. What is less well-known is the way in which young black men have become the unacknowledged locus of efforts to reform welfare through child support collections. Large proportions of black children are born out of wedlock, and high rates of poverty among such families have led national welfare reform debates to focus on establishing paternity and collecting child support from black men. (Hansen, 1999, pp. 1151–2)

More recently, researchers such as Elizabeth Cozzolino (2018; see also Cozzolino and Williams, 2017) have begun this much needed work, while government programmes have also revised the nature of enforcement measures that disproportionately jail poor Black men for non-compliance. The jailing of poor, Black men for child support non-compliance is a rare instance within child support programmes where disciplinary systems apply to men. However, rather than revealing child support as gender neutral, these processes reveal how the state acts in ways that preserve existing social hierarchies, be they racial or gendered.

Returning to establishing an order, determining paternity is one of the few sites in the child support process where fathers' autonomy and authority may be curtailed by the court, and where women are ushered through the leaky pipeline. For example, in Australia, if a purported father does not agree to take a paternity test, a court may deem them as the parent (Victoria Legal Aid, 2020). Similarly, in Germany, if a purported father does not engage in court processes to establish paternity, a judge will rely on the mother's account. Only by actively engaging in the process – such as by providing a DNA sample or other proof that he could not be the father – can fathers influence the decision. In both cases, fathers' rights are usurped by the rights of the child to know and be supported by their father, enshrined in the UNCRC, rather than any reference to mothers. The German legal informant explains:

Interviewee: The competent court is in Germany, according to German law and according to European law. It is possible for a judge to say it is the father, even if there's no DNA proof.

Facilitator: But there would be a lot of places, I assume, where they don't agree that …

Interviewee: They don't show. Mostly they don't show, they don't go to the court.

Facilitator: [Are there] cases where the judge says, 'I'm not equipped to be able to definitively say that that's the father?'

Interviewee: Then the law decides. Because there has to be a decision in the end. … But if it is clear that – if nobody says something to the opposite, and if she says, 'It was the only man I had sexual relations with in this period of time', and nobody else says, 'No, it's not true', then the judge will say, 'Okay' … because the interests of the child to have a father comes first. Because if the father says, 'No, that's not true', he still has the possibility to protest and then he has to bring a DNA [test].

The court's prioritisation of children's rights to know and to be supported by both parents is a rare example of the curtailment of fathers' autonomy and authority. More often, however, fathers are able to define the terms of child support arrangements through their disengagement or failure to participate in processes. In such instances, it is the mother's responsibility to enact the child support system, often in the face of a lack of information and even hostility from state systems and their ex-partner. In the face of such barriers, there are significant opportunities for women to fall out of the process along the way.

The costs and work of seeking child support

As the interviews revealed, the cost of accessing the child support system is prohibitive across a range of court-based systems. In almost all jurisdictions reviewed here, it is the mother's responsibility to initiate the child support process, whether through the courts, the state, mediators or privately.

> 'Usually mothers in [South] Korea, mothers always have to initiate all the process. As I discussed, mothers are usually responsible for identifying where the father is and where the father works, much of the information needs to be verified by the mother.' (South Korea)

> 'Then other problems are – so they – you see, the recipient parent attempts will then consider the cost of getting a lawyer, because of investigating all these leads, the cost of tracking the properties down – and there will be options. I do know that by the end of the day and judge says, "send me a copy" – "no, I can't". Even if I'm in court, and

> the paying parent has the financial capacity to hire a special lawyer, and to maybe hope for equal custody, it could drag on for ten years, with the mother filing new applications at every point. No concern for the interests of the child involved.' (Nigeria)

Across countries, women face knowledge, financial, geographic, cultural and emotional barriers to entering the child support system, as will be described in more detail as this chapter progresses. However, when they do enter the system, women are charged with collecting, assembling and presenting information about their financial needs and the resources of their ex-partners. Fathers are typically not compelled to engage in these processes, and in most cases, fathers' failure to engage confers financial benefits upon them, as incomes can be obscured and payments are made more difficult. For example, returning to paternity, in some Southeast Asian and African countries, mothers' claims 'become difficult because of the rigid evidentiary requirements for proving paternity' (Goonesekere, 2006, p. 266). For other forms of evidence, women may also face significant emotional and relational work, such as requiring corroboration by others, often including their recalcitrant ex-partners (Armstrong, 1992). Again, these difficulties are not confined to countries with less well-developed child support systems. They are, however, illustrative of issues that do not attract policymakers' attention in more advanced regimes.

For women, their responsibility for driving child support processes means that they also bear the cost of engaging with state systems. As the informant on Germany described, "yes, always when there are costs, it's the mother who has to pay", whereas the Malaysian informant noted, "Usually the people that can afford litigation are the people that litigate the most. Unfortunately, if you're a very low-income – people don't really understand the court system, they don't want to get involved in it." These costs may be direct, such as court fees, or the cost of obtaining, copying and posting documents such as birth certificates, bank statements or other proof of their ex-partner's income and assets. In addition, women face indirect costs, such as the opportunity costs of lost wages when they are required to attend court hearings or agency appointments. These appointments then place further costs on women, such as childcare and travel.

> 'Women – especially if you're a single mum raising three kids, let's say, or even one kid, they can't – they just can't have the time to divide themselves between the childcare and work. Then, on top of that, you have to add going through the court, which usually tends to be far away from where they live, so it's very hard to get permission to go, because their jobs are also very unstable.' (Peru)

The barriers of time and money, however, are not exclusively the consequences of antiquated or poorly funded systems in countries with poor infrastructure. In Australia, for example, there are no physical child support system branches for women to attend. Call centre queues are prohibitively long, with long waits to speak to departmental staff (Australian National Audit Office, 2015; Department of Human Services, 2018). When women make contact, they report that forms are often lost or ignored (Natalier et al, 2016; Cook et al, 2019). At the end of the application process, across countries, child support is often not guaranteed, while entering the system can cause the mother more problems.

While financial barriers are one of the main reasons for women not accessing court systems in countries without free access or facilitation services, the temporal, social and emotional barriers women face are also pressing problems. These problems are experienced across the board, in both administrative and court-based systems. In South Korea, for example, Confucian values shape the extent to which it is acceptable to pursue child support, as an academic informant explains:

> 'I don't think a lot of people really apply for orders to begin with because of some cultural influence. In [South] Korea because of the influence of the Confucian culture it is more acceptable not to pay child support in [South] Korea because there's some – the notion that male head can define who's included in your family and whether he will – the discretion of the fathers matters much more in [South] Korea. Since it is more acceptable not to pay child support and the system is new and the cultural acceptance of non-payments. There is more cost for mothers to pursue child support. A lot of people don't really bother applying for – well, doing all the dispute and pursuing child support.' (South Korea)

As in South Korea, social barriers that prevent mothers from accessing financial support from their children's father exist across systems. McKenzie's (2012) qualitative research with Australian separated mothers found that women give up seeking child support when the emotional costs exceed any likely financial returns. Evidence of such decision-making was widespread across the interviews. Women across countries were reported as either 'going through the motions' of seeking child support with no prospect of receiving payments, or avoiding seeking payments in order to cut their losses. As the Hong Kong legal informant explained:

> 'Another statistic is about 40 per cent of those who got a maintenance order from the court did not receive the maintenance. A high

> percentage cannot receive it. So, if it's so difficult people [women] just don't bother, though they have the need. They want to reduce their trouble or the conflict, all kind of consideration. They just decide not to apply for the order.' (Hong Kong)

Similarly, in Japan, when fathers with court-ordered child support have salaried jobs, the system works reasonably well. But when fathers own their own businesses or work 'cash-in-hand', or when mothers have not done sufficient investigative work to provide information to the authorities, payments are unlikely:

> 'I mean if the father works for the company, it's – I mean by the enforcement measures they can assess the salary of the father and get the child support from the ex-husband's salary. So that works very well. But if the husband doesn't work for a company, works independent[ly] or doesn't know where he works, in that case it's difficult to enforce.' (Japan)

In Malaysia, two court-based systems of child support operate, providing a Shariah law system for Muslim parents and another legal system for non-Muslims. In the Shariah law system, there are provisions for child support following relationship breakdown (Hadjian, 2013; Nor et al, 2018, 2019, 2020; Ahmad et al, 2020). As Hadjian (2013, p. 38) explains, 'In several verses, the Koran calls on Muslim fathers to support their children after dissolution of marriage. Sunni and Shi'a jurisprudence agree that during and after termination of the marriage, the father must maintain the children whether the wife is poor or rich.' However, despite these provisions, the Malaysian academic informant noted,

> 'They [mothers] feel anything that's going into court, even if it's in their advantage, is trouble and they just want to do their own thing and not be bothered. Just going to court, because even though it's the public prosecution dealing with the proceedings, they may be called into court just to give a statement. They just don't want that. Now more and more you get family mediation centres that can actually try to get parties to agree. Even though both parties need to agree to mediation and usually the stronger party doesn't want that, especially if they're high-income, they'll just [say], "No, if you want to discuss it, you go to court."' (Malaysia)

Both in Malaysia and Portugal, as the Portuguese informant described earlier, informants spoke of the 'trouble' that women want to avoid with their ex-partners. They are willing to accept less or no child support in order to keep the peace. As described with respect to the Malaysian case, the 'stronger party' can refuse to take part in mediation, while in Hong Kong, the party who has the need 'doesn't bother' in order to reduce their trouble or conflict. Here, gendered hierarchies of authority and autonomy are at play. Both mothers and fathers can opt out of child support processes, but on different terms, and – when welfare systems are involved – with differing degrees of choice and constraint. Fathers can subvert mothers' wishes to seek child support by not engaging or not paying. Mothers can acquiesce and cease proceedings. However, the beneficiaries in both cases are liable fathers. The losers in both scenarios are mothers and their children, 'though they have the need'. The state's role in turning a blind eye to fathers' abilities to subvert state legal and administrative processes through inaction is a key focus of this book. These processes are especially evident in instances of domestic violence where women are almost certain to exit the child support system.

Avoiding seeking support from violent ex-partners

Women with a violent ex-partner are especially likely to not seek child support payments. However, rather than child support avoidance being confined to 'opt-in' court-based systems, women who have experienced domestic violence are enabled – and indeed encouraged – to avoid the child support system in a range of contexts. For example, in Australia, women can be exempt from seeking child support without welfare benefit penalties (Patrick et al, 2007, 2008; Douglas and Nagesh, 2019). Similar provisions apply in a range of countries where child support is mandatory for benefit calculations. The gendered logic inherent within such exemptions is that it is too dangerous for women to engage personally with violent ex-partners, reflecting the individualisation of child support across countries. The state offers vulnerable women no support in seeking payments and does not seek payments on their behalf. As a result, violent fathers are freed from their financial responsibility to their children while mothers fall out of child support's leaky pipeline. While the financial and emotional effects of non-seeking or exemptions are not the focus in this chapter, as they are explored in Chapter 8, these processes are telling in terms of gender relations and what child support is meant to achieve post-separation.

Within child support systems internationally, women who have endured violent relationships – who are at most risk of violence immediately following physical or emotional separation (DeKeseredy et al, 2017) – have the following four 'choices': 1) private bargaining, 2) enter an adversarial system, 3) avoid child support, 4) seek an exemption from entering the system in cases where entry is mandatory. Choices one to three are evident across countries, as the following excerpts from the key informant interviews and research studies illustrate, while choice four is included only in mandatory systems. What is not typically available is a fifth option, which is to collect payments from the child(ren)'s father while being protected from direct contact and violence.

> 'In the old days here, when families getting income assistance or welfare had to get a support order, they were often exempted when there had been violence from getting that order. Now that they don't have to [seek child support as a condition of benefit eligibility] it's entirely their choice as to whether or not they do it. If they go through a service, we have what's called family justice counsellors that help people reach agreements or if they can't reach an agreement, provide them with some assistance going through the court process. They have extremely comprehensive screening for violence, work on safety plans et cetera, et cetera. But the ultimate decision as to whether to proceed through to get an order rests with the parent themselves.' (Canada)

> 'In addition to this there are a lot of women, which don't go to this body or child support to collect the money, because they are scared, because they know that if they will do something that … I need to say something about the violence according to this. It's not only that she's afraid that he will hurt her, or – she's also afraid that he wants custody of the children. He tells her a lot of times, "If you go to court or if you try to collect the child support, then I'm going away, you won't see me, I want to take the children."' (Israel)

> 'The other is, oftentimes quite frankly the mom has been threatened – I'm sure you've heard this before – has been threatened by the dad. "Don't get me hooked up with those people or with the government, so lie or tell them you don't know who the father is."' (US, state level)

Sweden does provide a limited example of the fifth case, where women at risk of violence can seek an exemption from being removed from the state system which can guarantee state support if fathers do not pay. However, as Fernqvist and Sépulchre's (2021) analysis of the 2016 reform revealed, mothers often did not know about the exemption and thus were more vulnerable to the risks that individualised child support posed. The Swedish official similarly noted how women fell out of the system despite likely being eligible for an exemption. It was only when the system failed women and placed them at risk that their vulnerabilities became visible.

> 'I don't know why the government decided to pass the legislation, but I know that we have big issues now that we are working with. The first one is all the incidents of conflict and domestic violence, threats, economical, control that the fathers are exerting over the mothers, all

of that has risen to the surface now and has come to our attention in different ways than before. Because they've been safe and secure inside the [child support] system and now when they're thrown out, all that rises and they tell us about it.' (Sweden)

As these excerpts reveal, women can bargain privately with their abuser, enter the adversarial legal or administrative child support system (which can be taken by their abuser as a provocation), seek an exemption by proving that they are at risk, or avoid the child support system, which may mean that they also miss out on other state benefits. All of these 'choices' disempower and punish the victims of domestic violence, including children, by rendering women subordinate to men's autonomy and authority. These 'choices' see women making agreements privately, being forcibly entered into the child support system, or acquiescing to men's autonomy. In none of the countries researched here did the state intervene to enforce payments from violent men while protecting women from them. Women were afforded the 'choice' to enter the system or to decline child support payments. There was no choice to receive payments made by fathers in a safe manner.

Falling out of the system over payment terms

For those women who enter the child support system, the next point in the leaky pipeline where they may fall out is agreeing to the terms of their child support payments. In many countries that have administrative systems, including Norway, the UK, Australia and others, governments claim that the 'easiest' way to establish an order is for parents to agree between themselves. For example, the Norwegian government administrator described:

'Well, in Norway, we try to encourage parents to agree privately on the child support. A private agreement is made very easily. It's just basically they just write it on a piece of paper what they want and both sign it. As long as they have done that in writing, it can also be collected through the collection agency.' (Norway)

The private system is 'easy' for states who bear no cost or responsibility for the process or outcomes. For parents, this method can also be easy if they have a good relationship and no ongoing disputes. But defaulting to the private system can also make life difficult for separated mothers as there is a normative expectation that parents 'should' be able to agree. However, research suggests that the payment and non-payment of child support has meaning beyond its material significance, as it reflects or reinforces gendered power and traditional fathering/mothering roles (Dudová, 2006; Natalier and Hewitt, 2010; Natalier, 2012; Cozzolino and Williams, 2017; Keil and

Elizabeth, 2017). An emerging area of research also examines how cultural factors shape the appropriateness of seeking and collecting child support payments (Keil and Elizabeth, 2017, 2019; Chung and Kim, 2019), although far more research is required here.

In summary, private agreements can work for parents who need child support systems the least. However, for women who need state support, the promotion of private agreements downloads responsibility on to individual women, as is explored further in Chapter 8. To secure a private agreement, women must take conciliatory action to make themselves and their children worthy of support, and to accept forms and terms of payment acceptable to the payer. Here, states abrogate their responsibility to ensure both parents support their children. Within private agreements, fathers are in the position most able to define payment terms, but there are no mechanisms available to ensure that they are held responsible for providing payments. Mothers, by contrast, are held responsible for establishing private agreements, despite their financial need (and gender norms) rendering them the weaker party in these negotiations. Within this context, it is no wonder that women fall out of the private child support system.

Failing to enforce payments

Summarising the leaky pipeline – across countries – to this point: in order to be in a position to receive payments, women need to identify the liable father, not be afraid of or prevented from pursuing an order, have a payment amount determined that is of sufficient value to make it worth pursuing – whether arrived at through private negotiation or with the assistance of administrative or legal entities – and have a child support order established. While many women are diverted into private negotiations, when the state is involved in establishing agreements its involvement ceases once an order is made. This is especially the case in court-based systems where overcoming barriers to enter the court system and have a child support order established do not necessarily translate into payments being made. The Nigerian academic informant provides an example:

> 'Sometimes when the people go to court they'll have the order, but it's one thing to have – to get the order from court – it's another thing to ensure the order. It gives the same hassle. Now, it is a problem that when she can go to court to have the order made, and then it's another business to enforce the order.' (Nigeria)

Should mothers make it through the system to the enforcing of child support payments, there are then two enforcement logics. Either the state can take on responsibility for ensuring payments, or this responsibility can be left to mothers. The allocation of responsibility to fathers is absent here. They may autonomously choose to take up this responsibility, but there is no system in which fathers bear responsibility for reporting their payment amounts and frequency and any deviation from child support orders. Fathers also face no responsibility to take action to devise or initiate debt repayment processes should payments be in arrears. This responsibility falls either on the state, who often fails to take up this responsibility, or on women, who often do not have the capacity to effect enforcement. However, in some systems, women can ask the state to take action on their behalf, as a Canadian government informant describes:

> 'Parents can enrol in our enforcement programme voluntarily, okay. They're not required to enrol. Obviously one of them enrols voluntarily and the other one we might call it an involuntary enrolment of their ex-partner, but they're not required to enrol. Some of the Canadian provinces they are enrolled and then they can try to opt out. In our experience … I guess we can't say 100 per cent, but 99.99 per cent of the people who enrol, enrol because they're not getting their money.' (Canada)

In the Canadian example, a voluntary – and thus emotionally contextualised – enforcement programme operates as the primary means of enforcement. This is similar to other programmes, where mothers have to report non-compliant fathers to programme administrators.

As described previously, fathers deemed to be non-compliant can be jailed in some contexts – action which would cease further payments to the mother due to the father's lack of income. However, the incentives for mothers to vigorously pursue payments in such scenarios are negligible.

> 'With regards – for a more sustained period that requirement is for the criminal proceedings. For the enforcement, you can enforce it straight away. What happens is that because enforcement proceedings are expensive and most people in Portugal you need to pay your own costs and costs are paid up front. … Each party needs to pay their own lawyers or either they're entitled to Legal Aid and then depending on the type of Legal Aid they will get a Legal Aid lawyer appointed to them by the Law Society. If not, they need to pay upfront. They will need to make a provision with law firm to pay their legal fees and to pay court costs. In cases of enforcement proceedings, because they are separate court proceedings, they will also need to pay the enforcement agencies. It's still an expensive procedure.' (Portugal)

The pursuance of non-compliance is perhaps the most revealing element of child support practice as a gendered governance practice. While the previous sections illustrate both more and less functional arrangements, no country deals well with non-compliance – despite the fact that non-compliance is rife, under-reported and largely ignored by policymakers in ways that have inadvertent or deliberate negative consequences for women. Malta, for example, was described previously as having a system that enabled women to move through the various points in the 'leaky pipe', yet it concurrently also positions women as responsible for enacting the system in the face of systemic and gendered barriers. While women can more easily establish an order and have a reasonable amount determined to be paid, non-compliance is largely left as the unspoken reality of Malta's child support programme, as a government administrator describes:

Interviewee:	Now I'm going to flip to the barriers or the negatives. One of them is the police force, when they go to report that maintenance hasn't been paid …
Facilitator:	Oh, so the mother can go to the police to report that maintenance hasn't been paid?
Interviewee:	Yes, to take the father to court. There is a lot of hegemonic masculinity, so either at the very best – but still it would not be good – the police would say for example – even in cases of violence – 'Kind of try and make peace or patch things up and go home and try to placate the situation'.

However, the experience described here is by no means confined to Malta. Most countries place responsibility for the reporting of non-compliance on individual women, which either results in enforcement action that could endanger women or exacerbate relational problems, or in inaction.

> 'It's not in most cases, because some of them do have the court order, but they [fathers] didn't pay. The punishment is – [mothers] have it on paper, but there's no enforcement to those who don't want to pay. That's why there are so many problems here for those [women] from low-income group. They don't really have the means to go after the payment, or the process is too difficult … then sometimes the husband will check the mother if they appeal, and then he will take away the children.' (Malaysia)

In the UK, which offers a more extreme example of pricing state enforcement activity, a legal informant described how women have to pay to enter the child support enforcement system. This policy measure, like many others across countries, holds women responsible for pursuing non-compliance, despite making it difficult for them to do so: "One of the things that came in the 2012 scheme was you, that you paid £20 to get your enforcement done. Which doesn't sound a lot of money, but if you've got no money in the first place, why should that person have to pay for that?" (UK). At other times, women are advised – or understand – that they must take on collection functions themselves, as the state will provide no support.

> 'There are a lot of fathers who work in Israel in [the] cash economy, and they have nowhere – and you can't find where they work, and you can't actually take money from their salaries because of that. … It's part of the problem, because most of the time she doesn't know and she can't be the investigator. That's why most of the time it seems very hard to collect the money. Because if she doesn't know and the state is not taking a private investigator in order to find it, so the situation is – there is nowhere money that is found.' (Israel)

> 'There's no enforcing here at the police station, because they're saying, "This is a family affair, we have to ensure you protect the family", like this, and now, "This is a family fight", and all those thoughts.' (Nigeria)

At the other end of the child support spectrum, some Nordic and continental European countries provide guaranteed (also known as advanced) maintenance.

> 'So, if the recipient lives in Norway, she's entitled to what's called an advanced payment of child support from the state. That depends on the income. So, if she has a very low income, she'll get a fairly large amount. If she has a very high income, she might get nothing. Then there's two – sort of there's three – different rates depending on the income. So, once they apply for that, they also then have to apply for child support to be established.' (Norway)

In Sweden, which prior to 2016 was conceived of as a generous state with guaranteed maintenance provisions, collecting child support payments can actually reduce women's financial security. If payers have been compliant within the state system for six months, the case is transferred to a private arrangement, removing state oversight and assurance (Fernqvist and Sépulchre, 2021). As a government administrator noted:

> 'If I'm blunt, you're thrown out of the system because the government says then if he can pay to a government agency for six months without delays and without – just doing it correctly for six months – then he might as well do it [pay privately] to the other party.' (Sweden)

By removing itself from the process when fathers have made six consecutive payments, the Swedish state assumes that parents will continue in this manner without any oversight. The state assumes no role in assisting with compliance. The cause of compliance, rather, is moved away from the system to the behaviour and attitudes of individual parents themselves: parents who pay will continue to pay irrespective of the system.

To states, child support administration is a financial outlay. Money spent pursuing payments is money that could be diverted elsewhere – either directly to parents, or to other budgetary areas. The key informant from Hong Kong candidly exemplified such government deliberations over whether to enforce their own child support laws:

> 'Because I think the Hong Kong government consider if they take an interventionalist approach to help the single mother to make their ex-spouse to pay the child support and maintenance it costs much. They directly give the money to the single mother and the child. The administrative fee is high for them … because it's quite difficult to make those who not willing to pay the money, to pay the money.' (Hong Kong)

While no interviewees in liberal welfare states were as candid, the financial cost-benefit calculation of enforcing child support payments can be revealed by examining who is the ultimate recipient of private child support. I argue that when this ultimate recipient is the state, child support debts are more vigorously pursued. For example, in New Zealand, all child support money collected on behalf of benefit recipients is retained by the state (Fletcher, 2016; Keil and Elizabeth, 2017, 2019). Unpaid liabilities are thus owed to the state and so enforcement actions feature prominently in New Zealand child support policy. Mothers and their children, however, are no better off. By contrast, in the UK, all child support money is private. Payments do not interact with welfare benefits. In this light, the imposition of fees can be seen as a government cost-shifting exercise. As such, it is mothers' responsibility to take action unless they pay for the government's support.

Australia offers a far more punitive approach. Irrespective of whether child support payments are received, mothers who collect child support privately are deemed to have received this money in full. Their welfare benefits are then reduced on this basis – often leaving low-income mothers short of both child support and benefit payments. Recently introduced measures then enabled vigorous methods to recoup 'overpaid' benefit payments from low-income mothers on the retrospective application of child support calculations (Department of Social Services, 2020). New Zealand, the UK and Australia provide stark examples of the state's interest in child support enforcement – but they also reveal the limits of the state's interest, whereby there is often little appetite for ensuring separated mothers and their children receive child support. Rather, there is an almost exclusive focus on ensuring that the state is minimising its benefit-related and administrative expenditure. These processes alone reveal the gender of the state and the implicit valuation of supports provided to separated mothers. Across countries, women are held responsible for men's non-compliance, and the individualising of negotiations is seen as the solution.

At the other end of the leaky pipeline

Across countries, there are different – yet systemically similar – ways through which women are dissuaded or prevented from accessing and enacting the child support system. Child support systems, irrespective of their technical enactment by a court or agency, require separated mothers to expend their limited resources to pursue the promise of additional, ongoing funds from their ex-partners. For many women, however, this promise is empty and the cost-benefit calculation of expending time, effort and resources on an unlikely outcome is often unfavourable. First, the systems reviewed here do not recognise women's time poverty, and instead place the onus on already time-poor women to meet significant administrative demands to enter the system. As a result, many women are excluded – a problem then cast as their own personal failure. Second, the systems typically do not acknowledge women's vulnerable physical, financial and emotional position vis-à-vis their ex-partner from whom they are expected to request money. When states do recognise women's vulnerability, they consider only her physical risks and fail to ensure her financial and emotional well-being.

The failure of states to understand or acknowledge women's relative powerlessness in general, and in the context of seeking post-separation payments in particular, is perhaps the most significant failure of child support in all countries without guaranteed payments. The intractability and common nature of these problems are functions of child support existing within gendered legal (Graycar and Morgan, 2002), administrative (Smith, 1999) and policy (Bacchi, 1999) systems. To use Stone's (1989, p. 285) parlance, these individually 'unplanned' barriers combine in ways that structure women's oppression. When taken together and viewed through a governmental policy analysis lens, the overly common and numerous barriers that women face when seeking child support can be seen not as the accidental outcomes of misguided action, but more as the intended and purposeful outcomes of gendered, classed and racialised states. Given these barriers, it is no wonder that women are dissuaded from applying for child support when seeking payment is not compulsory. However, women often are compelled to enter systems, yet face barriers or harm as a result of doing so. To explore these issues in more detail, in Chapter 5 I turn to examine how states see, or fail to see, women's needs, and instead position women as responsible for enacting a system in ways that serve the interests of the state. I then explore whose interests are central to the design and conduct of child support and the evaluations of system success in Chapter 6.

5

Divergent views of success and failure

The previous chapter set out some of the points in the child support process where women may fall out of the leaky pipeline, across a range of international settings. The purpose was to construct a general understanding of how the child support process works across countries, and more importantly does not work, to distribute finances from non-resident parents to their children's household. In this chapter, the attention turns to examine how states can make claims regarding the success of child support policy and how they are enabled to remain silent on its failures. I draw on the work of critical policy scholars (Stone, 1989; Jamrozik and Nocella, 1998; Bacchi, 1999) to examine problem framing and the construction of problem absence. These theorists provide a framework through which noticing or not noticing social problems can be understood, which provides insight into the different views that child support clients, front-line service staff, policy administrators and politicians will have. The process outlined in Chapter 4 provided key insight into women's experiences as child support seekers, but from the perspective of service staff, policy administrators and researchers who work with or implement programmes for such women. However, the informants drawn on in Chapter 4 must work within the laws and policies that governments have provided. While technical amendments to procedure and practice can be quite easily achieved, questions of the overall purpose, nature and process of child support require political engagement and public support. As such, child support is inherently political, and sits within intersectional relations of gender, class and race. The contention of this chapter is that within these political considerations, the concerns of women as child support recipients are not likely to be noticed or regarded as warranting significant political concern.

The analysis presented in this chapter again sets out the governance of child support as a process, but as a political rather than technical process, beginning with how child support policy problems are 'noticed'. As Bacchi's (2009) work reveals, how problems are brought into the public imaginary shapes the array of solutions that are available to address them. When the state can manage and contain social problems through technical and political means (Stone, 1989; Li, 2007), there is less reason for states to intervene to address their underpinning social causes. In this chapter, I delve into how child support policy problems are expressed in the literature, policy documents and interviews with key informants in order to examine the gendered nature of child support policy problems and their solutions and explore how such problems come to be seen or remain unseen. In doing so, I examine the viewpoints of recipient women, researchers, administrators and policymakers to explore how these views shape and are acknowledged within child support solutions. However, the purpose is not to develop a typology of problems. Rather, this chapter serves as an intermediary step in developing an explanatory model of the failures of child support at a systemic, global level. The aim is to identify the gendered processes that feed into the state's identification of harms and difficulties, and to whom, within the state–payer–payee triad of child support relations, these problems apply. Further, by identifying how child support harms and burdens are viewed and thus conceived, this chapter offers insight into how child support failures transcend national systems and their action or inaction. These issues are then examined more fully in Chapters 6 and 7, where state interests and administrative tools are addressed, respectively. To begin this analysis, however, I now turn to outline child support's position as both a public and a private issue and the way that this status complicates the identification of policy problems and their solutions.

The public and private nature of child support

The enactment of child support policy, and the administrative and legal procedures that give life to child support law, are constructed as appropriate responses to the problems to be solved. All such developments are shaped by power, as those who control the agenda control how both problems and their solutions can be understood and managed. These processes, be they legal, administrative or political, exist within a gendered context, in that men's positions, worldview and interests are taken as 'natural' and universal. As a result, laws (Smart, 1989; Graycar and Morgan, 2002), policies (Bacchi, 1999), institutions (Smith, 1999) and administrative procedures (Cook et al, 2015b; Cook, 2021a) typically acknowledge, reference and respond in ways that buttress rather than challenge the existing gendered social order. In the context of child support, the social order references men's 'natural' position as superordinate to women, separated fathers' higher class position vis-à-vis their ex-partners, and in some countries also racial dimensions – for example, positioning Black American families as more in need of 'governing' than their White American counterparts.

Speaking with respect to class, Jamrozik and Nocella (1998) outline two types of state responses to social problems. First are programmes and services designed to meet the needs of people conceived of as aspirational and responsible, to be taken up on a voluntary basis. State responses in this domain acknowledge their responsibility to intervene and eliminate or minimise the problems that stand in such people's way. For a second group of state program recipients, however, programmes assume that the problems to be addressed by government stem from recipients' inability or unwillingness to meet their own needs and obligations. Here, mandatory programmes are required to modify deviant population behaviour. Thus, the causes of policy problems for the former group lie in the public sphere, whereas the causes of the problems experienced by the latter lie in their own personal failings. When applied to child support, these two types of programmes are designed and administered in deeply gendered ways.

The solutions to child support policy problems flip the public and private positions outlined by Jamrozik and Nocella (1998). Voluntary programmes of child support agreements and payments – for responsible citizens – occur in private, without state surveillance. The private failings of the second group, however, are managed publicly, whereby the state plays an active role in compelling, monitoring and evaluating the behaviour of those deemed unable or unwilling. As such, the causes of child support problems and their solutions can be divided into two types: removing barriers for the responsible or compelling the unwilling. However, who is deemed as facing barriers or needing compulsion occurs within a socio-political context whereby those in power are the ultimate arbiters.

Catherine MacKinnon (1989, p. 35) suggests that the division between the public and the private marks an artificial boundary that precludes an examination of the structural organisation of both 'public' and 'private' and women's role therein, whereby the construction of the home, family and associated relations are rendered 'private' and thus not open to scrutiny, critique or ultimately change. Only those relations in the public sphere can be made visible and thus subject to intervention. Child support is one point where 'noticing' social problems that have been rendered private is possible. But the possibilities to make women's concerns explicit are shaped by power and the interests of those who wield it. The more that child support can be confined to the private sphere, such as through private agreements and payments, the less open to scrutiny – and thus intervention – it becomes.

As states with less developed and typically court-based systems seek to maintain child support largely within the private realm, and other states with highly developed administrative systems seek to re-privatise aspects of the child support process, the private sphere can be seen as both useful and productive. The contention of this book is that the maintenance or re-privatisation of child support is productive of outcomes that buttress the extant gender order. As Brush (2003, p. 27) contends, 'social policies [such as child support] … and male dominance are unlikely to be cancelled due to lack of interest. They will not wither away simply because people refuse to pay attention to them'. Rather, the lack of attention paid to child support transfers conducted (or not) in the private sphere serves a social function: maintaining extant social relations. The construction of child support as a private matter for parents, often irrespective of whether child support is integrated with public benefit systems, is productive in perpetuating these relations. Within this context, what is of interest in this chapter is identifying how child support problems come to be noticed, and how the causes of child support problems are framed in ways that either construct or obscure the need for reform. Chapter 6 takes furthers this analysis by assessing how these framings serve as 'nonperformatives' (Ahmed, 2006), in that they render permanent women's problems with child support, such as those problems outlined in Chapter 4.

Returning to Jamrozik and Nocella's (1998) two types of citizens and applying them to child support policy, they can be seen to divide neatly into the ways that states manage fathers and mothers as child support payers and claimants, respectively. The barriers to child support outlined in Chapter 4 do not often feature in child support reforms. In contrast, when interventions are made to 'improve' the child support process, it is women as child support recipients who are most often compelled to engage in these interventions, typically as a requirement of benefit receipt. The assumption underpinning such compulsion is that women would choose not to seek child support if they had the chance, and thus they must be forced to do so – often with financial penalties should they not comply. By contrast, in some systems, avoiding the system is fine, so long as the problem that child support seeks to manage – primarily child poverty – does not emerge elsewhere in ways that require state action. In short, in some countries women are free to not seek child support so long as this does not cause them to seek state support instead. Fathers, on the other hand, typically face no compulsory child support requirements to establish child support orders. Other than for poor fathers in the US, men's compliance with payment terms, while 'ordered', is often untracked or not rigorously followed up on. Payment terms and conditions imposed by fathers often remain in the private realm, with little state interest or scrutiny. In some policymaking contexts, the assumption is that if orders were made more voluntary, fathers would comply.

Returning to Jamrozik and Nocella's (1998) important categorisation, I would also add a third type of state response. This occurs when the state fails to take up the methods of the first, 'public' type of response and, in doing so, structurally entrenches the effects of the second, 'private' type. This third type of state response sees mothers who receive no state solutions to the systemic child support problems they experience held responsible for their failure to collect payments. In some countries, most notably the UK, Sweden and Australia, there have been moves to 'wind back' state oversight of child support. These privatised state child support programmes may require women's engagement but place the enactment and management of the payment terms within the private domain. As a result, the problems that women experience within private child support systems are invisible to the public system. The failure to see the problems that women experience means that there is no requirement for states to act – although states cannot be marked out as failing women, as there is no record of the problem that they have failed to address. For example, there is no record or public outcry over non-compliance in private child support programmes. Indeed, on the contrary, policymakers suggest that private payments are preferable as payers will be more willing to pay (House of Representatives Standing Committee on Family and Community Affairs, 2003). However, an analysis of the UK's move towards private collections (Allbeson, 2017) suggests that private payments also make women more likely to give up. The following chapter examines the interests served by this third type in more detail, where I draw on Ahmed's (2006, 2007) work on institutional 'nonperformatives' to explain and illustrate how and why the state may fail to intervene in 'problems' with child support systems. For now, rather, the focus is on how states view the failures of child support that women experience, particularly in the majority of court-based systems and several administrative regimes where these transfers occur in private.

Child support law and policy reveal the state's role in compelling a private intended recipient to seek a payment from another private individual. Simultaneously, such policies compel the payment of private money by one private party to another, of an amount determined by the state. In child support, it is typically women's reproductive labour spent caring for children that is being exchanged for men's wages in the form of child support, obtained through their employment income. Here, child support is, has been and should be regarded as a feminist intervention to recognise women's unpaid labour post-separation: making the cost of women's labour visible (Waring, 1999). In these terms, child support policy can be seen as revolutionary, pioneering and thus ultimately marked out as 'trouble' within the existing gender order. Indeed, critics of child support also point to it as a feminist intervention (Morgan, 1995). But, child support has not been managed explicitly as a feminist intervention to recognise – and thus see – the value of unpaid labour upon the breakdown of the gender contract (Cook and Skinner, 2019). While states may attach a child support value to women's caring labour in order to compensate for the opportunity costs that children in such households experience as a result of their mother's caring work, the state's interest in doing so is often very limited. The state does not take an interest in the amount of work that women must undertake to enact the child support system, and the frequent futility of this work. The opportunity costs of engaging in the system – or not – are typically not calculated or made visible.

Making problems more or less explicit

According to the theorists outlined at the beginning of this chapter, social problems are only identified as such when they are conceived of as being amenable to action, and when they come to threaten the existing social order. The social problem that preceded the development of child support policy was the rapidly increasingly number of lone-parent families and the high rates of child and single-mother poverty that follow escalations in divorces and separations, in some countries resulting from the introduction of no-fault divorce. While single-parent benefits had been introduced in many countries prior to the institutional introduction of child support, the state was primed to 'notice' the increasing number of such households and the cost of supporting them, given the burgeoning expenditure on this group and relatively low rates of lone-parent employment in English-speaking countries (Bradshaw, 1996). As such, the social nature of the problem was at the fore; its cause was seen as structural, social and systemic, and a state response was seen as possible and manageable.

Causal stories (Stone, 1989) describe the rhetoric that governments take up to explain why particular solutions are required. These stories set out the 'type' of problem that states are dealing with, and thus the type of solutions likely to provide effective relief. However, as this conceptualisation suggests, these are stories, and thus their telling – and who can tell them – are controlled by social and political elites. As Jamrozik and Nocella (1998) note, the worldview of policymakers is ontologically different from the worldview of those who experience the programmes and services they design. As a result, elites' descriptions of the problems to be solved – and thus the causes of these problems – may exist independent of the reality of parents' child support experiences. Similarly, programme administrators have different views of child support problems, as do front-line agency staff. As a result, the 'solutions' to the 'problems' described by policymakers may or may not solve any of the problems of those they serve. As Stone (1989, p. 282, emphasis added) suggests,

> Political actors *deliberately* portray [problems] in ways calculated to gain support from their side. And political actors, in turn, do not simply accept causal models that are given from science or popular culture or any other source. They compose stories that describe harms and difficulties, attribute them to actions of other individuals or organizations, and thereby claim the right to invoke government power to stop the harm.

What Stone's account does not provide, however, is a gender overlay. While her theory applies to policymaking in general, the gender of law and policy (Bacchi, 1999; Graycar and Morgan, 2002) suggests that the harms and difficulties that are used to define problems, and their solutions posed, will be gendered. Child support provides a prime example of the socially constructed nature of attributing cause, blame and responsibility and – more particularly – the gender of these processes.

While the solution by some states to provide guaranteed maintenance in cases of non-compliance may serve as a counterpoint to the gender of child support policymaking, the provision of money by the state still 'covers' for men's failures and the failure of child support as a system. Guaranteed payments, when examined through the lens of gendered governance, can be seen as an active tool in absolving men of their financial responsibility for children post-separation. As the Norwegian informant explained: "I think because they [mothers] do receive these advanced payments, maybe people complain less and people get some [money]" (Norway). Here, providing guaranteed payments is positioned as a tool to make people 'complain less'. Irrespective of their original intention, these payments cover for the reality of non-compliance and lessen the state's need to take action to ensure that fathers pay. Similarly, in Sweden it was stated that mothers do not fight their ex-partners or the system to seek child support payments higher than the guaranteed payment amount. While it is not a problem logic that informs Swedish policymaking, there is some acknowledgment that women will not know about the system or avoid it due to its relational and physical risks.

> 'In 2006 it [child support] was changed a little bit again to be even more incorporated or even more structural, I would say. … Today [in 2017] we have realised I think – the government has realised, the parents have to a certain extent realised and the social security agency has realised – that parents [mothers] are not actually using the option of going to court or agreeing on a private agreement because they don't know they can do that. They don't know that the amount can be higher if they go that direction– or they have conflict that they don't want to surface. They're [mothers are] content with the lower amount [referenced to the guaranteed payment amount] because they feel more secure that way and have you a buffer.' (Sweden)

In Sweden, while establishing child support is a routine procedural matter, knowing that you can be entitled to an amount higher than that provided within the guaranteed system is largely unknown, even after reforms to move compliant payers to private arrangements. As a result, the amount typically awarded to be paid does not reference fathers' capacity to pay and children receive far less support from their non-resident parent than they are entitled to. Rather, parents' bureaucratic ease is prioritised at the expense of mothers and their children, and to the advantage of non-resident parents. In both Sweden and Norway, men's financial autonomy is preserved to the greatest extent possible. The state stays out of men's financial business unless women do the difficult, time consuming, emotional and relational work to pursue private payments. By locating the path to solutions to 'solve' inappropriately small orders or fathers' non-compliance with women (who must complain or know that they can ask for more) the problems with child support are also located with women. The role of the state or of individual fathers in enacting the private transfer of child support is invisible and thus not amenable to solutions. In countries where guaranteed payments are not possible, however, there are also administrative means of minimising the necessity for fathers to pay, or to pay a sufficient amount. But the wilful blindness of states to women's experiences of child support shields the state from having to address systemic failures.

Failing to notice problems that are inconvenient to the status quo entrenches gendered patterns of interaction that afford fathers greater power over mothers in child support deliberations. Malta provides a significant example of how such processes operate:

> 'Then, in terms of mediation, the downside or the flip side is that there are complaints that they [mediators] are not trained to deal with violence and power differentials and, in fact, actually it's not real common – even a lot of lawyers – but in Malta, because it's compulsory for everyone, they all have to go through it. There are no clear protocols for mediators – how to deal with this, whether to stop the mediation, to ask for it to be stopped. From the work I've read, they all tackle it on a personal basis – each mediator. I've had mothers saying, "I don't know why I went to mediation, the meditator was – his or her mouth was shut. She didn't say anything. She accepted what my ex-husband said or didn't challenge him." Mediators have to be trained in high conflict or else there should be clearer protocols for what to do when there are real cases of violence. At the same time, the minster didn't want to – he said, "Because if we do that [recognise violence], everybody will claim violence or that they evade the mediation." So there are a lot of dilemmas, but the situation as it is, needs to reach some kind of resolution.' (Malta)

Here, the key informant notes that the government explicitly acknowledges that the violence experienced by women would be a risk to the government. Their assertion is that 'everybody' will claim violence to avoid mediation. The 'everybody' referred to here are women. The underpinning logic is that mediation in its present form does not provide a just outcome, so women will concoct tales of violence to avoid it. It is the same claim made by countries with child support–welfare interactions – that women will avoid seeking child support unless they are compelled to do so. Why this may be the case is not interrogated. Returning to Malta, rather than acknowledging that the mediation process is fraught for women, and that at least some women will enter the mediation process having escaped a violent ex-partner, the government's position is to continue with a process that is regarded by the key informant as accepting the husband's version of financial and family claims. The benefits to individual fathers are obvious. But, for the state, the benefit is that the system of mediation is 'working' – albeit in ways that do nothing to disrupt the gender order. These processes reveal the gendered moral rationality which often underpins mothers' decision-making (Edwards and Duncan, 1996). Here, it is often more reasonable for women to avoid child support than pursue a recalcitrant – and perhaps also violent – ex-partner. As the Hong Kong informant explains:

> 'They want the money but they think it's too painful to ask the ex-spouse for the money because they can predict the resistance of the other party to give them the money even if the court order them for the money. They just want to save themselves from the painful struggle with the ex-spouse. Because I think in the marriage they have more than enough painful experience, encounter with the other party. They just want to leave the ex-spouse so they have this kind of financial arrangement [for child support orders of one Hong Kong dollar] to make their connection – to minimise the connection and contact with the other party.' (Hong Kong)

The questions asked in this book, however, centre on whose responsibility it *should* be to arrange payments, how current arrangements align with women's and children's well-being, and what the consequences are of continuing with current practice. My argument is that it is often women's interests that are sidelined in child support processes, despite them being positioned as responsible for enacting these irresponsible systems. While women could expend additional time, energy and resources to pursue payments, institutional weaknesses, barriers to access, individualising processes in the context of hostile relationships and limited economic returns all work to routinise women's non-pursuance and non-collection. As Gill et al (2017, p. 11) note with respect to consumer choice in 'caring' policy,

> Policies designed to protect and to nurture can often be perverse, inadvertently harbouring and promoting relations of harm. Policies aiming to promote choice may, at the same time, transfer responsibility and deny accountability of institutions. Policies promoting equality and citizenship may also promote specific aspirations and normativities such as active participation and in turn exclude alternative subjectivities. Moreover, policies designed to protect those in most need of care may resort to overly protective measures of sensitivity or control that deny individual needs and differences.

The promotion of 'choice' within child support policy and the harms that this can enact are most problematic, yet evident, in cases where there has been a history of violence in the relationship. For example, my examination of mothers' experiences of Australian child support and related benefit forms and information (Cook, 2021a) found that women were ushered into the most financially disadvantageous arrangements, albeit ones that provided the most financial benefit to the state. At the same time, women's disadvantageous administrative circumstances were regarded in policy documentation and by departmental officials as their personal choice. As a result, of these individualising processes, scrutiny of the ethics of state settings or the duty of care provided to domestic violence victims was absent.

Child support cases that reference a history of domestic violence warrant special consideration within legal or administrative settings, but the solutions provided by the child support process are rarely satisfactory, and can instead be used to inflict further financial or emotional harm (Australian Law Reform Commission, 2012). As DeKeseredy et al (2017, p. 117) note, research has found that abusive ex-partners drag out post-separation proceedings as a way to drain women of funds, regain control, avoid paying child support and negotiate unfair financial settlements with women who 'just want closure'. Opportunities for ongoing coercive control and abuse can be enabled by child support processes. At other times, the barriers to entering the system, including the very real threat of violence and the futility of the result, often mean that women do not even begin to initiate the child support process. As a result, financial benefits accrue to abusive fathers from women not entering the system. As the Israeli informant explained:

> 'Some of them [single mothers] are not going through suing [for] child support, because they are afraid from the fathers because there is violence in their relationship. The fathers tell them that, "If you're going to take me to court then I'm going to kill you", or, "You will be sorry", or stuff like that, and they are afraid to do it.' (Israel)

With respect to establishing a child support order, or justifying their 'failure' to do so, in some countries mothers must prove that they are seeking child support, or that there is no father or that he is violent. When fathers are violent, the law excuses women from seeking child support from such dangerous men. The state does not compel these men to provide for their children and does not facilitate women's access to financial security by acting as an intermediary. The reflections of the Canadian key informants provide further insight into how this issue is being managed in North American contexts:

> 'I think on the domestic violence what we're coming to realise is – and I think is, you know, this is perhaps happening around the world – the more we really learn about domestic violence, our numbers are really, really low in terms of disclosed domestic violence. So, to what extent are we being really … do[ing] a really good job of making it okay for victims of violence to disclose … I think that, like, in a number of other programmes, certainly in the US, we're wondering whether we really are, by the way we ask the questions and by the way we're set up, are we sort of, you know, again doing things which would suggest, perhaps if there are concerns about domestic violence, "don't even bother coming to us [the child support programme]", because they can't be sure we'll protect them.' (Canada)

The benefit and usefulness of child support to women is a point that will be taken up throughout the remainder of the book, as it is illustrative of child support as a governance practice. The point to be taken in this chapter, however, is that these women do not enter into the child support system and thus their experiences are excluded from the policymaking gaze. Some countries have sought to understand how domestic violence intersects with child support, such as Australia, which exempts mothers from seeking support from violent ex-partners (Department of Social Services, 2020), but they are then locked out of the financial benefits that child support offers. As such, women are in a difficult bind as to whether they seek or avoid child support, or conceal their violent ex-partner's behaviour. What reveals child support as a practice to govern 'bad women' is that there are countless requirements placed on women who have very little control over whether payments are made; this is especially the case in instances where ex-partners have exercised physical, psychological and financial means of power and control. At the same time, rather than taking all steps necessary to ensure that children in separated households receive payments, systems that have sought to respond to policy 'problems' have failed to notice or have ignored or excused violent men's behaviour, instead placing more requirements on low-income women who are the victims of such abuse. Often, fathers' poor child support behaviour or women's child support avoidance is unknown because data are not collected to evidence women's experiences.

The gender of data and the absence of women's concerns

Within feminist discussions on the limitations of quantitative research in capturing women's lived experience, and the array of feminist methodological responses (see, for example, Graham, 1983; Smith,

1987), there is an emerging discussion of the way that over-simplified, technocratic views of administrative data limit the views possible within technical systems (Postman, 1993). In the field of social welfare research in particular, technical data collection processes have been examined with respect to how they produce and reproduce textually mediated ruling relations. Within institutions, data collection and reporting systems organise what can be seen as real (Smith, 2001; Cook et al, 2015b; Singh, 2017; Hansen et al, 2018). These processes construct a particular view that is a selective, masculinised account of child support problems and who experiences them. As a result, knowledge of a particular problem is framed with reference to men's interests because 'women have been largely excluded from the work of producing forms of thought and the images and symbols in which thought is expressed and ordered' (Smith, 1987, p. 33). For example, as the Swedish informant noted with respect to their system's data blind spots:

> 'I was just going to say that we don't know – if the people don't come back, we don't know if it is because it's been working or if it is because they don't feel that they want to put the effort into trying again. If that just means that they say, "Oh fine, I'm not going to deal with it anymore. Just let him have it. I'll be okay." They don't pursue it anymore.' (Sweden)

Similar concerns have been previously documented by feminist researchers who have noted how a lack of data has been used as a justification to not act on issues of concern to women, but has provided an impetus for action on issues of concern to men. A striking example of the power of partial and selective accounts of child support experience is described by Millward and Fehlberg (2013). They examined how the post-separation contact arrangements and their attendant infrastructure costs were determined in Australia using a yes/no checklist of items completed by non-resident fathers, rather than requiring an estimate of expenditure on each item. Despite its limitations, the 'Expenditure Index' constructed by Woods (1999) for the Department of Family and Community Services, and research that used this study as a basis (Henman and Mitchell, 2001; Henman et al, 2007), played a major role in the recalibration of the Australian child support formula (House of Representatives Standing Committee on Family and Community Affairs, 2003; Ministerial Taskforce on Child Support, 2005). This change saw non-resident fathers given child support 'discounts' to recognise the costs of care, despite women's reports that child support was often not paid in full, on time or at all, and that reports of non-resident care often did not reflect the actual (mis)workings of payment and receipt.

At the same time, women's knowledge and experiences of child support failures are largely omitted from research and policy reviews, but this does not mean that they do not exist. Relating these gendered processes to 'epistemic practice', Cavaghan (2013, p. 411) remarks that: 'Knowledge does not become more popular or frequently referred to purely on the basis that it is "truer", and epistemic practices do not become more established because they produce better knowledge. Rather, material resources influence the dominance or marginalization of particular knowledge.' The marginalisation of women's experience from the design, evaluation and reform of child support practice is a consequence of epistemic lenses that frame the world, its problems and its solutions in reference to men's understandings and thus men's interests (Bacchi, 1999). Here, the failure to recognise women's experience provides a patriarchal dividend to fathers, and also the state, which does not have to manage the child support problems that women espouse. These epistemic lenses frame how child support can be viewed and understood. These lenses shape what administrative data are sought and how child support is researched. The realities constructed by these datasets exclude women's experiences and understandings.

Technical data and the limited scope of child support reality

The processes through which child support reality is coded in administrative datasets renders invisible or silences women's claims for recognition of their lived reality. This codification of women's experiences through surveys and administration thus 'offers a glimpse of the material stuff that coordinates everyday life, defines the structure and operations of machines and software tools, drives the routines of logistical systems and even defines and thus controls the obligations, rights and responsibilities of individuals, organisations and institutions of governance' (McCosker and Milne, 2014, p. 5).

As women's reports of their child support experiences cannot fit into the administrative technologies used to manage them, their experiences become lost to possible system reform. Changes to child support systems, while often conducted in the name of 'improving' child support systems, have not had a major impact on child support compliance rates or payment amounts (Allbeson, 2017). For example, in Australia, child support reforms were shown to have negative financial consequences for low-income single mothers in particular, while high-income fathers were shown to be better off as a result (Smyth and Henman, 2010; Son et al, 2014). There are few more striking examples of the gender of governance than this.

In some countries, changes to child support law and the financial outcomes for mothers and fathers following separation have occurred alongside other policy developments, particularly the uptake of 'active labour market programmes', also known as 'workfare' or 'welfare-to-work'. Such programmes seek to lessen women's dependence on both the state and their ex-partner, reshaping the symbolic and financial role that child support is purported to play in the lives of separated mothers. The central argument that I am making is that child support policy, sometimes in tandem with welfare-to-work, plays an active role in the gendered reconfiguration of separated parents' financial responsibilities to children. Within this conceptualisation, child support law or policy is an active force in the repositioning of the market – as opposed to the state or ex-partners – as the most appropriate source of women's financial dependence. This marks a fundamental shift in the original purpose and symbolic aims of child support to reduce child poverty, yet it is consistent with what is suggested by the 'responsibilisation' discourse (Clarke, 2005, p. 451) that positions separated mothers as responsible for 'the conditions of [their] own independence – ideally by becoming a "hard working" individual or family member'. Within such rhetoric, separated mothers should be independent, not dependent on either their ex-partner or the state. They should turn to the market to meet their family's financial needs.

The reconfiguration of gender roles and responsibilities also speaks to important symbolic and material consequences for children and parents post-separation. Through their reduced financial contribution, and the requirements placed on mothers to be financially self-sufficient, fathers without high incomes or unusually high levels of child-contact are positioned as increasingly irrelevant to post-separation family life. For the separated-mother 'target' of welfare-to-work requirements, the policy positions women who were previously identified as 'carers' as would-be 'workers' who are increasingly responsible for generating employment income. By removing the choice to be a 'stay-at-home' mother, welfare-to-work policy plays an active role in shaping contemporary low-income separated mothers' parenting practices. At the same time, non-resident fathers' responsibilities to children have remained largely invisible within welfare policy, reinforcing the construction of separated fathers as unencumbered individuals both within families and welfare regimes. Such invisibility has likely fuelled the men's rights lobby's push for recognition in other – and arguably unhelpful – ways with respect to achieving gender equality. However, state interventions into family roles and responsibilities most often fall on low-income parents who are engaged with the welfare state, confining these processes and their outcomes largely to poor and middle-class separated families. What is largely absent within welfare-focused analyses is an examination of how family-focused policies recognise, respond to and produce gender roles and class interests.

6

The interests served by failure

This chapter reflects on the sites of child support failure outlined in Chapter 4 and locates these within the issues discussed in Chapter 5 regarding the failure to notice child support problems, particularly those that are experienced by women who must enact the child support system and then encounter the consequences of its failures. In this chapter, I advance the discussion by examining who benefits from the ways that child support fails, and the interests served at institutional and interactional levels. The assumption, developed in the previous chapters, is that child support systems inhere the subordination of women to masculinist norms. The failure to take meaningful action to collect and transfer payments confers benefits to individual men, fathers as a group, and the state as a gendered institution. My contention is that, across cases, the logics of child support action and inaction are underpinned by the gendered social processes of maintaining, restoring or increasing men's financial autonomy and authority over mothers following separation. At a systemic level, child support – as a process of transferring payments – can fail irrespective of whether states are busy implementing ongoing rounds of review and reform or are seemingly indifferent to the problems of sole parent poverty and parental irresponsibility that lie before them. The 'theatre' of operating a child support system can distract from the failure to ensure child support payments. The existence of a child support system – irrespective of its technical advancement or relative under-development – ultimately provides cover to the state's advancement of its own interests above those of the people it purportedly seeks to serve.

Preserving masculine interests

There are two types of policy 'solutions' available to states, given the way that child support 'problems' have been noticed or not. When child support is framed as problematic, solutions become more technically complex, and as a result more contested, as they must seek to remedy all of the problems that the system brings to the public's attention. Alternatively, the status quo can be maintained by rendering invisible the problems that child support fails to identify and resolve. This dichotomy – of systems that seek to reform or preserve the status quo – sits in the background of subsequent chapters that examine how child support reform has proceeded and how, despite different logics, systems and levels of activity, the interests that are served by action or inaction are remarkably similar.

Across systems, failure to act – or failure to act effectively when action is taken – manifests in a variety of ways, as illustrated in Chapter 4. Women may be logistically prevented or socially dissuaded from accessing the child support system, or the transfer and enforcement of payments may be so onerous or unsupported as to render these fictional. In some systems, there is no acknowledgement or recognition of the problems that women face, and as such, there is no scope to address these. In other systems that seek to 'solve' child support problems, policy processes typically identify these problems and their solutions from men's perspectives. Systems and financial logics that benefit state interests are used to manage problems through technical means. Women's interests are often 'out of scope' and thus excluded from reform processes. As a result, their experiences of child support are rendered invisible. Thus, child support reforms typically tighten the state's hand of governance and move to shape what was often originally a feminist intervention into its masculinist image. In both types of system, women are disciplined to accept what is on offer and not 'make waves', as doing so can result in individual, institutional and financial harms. In some cases, such as in Australia, men's rights groups have rallied against child support systems and their feminist roots, demanding that systems be made less effective. However, backlash has been muted in most countries – perhaps because child support systems have already been rendered so ineffective that the amount of money due is insignificant, or only those willing to contribute voluntarily do so.

For child support programmes internationally – including both court-based processes that can be avoided if substituted with individualised bargaining and administrative programmes that are incrementally being returned to more privatised agreements – individuals are regarded as the most appropriate locus of deliberation and agreement. These issues are taken up further in Chapter 8, which examines how social problems are ultimately residualised into personal problems in ways that divert attention away from addressing the causal social problems (Jamrozik and Nocella, 1998). In this chapter, by contrast, the focus is on how child support systems engage in processes of masculinism (Nicholas and Agius, 2018) and, in doing so, buttress the existing gender order that sees men's interests prioritised over those of low-income women and their children. Men's interests, expressed as financial autonomy and authority, are referenced and reinforced in interactions between parents as they work to arrange or seek payments privately, by institutional requirements and demands that are placed on mothers but rarely applied to fathers (Natalier, 2018; Natalier et al, 2018), and within cultural conventions that shape what is considered appropriate and acceptable behaviour for parents post-separation (Fogarty and Augoustinos, 2008; Cozzolino and Williams, 2017).

Child support as a threat to institutionalised masculinism and to individual men

As described in Chapter 1, child support policy – as opposed to law which has existed for a much longer period – was first introduced in the US in 1975. In the context of social policy, child support marks the beginning of welfare conditionality for single mothers. As Luzkow (2016) describes, the expansion of the middle classes is central to both support of the welfare state and its demise. As the author describes, the welfare state depends on a sense of shared purpose, solidarity and trust. At a political level, those paying for the welfare system, largely the middle classes, must identify themselves as current or potential future beneficiaries. Following the ravages of the Great Depression and World War II, citizens' right to state support was positioned as inalienable (Titmuss, 1950). Thus, it became the state's duty to provide welfare as a social citizenship entitlement (Marshall, 1950). The return on the nation's investment was that it enhanced collective well-being and promoted the common good. In Beveridge's UK welfare model, including the middle classes as beneficiaries of the welfare state not only located their tax contributions as fulfilling their own interests, but built the necessary collective identity that underpinned the system. As a result of the Keynesian welfare state, a great levelling was to occur. But, importantly, for the middle classes who largely funded this exercise, the result would be that they 'levelled up' (Luzkow, 2016).

However, Keynes's welfare state – and the time in which it was introduced – was devoid of gender analysis. As a result, the collectivist activity of redistribution that Keynes described naturalised gender roles through its focus on wage-earning males and their dependants within their nuclear families. 'Levelling up' in this context occurred at a family level. But rapid family reconfigurations that occurred in the late 1970s and 1980s following the introduction of no-fault divorce legislation undermined the social contract on which the male breadwinner's welfare state was based. For example, the introduction of single parent pensions saw a rapid expansion in the cost of welfare programmes. Trust, shared purpose and solidarity were eroded. Middle-class nuclear families – and more importantly the breadwinners therein – had little to gain from the welfare state providing benefits to single-mother-headed families. Even further, the welfare state now posed a threat to their normative, male-breadwinner nuclear family life. Single-parent benefits were not accessible to the masses – as was the basis of the Beveridge model – and as such these costly benefits provided no advantage to those paying into the system, and offered no means for contributing wage earners to 'level up'. Those who did stand to 'level up' as a result of single-parent benefits were those who had not contributed directly, and who in some cases had broken the gender contract with their previous male breadwinner. Given the lack of shared purpose and solidarity with single-parent benefit recipients, it is little wonder that the welfare state as a whole has come under attack in liberal democracies such as the Canada, the US and Australia, where individualising rhetoric has come to predominate. The individualised notion of child support then provides a further blow to both the shared purpose of the welfare state and individual men's masculinist sensibilities.

While welfare conditionality and work tests were introduced for single mothers in Canada, the US and Australia in 1995, 1996 and 2006, respectively (see Edin and Lein, 1997; Gorlick and Brethour, 1998; Costello, 2005), I contend that the introduction of child support policy also played a significant role in the demise of welfare state solidarity. A decade or more prior to the introduction of conditional welfare benefits for single parents, child support policies fundamentally shifted the sources of support for single parents away from the state and back onto individual family members. This, I argue, was key to the backlash that child support has experienced in these individualising liberal welfare states.

In the Keynesian welfare era, the state intervened to do what families had done previously: take care of members who could not take care of themselves. The introduction of child support, by contrast, undoes this, and places the onus back on individual family members, described by Sevenhuijsen (1986) as the eternal biological family. However, these enlisted family members, namely non-resident fathers, may be reluctant to resume their breadwinning role and may have, indeed, already abrogated their responsibilities.

With the introduction of child support and the subsequent erosion of the welfare state, child support can be increasingly seen as 'levelling down' for contributing male breadwinners. Not only are their taxes supporting single parent benefits at a generalised level, but they must contribute directly to ex-partners who have broken the gender contract (Cook and Skinner, 2020). In both cases, there is no sense of shared purpose, solidarity or trust. Both child support and lone-parent benefits are open to challenge and reform. Both systems must be brought under neoliberal regulation that places increasing emphasis on single mothers' self-reliance, self-disciplining and regulation through new, yet familiar, forms of governance. These personalised governance relations mean that women must again conform to men's requirements, albeit the requirements of their ex-partner rather than their husband as may have previously been the case within the nuclear family.

Given that child support programmes 'levelled down' non-resident, breadwinning, taxpaying male parents, especially when combined with welfare state transfers to single parents, there was a need to challenge these programmes. Indeed, in the US, moving child support from a largely ineffective individualised system to a nation-wide state-based system was initially opposed by both sides of politics (Garfinkel et al, 1998). According to the authors, the right viewed child support as an infringement on family privacy whereas the left argued that child support punished poor fathers and may expose mothers to danger. However, strongly held notions of individual responsibility and the need to provide some form of economic security to poor women assuaged both the Left's and the Right's concerns to the extent where legislation was possible. As Crowley (2003) describes, the introduction of the Personal Responsibility and Work Opportunity Reconciliation Act 1996 (PRWORA) in the US advanced efforts to tighten child support enforcement that had begun with feminist efforts associated with the previous Aid to Families with Dependent Children legislation in 1984 (Crowley, 2003). But pragmatic political backing for child support does not mean that individual resentment and challenge were quashed. While the National Child Support Enforcement Agency programme enjoyed, and continues to enjoy, strong bipartisan political support, opposition to child support enforcement came 'from middle- and upper-income fathers who argue that they are not being treated fairly by the courts, that they lack sufficient access to their children and/or their new families are suffering because their order levels are set too big' (Garfinkel et al, 1998, pp. 18–19). Through this argument, I am not suggesting that child support is an issue upon which voter behaviour or elections are fought. Such issues rarely feature in policy campaigns. Rather, men's dissatisfaction with child support works at a cultural level – eroding trust in public institutions such as the family court, child support and benefit systems. Policymakers and politicians, however, appease such disgruntled publics pandering to vocal individuals' concerns, such as order values that are too high, for example. Such responses entrench the individualism with the child support system, doing little to acknowledge or address the social and economic shifts that underpin men's concerns.

Since the introduction of child support in the US, as Garfinkel et al (1998) describe, the value of single-parent welfare payments declined by 30 per cent. However, rather than being viewed as the collective burden of taxpayers, the responsibility for supporting children in such families was increasingly reframed as fathers' personal responsibility. But, as Garfinkel et al (1998, p. 15) go on to state, 'some fathers who could afford a good lawyer were able to avoid a child support order'. As such, while the nature of financial welfare in the US became increasingly economically rationalised, so too did the responsibility to pay child support. If a father's resources enabled him to avoid payment, then this was an economically rational course of action. At the same time, poor fathers often remained saddled with large child support obligations due to class and racial perversities in access to justice and thus the setting of child support orders. As the state kept all of the money paid to offset poor mothers' benefit payments, poor fathers 'had very little incentive to pay child support, and many of these men simply disappeared' (Garfinkel et al, 1998, p. 16). At the same time as being able to avoid payment through a range of means, men have been vocal critics of child support, internationally.

The complaints described in the US have been echoed across countries and over time and have been particularly successful in shaping child support policy reform. How these neoliberal forces play out in non-liberal regimes, such as in developing systems, is yet to be seen. As the Swedish child support case reveals, however, these forces may be at play in rolling back child support in Nordic contexts. What underpins the rolling back of child support – or its non-implementation or structured failure – is backlash, or the threat of backlash.

The political success of child support backlash

As Walby (1993) describes, 'backlash' represents both an active resistance against feminist interventions, such as child support, and an effort to maintain and reinforce existing gender relations. Her analysis reveals tactics to actively resist as well as deny action. In the context of child support backlash, there have been both active and passive strategies used to challenge or resist legal, administrative or social changes to child support that would enhance women's advancement (Boyd, 2004). In some countries, child support policy problems have been framed and pursued most vigorously by the vocal men's rights lobby. The reforms that occurred as a result of fathers' rights activist lobbying have been shown to undermine the original purpose of child support, reframing the problems in terms of women's equal responsibility to earn and men's equal right to care. The application of such tactics in Australia, for example, has seen fathers co-opt gender equality rhetoric to frame solutions to child support unfairness in terms of equal treatment (Cook and Skinner, 2019). Fathers' suggestions for reform, however, remained couched within the logic of the existing, technical systems (Cook and Skinner, 2020) and gender hierarchies of earning and caring (Cook and Skinner, 2019), which would see men reinstated as the authority over when and how money could be spent.

However, the tactics of child support's opponents are diverse, as Crowley's (2003) analysis of the entrepreneurial tactics of child support policy development describes. With respect to the early male advocacy groups that pre-dated US child support opposition, Crowley (2003, p. 189) describes their tactics as involving three prominent themes: 1) the sexual degradation of women, 2) the portrayal of all women as 'gold diggers', and 3) the suggestion that all women are financially irresponsible. These tactics ultimately proved unsuccessful in the US, and they now seem out of step with gender roles and expectations. But I argue that while these themes may no longer hold political promise, they remain evident to varying degrees in the psyche of fathers disaffected by child support. For example, the term 'gold digger' has remained in popular culture and normative understandings of mothers' purportedly inappropriate access to and use of child support (Goodall and Cook, 2020).

Researchers in Australia, the UK, Canada and the US have noted men's issues with women's promiscuity and re-partnering, seeking more money than they are entitled to and using child support money inappropriately (Uviller, 1978; Bertoia and Drakich, 1993; Kaye and Tolmie, 1998; Crowley, 2003; Fogarty and Augoustinos, 2008; Cook and Skinner, 2020; Goodall and Cook, 2020). These studies span the entirety of child support policymaking, showing few signs of change across technical or policy contexts. What these repeated instances illustrate, rather, is the social order that 'fathers' rights' arguments seek to preserve: the dominant, facilitated and autonomous position of fathers within households, and their continuation of such freedoms across households.

While Crowley's (2003) historical analysis notes the limitations of fathers' rights groups' initial anti-women stance, the question for disgruntled taxpaying fathers then became how to achieve their aims without marking oneself out as self-interested, misogynistic and out of step with a progressive agenda. The answer for those seeking political action has been through the rational, detached and purportedly gender-neutral deployment of 'expertise'. Expertise and evidence on the harms of child support have been deployed by middle-class fathers and their representatives in fathers' rights groups to achieve technical reforms that effectively dismantle the benefits of child support (Cook and Natalier, 2016).

In the US, the PRWORA legislation introduced measures – and, importantly, the human and administrative resources to enact them – to identify delinquent payers and penalise those who fell behind in payments. Draconian measures such as denying food stamps and revoking driver's and other professional licences were enacted. But this did not mean that child support was widely taken up. Rather, fathers in the US were mobilised to protest child support, with claims centring upon their unequal treatment before the law, and the need for the state to assist men to 'get ahead', thus allowing them to better service their child support obligations (Crowley, 2003). As will be described in the following chapter, fathers' evidence has informed technical reforms that have served to buttress the interests of payers. Technical changes to child support policies and procedures have failed to address the social and structural issues regarding rapidly evolving work, family and gender regimes that have ostensibly left men's ability to choose intact. The changes to child support that fathers demand often either reduce fathers' liabilities, impose barriers for women within technical systems or institute nonperformative elements within system design. Across technically dominated and contested child support contexts, analyses reveal that the most vocal fathers would like to see child support abandoned or significantly lessened.

For activist fathers, their aims are, ideally, to dismantle any coercive and responsibilising elements of the child support programme in a given context and replace them with discretionary, unexamined processes that are enacted through individualised interaction. These processes return child support to the individualistic processes determined by social norms and conventions rather than notions of justice or equality that preceded formal child support systems (Wyss, 2001). While these individualising processes could be regarded as 'freeing' separated parents from the technical governance of their lives, as Chapter 8 describes, they remain inadequate for addressing the social problem of single-mother and child poverty, for which child support was originally enacted. Instead, any intervention relies on fathers' individual benevolence and the gift-worthiness of the recipient mother (Natalier and Hewitt, 2010; Keil and Elizabeth, 2017). Gender roles are reinforced. In the context of an erosion of trust in the benefit system, and increasingly individualised relations, reforms are required to bring both child support and lone parent benefits in line with social convention.

Rendering child support problems permanent

As a result of gendered, often classed and sometimes racialised interests, I argue that there is a 'permanence' that pervades child support systems. This permanence sees the same issues repeat over time, in ways that are seemingly intractable. For example, there is resignation to the fact that child support is an 'unsolvable Rubik's cube' (Smyth and Henman, 2010, p. 6). However, underpinning the acceptance of child support as 'unsolvable' is state silence, whereby the problems with child support are either deliberately or inadvertently unacknowledged, and thus actively made unresolvable. Both silence and deflection illustrate the 'causal stories' (Stone, 1989) that the state tells about child support's legal, policy and administrative problems. These accounts, and the permanence they produce, have material as well as symbolic consequences. As Stone (1989, p. 283) suggests,

> Causal stories have both an empirical and a moral dimension. On the empirical level, they purport to demonstrate the mechanism by which one set of people brings about harms to another set. On the normative level, they blame one set of people for causing the suffering of others. On both levels, causal stories move situations intellectually from the realm of fate to the realm of human agency.

While Stone's (1989) account describes harms that are actively brought upon another group of people, her work also describes the opposite – where causal stories obscure human agency, by locating the causes of the problem within complex social, historic and institutional systems, often described as 'wicked problems' (McConnell, 2018). Here, the failure of states to enforce child support and thus the low rates of poverty reduction that result (Hakovirta, 2011; OECD, 2011) are not the effects of state inaction, but rather, the 'unintended' consequences of complex systems. As Stone (1989, p. 292) suggests, 'complex cause is sometimes used as a strategy to avoid blame and the burdens of reform'. But the empirical and moral dimensions of avoidance are no less than those produced through active reform. The complex systems in which child support is embedded produce consequences such as non-compliance, enduring poverty and increased violence against women 'by accident'. From the state's perspective, these are not 'intended' consequences; rather, they are regarded as unintended and thus 'unforeseen' consequences of complex systems and sets of actors, rendering them beyond state control. This does not change the experience of financial abuse, poverty or violence for women and children, nor does it go any way to intervene to lessen these harms.

Identifying the causes of non-compliance, poverty and women's vulnerability as beyond control legitimises women's subordination and men's financial autonomy. It also illustrates the gender of the state in its enactment of laws, policies and institutions that willingly or inadvertently fail to recognise child support non-compliance as a social problem that is the outcome of the system's design. Some would regard this outcome as intentional, whereas others would regard it as inadvertent. In any case, drawing on Stone's (1989) model of the causes of policy problems, these consequences can be seen as a result of purposeful design in child support systems.

Brush (2003) describes how state practices speak to how power is exercised through who controls the rules, how problems are identified and understood, and how challenges to the rules are managed. In this case, these practices illustrate how child support policymaking, its administration and reform, and the management (or lack thereof) of compliance reference and reinforce traditional power structures which position men as financially independent and autonomous. Women, by contrast, are rendered financially subordinate and thus, ideally, grateful for whatever resources they receive. However, separated mothers are also increasingly expected to earn their own income – and, as examples presented in previous chapters have shown, are then punished for it in child support and benefit calculations – presenting contradictory messages. These are located in masculinised understandings of individual capacity to earn which do not map well onto mothers with caregiving responsibilities, but simultaneously frame single mothers as the opposite of passive, dependent, grateful recipients. But, despite the contradictory messages and expectations, the power of the state remains, given these low-income mothers' receipt of benefits or other payments.

The introduction of administrative child support systems has not achieved its aims, but rather has rendered women's poverty permanent.

These systems masked the extant power of the state to compel women's child support seeking and, in many cases, to retain all or part of any child support money paid. In cases where wage withholding is not an option, or where private arrangements are possible, it is often left to men's discretion as to whether they comply with child support orders or not. As such, the social problem of child poverty that child support sought to resolve was rhetorically achieved, but substantively left intact. As one Canadian bureaucrat conceded:

> 'They've gone from that, sort of, 30 years ago the feminist approach of 40 years ago – "He should pay because it's not fair that a woman would pick up all that" – to "Oh well this is life. He was a loser when we were together, he's a loser now and the system's for someone else. The system's not for us. It doesn't respond."' (Canada)

While the bureaucrat was describing the expectations and experiences of single mothers, this excerpt can apply equally to the system. For example, across the border in the US, a federal informant noted with respect to the US's high-value orders that:

> 'High orders [are] set on presumptions rather than evidence, and using a model that is really based on previously married, middle-class couple … I think the basic paradigm certainly works for many families. I mean, it certainly – there are many families in the child support caseload in the US that fit that basic structure of mostly middle-class, often divorced twice, so more complicated than one mother, one father, two point five kids.' (US, federal level)

Given their precarious financial position, single mothers must depend on income and in-kind contributions from a range of sources to ensure their financial survival, including the state, market, family and community. However, countries in the Anglosphere, including Australia, New Zealand, the US and the UK have been identified as having some of the lowest unemployment benefit rates of OECD countries, particularly for single-parent families, which have been eroded since the introduction of child support systems. In this context, I suggest that child support can be seen as the policy articulation of 'appropriate' income packages for single mothers, where the state intervenes to compel single mothers' activity in seeking state, market and family resources. As a result, private child support transfers from one parent to the other exist within the context of compelled governance practices that intersect with income secured from the state and the market. However, these unreliable income sources often fail to lift mothers above the poverty line.

Discussions of the role of the individual, a male breadwinner, the extended family and the welfare state are not confined to liberal democracies. Similar discussions were had across a range of contexts:

> 'I mean, in my impression, in many cases when the mother divorces, they go to their parents' home and they may not need to worry about their financial conditions. So, some people are just protected by the mother's parents. But certainly, if the mother doesn't have a parent or they have a problem, financial problem, in that case they have to – I mean the mother has to work and they have to raise children. Some mothers think that they have to be independent and they have to do it themselves; some people think like that.' (Japan)

> 'In terms of divorce things have also changed. For example, there was always an obligation almost on the husband being the stronger party to maintain the wife and to maintain the standard of living. Now the law has changed. Now the law has made it more equal in terms of treatment so the wife will – there's an obligation on the wife that doesn't work, for example, and if there's – if she doesn't have children or if she's not caring for the children but to find her own source of income, this in terms of spousal maintenance for example is very important. Before husbands would need to maintain their wives forever. Not only to maintain their wives but to maintain their standard of living, which is another thing that was eliminated in our new law.' (Portugal)

> 'Their [fathers'] salaries are much higher. So even if the women now goes to work and she is taking care of old people or taking care of small children in kindergarten or stuff like that, which enable her to be with her children as well, she doesn't make enough money to live from it. So, she is in poverty even though she is working. Most of the single parents, the single mothers they work. But it's not enough.' (Israel)

The extent to which child support laws and practices have followed social attitudinal changes is still playing out.

Reducing poverty or benefit payments

As discussed earlier, child support has been described as achieving one of three competing aims: reducing child poverty, reducing welfare expenditure, or enforcing paternal responsibility. Mothers are largely invisible here, despite being central to enacting the process. Additionally, the first two of these aims of child support locate its purview firmly within the welfare state. However, it is the third aim that problematises child support's location within welfare state policies and practices and renders child support unlike other policies within the social policy domain. The blurring of public and private responsibilities is child support's undoing, as mothers' private enforcement of fathers' publicly ordered parental responsibility largely goes without scrutiny. At the same time, states do not have the necessary tools to intervene in private affairs that lie outside of their social policy gaze. As a result, child support systems may be more of a theatrical device than a system for financial redistribution. They claim to transfer money from a non-resident to a resident parent, but very often do not.

By having a child support system, countries can claim how well they are doing at transferring payments, while not doing that at all. Sweden's pre-2016 system provides a stark example of the representation of a particular view of reality through a technical system and the way that this 'reality' has material implications. OECD (2011) data reports that 100 per cent of Swedish sole parents received child support in 2005. However, this figure is achieved by including all government-provided guaranteed maintenance in cases of non-compliance as 'child support'. The extent of non-compliance within the Swedish system was obscured, thus excusing non-compliant payers. Even within the post-2016 system, non-compliance is obscured, as payees can return to the guaranteed system if payments are not forthcoming. The Swedish informant describes how non-compliance is not pursued, as the money can instead be replaced by income from the welfare system.

> 'Then, if that [child support] agreement has a certain standard or formality, it's supposed to be signed or witnessed by two people and signed. Then you can take that to the enforcement agency and have it enforced if the father doesn't pay the way he's supposed to. But that is very rarely used. That has some historical reasons I suppose but, to not go into it too deeply, we have a big welfare system in Sweden.' (Sweden)

At the same time, the definition of child support, as discussed in Chapter 1, is broadened to include government payments. While this may provide a useful solution to the problem of sole parent and child poverty (indeed, the same OECD data reports that Swedish sole parent family poverty reduced from 21.2 per cent to 9.7 per cent as a result of the child support system), it addresses different 'causes' than those assumed within most child support systems. Applying Bacchi's (2009) problem framework to the Swedish system reveals that the causal mechanisms diverge from those in other countries depending on whether you begin from the problem (child poverty) and work through to the solution (advanced payments), or begin from the solution (advanced payments), and work from that to identify what problem it solves (non-payment of child support). The question to ask then becomes, why has the Swedish government invested significant state resources in covering for non-compliant fathers? Answering this question leads to an examination of the ideological tenets that underpin child support, which were evolving at the time of the interview with the key informant. Sweden is replacing its focus on ensuring single parents' financial well-being with a focus on individual responsibility. As a recent examination of the 2016 Swedish reform noted, as to why they could not engage in the private child support system, 'Prior to the reform, [state-provided] child maintenance was a universal benefit in the sense that any separated parent could apply for it. After the reform, this scheme became conditional on an exemption for "special reasons"' (Fernqvist and Sépulchre, 2021, p. 13). However, as is described further in Chapter 8, the institutional requirement in Sweden to privatise child support payments reinforces gendered individual and interactional norms. Which problems these personal solutions solve is also revealing. Moving payments into the private domain solves the problem of state oversight of payments. Welfare expenditure is reduced, at the expense of reducing child poverty.

What is of significance to this chapter is that the failures of child support, as described in Chapter 4, are enabled by a lack of state attention to their causes and a lack of regard for the consequences borne by individual mothers and their children. However, the invisibility of such problems and the inefficacy of the solutions does not mean that child support is unproductive. By contrast, child support can provide benefits and can serve as a useful device. In addition to the financial benefits that child support can provide when it is paid regularly, I argue that its other benefits confer primarily upon states with advanced, technical systems and upon individual fathers in countries with more rudimentary regimes. In highly technical systems, which often have an administrative as opposed to a legal bent, states have typically intervened to present child support as a response to burgeoning child poverty (Skinner and Hakovirta, 2020), and in some cases, such benefits are realised (Hakovirta, 2011; OECD, 2011). However, as is outlined later, poverty reduction effects are often quickly subsumed by state welfare expenditure reduction goals.

While child support can certainly reduce single parents' experiences of poverty, it is often ineffective as a poverty reduction mechanism. In many cases, this is due to the limited resources available to each parent when the economy of scale of a dual-parent household is lost upon separation. There is often simply not enough money to go around. For these cases, child support is a poor solution to the problem of child poverty. Individual fathers with low incomes cannot provide sufficient funds to keep themselves and a separate household above the poverty line (Hakovirta et al, 2019a). However, family separation and child support do not apply exclusively to the poor. For previously middle-class families, research has shown that across countries, in the years following separation, the economic consequences of divorce are far worse for mothers than they are for fathers (de Vaus et al, 2017; Fletcher et al, 2020), whose incomes have been shown in some cases to increase in the years following separation (de Vaus et al, 2017). Women and children in all families are failed by: 1) the leaky pipeline of child support, which is presented as a means of redistributing a male breadwinner's income across households to compensate mothers for the opportunity costs of their caring labour; and 2) by the inadequacy of funds that such families are often entitled to receive. In both cases, what then is child support for?

Bacchi's (1999, 2009) research suggests that the policy 'solution' of an administrative approach to child support – as has been taken up by various US states, Australia, New Zealand, Norway and the UK, and as is emerging in South Korea – is revealing of the policy 'problem' that it seeks to remedy. The introduction of an administrative regime in these countries suggests that parents in these countries experienced problems with the previous court-based approach. As Chapter 3 outlined, and as policy history has described (Edwards et al, 2001; Edwards, 2019), these problems included the barriers to accessing court-based systems and the difficulty that individual parents have in trying to enforce court orders. But, perhaps more importantly to states, a problem that administrative child support systems could solve was burgeoning welfare expenditure on single-parent families resulting from the introduction of no-fault divorce and the growth in single-mother-headed families who were unable to individually fulfil both breadwinning and caregiving roles. This costly demographic shift was a looming problem for states. By positioning fathers as responsible for providing income to children, states could offset some of their costs (see Skinner, 2012 for a description of the UK's child support policy history). Further, reductions in state welfare expenditure could be achieved more effectively when child support was brought into the same administrative domain as benefit payments.

In many US states, the state retains a proportion of all money paid, described as a child support 'clawback'. Many other jurisdictions compel single mothers to seek child support in order to be eligible for state benefits. In other systems, women choose between seeking benefits or seeking child support, as it is impossible to receive an income from both sources. In its most extreme form, as in New Zealand and South Korea for example, the government retains all child support money paid. As the South Korean informant explained:

> 'For families who [are] on welfare, a "dollar" transferred as child support will reduce a dollar from welfare support. Almost like the 100 per cent tax. Also, in terms of the determination of eligibility, and also the benefit amounts, it works like full disregard and none passed through. But we don't have a requirement for welfare recipients to be the client of the child support system. We don't have that.' (South Korea)

Given the full clawback of child support payments by the state, in South Korea, the key informant noted that women were likely to choose welfare benefits over child support payments, as they were more reliable. However, in New Zealand, women are compelled to enter the child support system, but the government still retains all of the money paid (up to the value of the benefit payment), as an academic informant explained.

> 'They only have to seek child support here if they're on a benefit. We don't have a pass-on provision, so if you're on a benefit and if you name the father then you have to pursue child support formally. Then the money that they get through child support is used to offset the cost of the benefit. So, they only receive child support if it's in excess of the amount that they receive through the benefit. So, then a lot of mothers don't realise that and so when they realise that they're like, "Oh, no, now I'm pursuing child – I'm on a benefit."' (New Zealand)

In other many other countries, where the state does not have a direct interest in the money received, what is left unquestioned and unchecked in child support programmes is whether mothers and their children actually receive payments.

Non-payment is often inconsequential to the operation of child support and eligibility for welfare payments in such countries. As Chapter 5 outlined, such considerations are typically not examined by governments or in research, and thus are not able to be evidenced. But rather than their invisibility ensuring that such issues remain unexamined, the unspoken and unacknowledged blind spots of child support are central to my analysis, where they can be understood as tools in preserving the existing social order.

Child support as nonperformative

There have been two primary processes through which child support policy has buttressed men's interests, which result in and are represented by a failure to transfer payments to single-mother-headed families. However, the promotion of masculine interest in child support involves more than a lack of enforcement. The two processes through which child support buttresses men's interests are states doing nothing, or very little, to address the problems with child support systems and active interventions that – rather than addressing the systemic failures of child support policy – embed structural disadvantages in the name of system 'improvement' (Li, 2007). The result of each process, however, is usually the same. Single-mother-headed families are typically no better off, and separated fathers are typically freed from their responsibilities to children unless they voluntarily choose to engage with state processes or engage privately on their own terms.

While Ahmed's (2006, 2007) work focuses on the nonperformativity of institutional processes, such as anti-racism policy in university settings, her work is useful for examining broader processes, such as how child support processes enable fathers' non-performance, which is then taken by states to 'stand in for' the enactment of the child support system. Failing to notice inconvenient problems, noticing only those problems that impede powerful interests – in this case, interests of the state and fathers – and presenting the existence of 'a solution' as the achievement of 'the solution' all serve to diffuse the need to act. These are processes of non-performance that enable states to do nothing, while simultaneously claiming that the problem has been solved. I argue that while child support was introduced as a measure to improve the material circumstances of children living in single-mother-headed households, it is because mothers receive these payments on behalf of their children that the system has been resisted. Rather than ensuring that fathers transfer payments to mothers to oversee on behalf of their children, the system often serves as a nonperformative. Through its very existence, child support 'works' by failing to bring about improvements in the material living standards of most single-mother-headed families. More importantly, however, child support 'works' because its very existence denies the need for greater intervention, as a system to solve the problem already exists. Failures in the system can then be attributed to an 'implementation gap' whereby the goals of the policy are not met due to inefficient or incomplete procedures. The remedy, in these cases, is to increase technical precision or identify solutions within the private realm (Jamrozik and Nocella, 1998). But, as will be shown in Chapter 7, technical reforms are also often nonperformative, or work against the interests of those they are purportedly designed to serve. Here, silence plays an important and productive role in attempts to resist identifying problems or introducing changes that foreground the experiences of mothers and their children.

Adding a further conceptual lens to Ahmed's work, the causal stories (Stone, 1989) told about the problems of child support frame how child support problems can be acted upon or ignored, thus leading to action or inaction. Of course, control of the causal story exists within gendered social and institutional hierarchies that limit women's ability to institute change and embolden men to resist and reframe any interventions that challenge their social and financial dominance (Bacchi, 1999; Smith, 2001; Graycar and Morgan, 2002). Jamrozik and Nocella's (1998) work on the sociology of social problems also covers similar conceptual terrain, as does Li's (2007, p. 8) practice of improvement described as 'antipolitics', which she defines as the design of programmes to contain a challenge to the status quo. Antipolitics shares many features of Ahmed's (2006) description of nonperformatives and Nicholas and Agius's (2018) description of 'doing nothing'. While these concepts have been identified and deployed from a range of theoretical and epistemological traditions, they each point to the role of power in designing social programmes and in defining their 'success'. In child support systems set on an agenda of review and reform, technologies of governance may be deployed to seemingly 'improve' child support, while simultaneously deflecting attention away from measures that would materially improve women and children's circumstances. Changes that are introduced are not designed to facilitate women's emancipation, but rather such changes are allowed because they entrench women's traditional roles and location in the gender order (Bacchi, 1999). To quote Ahmed (2006, p. 105), 'the nonperformative does not "fail to act" because of conditions that are external to the speech act: rather, it "works" because it fails to bring about what it names' (see also Masoumi, 2019).

In terms of how the status quo is entrenched and maintained, the nonperformativity of child support can involve either failing to acknowledge the problem, thus protecting the existing way of doing things, or acknowledging the problem without actually addressing it. States may do only enough to assuage the public and appear as if action is being taken – thus, performing action while achieving inaction. By doing little to make child support systems more equitable, by making changes to technical details while leaving structural barriers intact, or by doing nothing at all, states defer to their historical, gendered ways of doing things, which privilege men's interests and their ability to choose if and how to support their children. These processes align with Ahmed's (2007) work on performatives and nonperformatives, whereby dominant groups employ strategies of inaction in lieu of addressing a problem that threatens the extant social order. However, these nonperformative processes are not confined to rudimentary systems where the leaky pipe may be thought to be most evident. Such processes also exist in systems regarded as 'high functioning' or even 'world leading', such as Australia. To paraphrase Ahmed (2007, p. 597) having a 'good' child support policy – as Australia, for example, claims to have – becomes translated into being 'good at' child support. The remainder of this chapter steps through how and why this is not the case.

To begin the task of disentangling child support nonperformatives, I set out how child support governance has worked in two ways to protect masculine interests. First, the protection of masculine interests has occurred through the deployment of silence and inaction in order to resist identifying problems or introducing changes that recognise women's interests. Second, while child support has often been ineffective, there has been a gendered backlash against it. This backlash has not been led by women who do not receive payments, but rather by fathers whose complaints would suggest that they are the victims of their own privilege which is supported by child support's masculine worldview and the gendered interests of legal, policy and administrative processes. Australia's purportedly 'world-leading' approach provides a case in point. Thus, before addressing silence, inaction and backlash, I now set out how nonperformatives have been achieved in Australia and a range of other child support contexts.

The cautionary tale of Australia's child support policy 'success'

In Australia, child support is one of the most complained about government functions (Commonwealth Ombudsman, 2012, 2014), prompting almost continual review since its inception in 1988–89. Over this period, government reviews have been conducted repeatedly (House Standing Commmittee Family and Community Affairs, 2003; Ministerial Taskforce on Child Support, 2005; House of Representatives Standing Committee on Social Policy and Legal Affairs, 2015; Joint Select Committee on Australia's Family Law System, 2020).

Australia's highly technical and highly interventionist system provides unsurpassed insight into the governance of single mothers at the extreme, as it is in the justification of gendered (Cook and Natalier, 2013, 2014, 2016) and disadvantageous (Fehlberg and Maclean, 2009) reforms that the disciplining of single mothers is evident. In Australia, as Meredith Edwards (2019, p. 142), one of the original proponents of the scheme, describes, when Australia's child support system was introduced in 1989, 'the pay-as-you-earn system of collecting taxes would be used to collect child support payments'. But, within six years of the mandatory wage-withholding system being enshrined, its success in curtailing men's financial autonomy and authority led to it being recast as a voluntary option. As the Joint Select Committee on Certain Family Law Issues (1994, p. 229) noted, 'the effect of this [private transfers] would be to minimise the intervention of Government as well as the CSA's cost of administering the Scheme'. Here, the state's interest in minimising costs, and the gendered interest in minimising the state's 'intervention' in men's affairs is starkly evident. What led to the dismantling of the automatic system of wage-withholding was that it was performing as its 'femocrat' designers had intended. As a result, it needed to be reconstructed as a nonperformative in order to ensure its continued support. Despite the Joint Select Committee noting that 'one of the great successes' of the scheme was involuntary wage withholding, the committee recommended that 'private collection, rather than CSA collection, [be] encouraged as much as possible' (Joint Select Committee on Certain Family Law Issues, 1994, p. 192). Since then, private child support agreements in Australia have come to predominate (House of Representatives Standing Committee on Social Policy and Legal Affairs, 2015), which are then assumed in benefit interactions to be 100 per cent compliant. Taken together, and alongside minor administrative changes that have been ushered through parliament, these reviews have weakened Australia's system and have failed to address any of the concerns expressed by or on behalf of impoverished women and their children (Hancock, 1998; Australian Law Reform Commission, 2012; Cook and Natalier, 2013; Cook, 2020). As such, Australia's child support reform process can be read as a nonperformative for women, whereby no action is taken while 'nodding along' with women's concerns. Here, policy processes of quantification and the 'erasure of the social' (Frohmann, 1992, p. 376) have seen child support framed in men's terms, thus buttressing men's concerns. The resultant 'interventionist' formula changes that occurred in 2008 saw high-income men financially benefit (Smyth and Henman, 2010), while low-income women have seen their child support incomes fall (Summerfield et al, 2010) and their poverty increase (Son et al, 2014). Further, while non-compliance is purportedly a significant issue (Stewart, 2019), measures to improve collection and enforcement have been actively excluded from Australia's major reform process (Cook and Natalier, 2013). The only collection measure implemented in the last decade has been to collect benefit overpayments from low-income single mothers when child support is retrospectively increased (Department of Human Services, 2019). Introduced as a measure to 'improve child support compliance' this change is not only a nonperformative with respect to child support compliance, it also actively produces single mothers' disadvantage (Cook, 2021a).

Australia's position, spanning both an unwillingness to 'see' the problems of concern to women, and the active use of nonperformatives, demonstrates how these two forms of gendered processes are not discrete, but rather comprise a suite of tools enacted by states at particular times and in particular ways that align with their masculine worldviews and interests. The messiness of these categories does not render them irrelevant. Rather, it shows how an understanding of policy solutions – including non-solutions – is essential to identifying the purported 'problems' that precipitated them (Bacchi, 1999, 2009).

As has been discussed, policies, laws and their associated documentation can often come to stand in for the problems that they seek to resolve. By virtue of having a child support system, irrespective of its dysfunctions, the problems that the Australian child support system was supposed to alleviate are seen to have been overcome. There is no longer a need to vigorously pursue fathers to transfer payments to their previously dependent, caregiving partners. The system will do this. When mothers and their children remain in poverty, their solutions remain elsewhere, as it is easier to suggest that the child support system is not at fault. Either individual women are not trying hard enough to enter and engage in the system or with their ex-partners, or perhaps the system is biased against men by requiring that they pay too much, or that payments are not commensurate with their 'access'. In any case, it is not the system that is broken, but rather the more easily correctible techniques, or perhaps even the characteristics and behaviours of the applicants themselves. While this case study pertains exclusively to Australia, child support reforms serve more as nonperformatives than as measures to ensure that single mothers and their children receive payments.

Examples of state-initiated proceedings, the automatic inclusion of child support within divorce proceedings and wage-withholding may present a rosy picture of the nature and function of child support across countries. Indeed, individual states may hold up these examples as accounts of the benefits or high functioning of their systems. However, in a range of countries, while seemingly functional systems exist for entering parents into the child support system, few processes subsequently exist for actually collecting and transferring payments.

International nonperformativity

As has been a key theme of this chapter, one means of preserving state interests is by doing nothing. This tactic can be taken up by rudimentary systems that fail to identify or act on a problem, or by interventionist systems that seek to make 'improvements' but do so in ways that fail to intervene in the underlying causes. Examples of the nonperformativity of child support are evident across countries and throughout the child support process. For example, while Malta has mandatory provisions to establish child support, this only works when fathers can be subpoenaed to attend court proceedings, which is a significant failure:

> 'At the worst they [the police charged with subpoenaing parents to attend court] called you or the man, or they don't notify – if the court sends a notification to the father for example – they [the police] say he's not found at home. They collude. For example, I've had cases … because Malta is a very small country, very face-to-face, they might know them or be friends with them. She said he called him. He [the police officer] was joking with him – in this case she wanted to report violence as well – that he was joking with him about football, for example, so a lack of professionalisation in the police force. … I mean, there's no enforcement as such. … There are also in Maltese law a lot of loopholes with regards to enforceability. For example, time barring is one of them under criminal law. If it's 90 days, it's time barred. You can't – basically it [the case for enforcement] will fall. If the father isn't notified and miraculously isn't found, those 90 days elapse and that's it.' (Malta)

The Peruvian informant made similar observations, in that women were required to expend significant time, resources and energy to enter the child support system but men were freed from these obligations through inaction.

They noted that, "I think in the urban areas, women can give a fight a little bit longer with the scarce resources they have. Most of them. But, in rural areas in Peru, the situation is … it's very sad actually for many women." While they also noted that while "the Government has been promoting more women to ask for it [child support]", women who live outside major centres with child support offices cannot access the system. On these issues, the informant went on to note:

> 'However, I think it [encouraging child support] is very focussed on urban areas, of course. It's very hard to reach rural areas. In urban areas still there is a – some women have – the rates of women demanding for child support have increased in the past years, but – and the government can't – I mean the judiciary system is very small. We have – there are not many lawyers who can represent the women. They have – they're overloaded with cases.' (Peru)

As discussed earlier, state inaction maintains barriers to child support for women, be they geographic, literary, social, financial, temporal or procedural, which typify most systems except those with guaranteed (or advanced) maintenance schemes. While women must expend significant time, energy and costs to enact child support systems, fathers do not need to engage. By failing to acknowledge and act on these barriers, women's financial needs are rendered invisible and men are freed up to provide child support on their own terms, if at all.

The mandatory seeking of child support in many countries may provide women with additional resources, but these benefits only accrue if payments are made. Seeking child support may instead limit women's eligibility for state benefits, as it is included as income in eligibility calculations or reduces the amount of benefit outlays:

> 'But in order to get the living support and not the child support, she also has to prove that there is no father or that there is violence and this is why she is not suing the father in court. She can't just choose not to sue the father. If she has a court order that says that he needs to pay the money, even if he is not paying it, they usually think it's income in the – when they see her salary. Then she – and if she wants to get help with other support, then she needs to prove that she's not getting the money. She needs to sign a declaration or stuff like that, or to show her bank account to prove that she's not getting the money in order not to make it part of her income. … When it comes to the social security, there the state says, "I don't want to pay the money instead of the father". That's why she makes a lot of [unsuccessful claims] in this situation. You can't get the money with this situation.

You can't – because they don't want to give the money instead of the father.' (Israel)

Regardless of the type of state activity, the failures of child support typically remain. The permanence that child support reflects and affects does not lie in the legal, administrative or political structures, as there has often been great change within child support systems and settings. Rather, this permanence exists in the gendered and classed expectations placed on women who enter the child support system: the prioritising of gendered, masculinist worldviews (Nicholas and Agius, 2018), including a simultaneous blindness to feminine concerns (Cook et al, 2015b). The permanence of these gendered and classed expectations results in the permanence of gendered outcomes for women. These outcomes – in the form of child support laws, policies and processes – can increase women's risk of financial, legal, physical and emotional harm. Insidiously, these harms can often occur irrespective of whether child support is paid or received, and can be the result of women simply entering the system. These risks to women are often compelled by states. The alternative to this harm is for women to 'give up' on pursuing child support – ultimately absolving the children's father of all financial responsibility. In some contexts, women abrogating their children's right to support from the father due to safety concerns are then ineligible for state support. At the same time, women's reactions to these systems respond to and legitimise men's rights discourses that push back against seemingly 'feminist' agendas (Nicholas and Agius, 2018). As the examples in this book demonstrate, across countries, women are compelled by child support systems to act in ways that mark their actions out as contrary to the culturally assigned gender norms of passivity, docility and submissiveness to men's financial autonomy and authority. Women are enlisted through child support programmes to serve as facilitators of men's social and emotional needs.

As was discussed in Chapter 4, seeking payments may increase the risk of physical violence against women. In response, several countries that mandate the seeking of child support have exemption processes if women can demonstrate a history of abuse (Pearson et al, 2001; Douglas and Nagesh, 2019). Again, while the child support system is not enacted in these cases, the mere existence of a system – and of processes to exempt women from the compulsion to enter it – stands in for having a system that can ensure women's financial security after leaving a violent relationship. Women and children who have left abusive relationships are no less needy of financial support than those who have not; indeed, they may be more so. While exemptions do not alleviate women's financial need, they do expose the dangers for women inherent in individualised child support systems.

Exemption processes, however, typically only apply when women can prove that they are at risk of continuing violence (Douglas and Nagesh,

2019). Administrative processes typically do not consider how initiating the child support process may in itself precipitate violence by escalating tensions between parents. Such omissions identify that women's safety is not the primary concern of policymakers. For states, the mandatory requirement that low-income separated mothers seek child support serves to direct women to a source of income other than state benefits. This private money can reduce women's need for state support or reduce the value of benefit outlays. But, at the same time, while many child support systems with welfare benefit interactions compel mothers to establish orders, most systems do not have similar provisions to compel fathers' engagement. Again, doing nothing can result in financial reward. The rewards for fathers rely on inactive systems that do not compel men's activity, as well as gendered interpersonal power dynamics whereby women must appease fathers in order to coax payments (Natalier and Hewitt, 2010).

As the preceding discussion illustrates, men's worldviews and concerns have been effective in amending legislation to undermine the original purpose of child support. In doing so, child support in advanced, liberal regimes in particular has been reframed in terms of women's equal responsibility to earn and men's equal right to care (Cook and Skinner, 2019). But, while gender equality arguments are laudable, they focus on equal rights without addressing the structural issues regarding rapidly evolving work, family and gender regimes. As a result, fathers have been able to use this discourse to support their right to 'choose' how and whether to engage in care, while mothers are left responsible for picking up any care not taken up by fathers, while also often being compelled to engage in work through welfare-to-work programmes. Here, fathers have been successful in deploying personal experiences of injustice to effect policy reform, while mothers have been excluded from and silenced within policymaking processes. These issues are examined in more detail in Chapter 8, while attention now turns to the technical means through which child support is enacted and the ways in which these technical systems render separated mothers responsible for: 1) the actions of fathers, 2) the enactment of the system, and 3) achieving the interests of the state.

7

Rendering gendered social problems technical

This chapter returns to Jamrozik and Nocella's (1998) theory of the residualisation of social problems into technical and personal concerns, locating the evolution of purportedly 'advanced' child support systems within Li's (2007) process of 'rendering technical'. The purpose is to identify how the social problems that child support purportedly solves are translated into a series of technical criteria, procedures and formulae that draw attention away from the issues at hand. At the same time, it is women as recipients of child support who have to enact these technical measures. In doing so, women are rendered responsible for the 'correct' enactment of the system, despite the system often failing to deliver child support payments as a result.

Through child support, the problem of single parents' and their children's poverty is positioned as possible to address by increasing non-resident parent responsibility for providing direct payments, pursuing non-resident parent contributions to the state to subsidise increased benefit provisions, or a combination of both. However, these techniques add another layer of complexity to understanding the 'problem' to be solved and move the critical gaze away from the underlying social problem to focus on the technical means. Child poverty is obscured from the gaze of researchers and governments, who instead focus on technical and operational concerns. For example, in the US, which leads the world in the technical management of child support, governments and thus researchers focus on such issues as 'right sizing orders', determining under what conditions fathers are more likely to pay, and at what point compliance measures move from being motivational to punitive (Oldham and Smyth, 2018; Cancian et al, 2019; Hodges et al, 2020; Vogel, 2020a, 2020b). These concerns shift the focus away from the 'feminist' concerns that led to the establishment of child support programmes and move them into the gaze of the masculine bureaucracy, legal system or policy process. Within these systems, the concern of government becomes not one of children's financial welfare, but one of reducing welfare expenditure and, implicitly, working to buttress men's financial autonomy and discretion.

The prioritisation of technical concerns sees such changes as the introduction of paternity tests and legal hurdles to ensure women are not inappropriately claiming, caps on and amendments to child support formulae to ensure the 'right sizing' of orders to meet men's needs, and the 'clawback' of child support to recoup benefit expenditures. These changes do not begin from the position of reducing women's and children's poverty but begin from the interests of men and the state. As such, the technical tools introduced to manage child support may serve more to deflect attention away from the underlying social problem of women's and children's poverty following parental separation. Technical responses to ensure 'fairness' and 'integrity' in child support systems may, in fact, do the opposite of what they purport. They may preclude women from entering the child support system by imposing barriers to access, or limit women's access to child support by clawing back or reducing the value of payments. In this way, technical child support responses may be nonperformative with respect to addressing the problem of child poverty.

Following the trajectory of the management of social problems outlined by Jamrozik and Nocella (1998), child support in many countries has shifted its focus away from how best to address single-parent and child poverty to how best it can implement child support programmes. For example, in Australia, once the child support system was established, the discussion of problems was confined to the scheme's technical remit. The first review of the scheme, in 1992, noted the narrowing of the government's interests:

> The debate now is not whether child support should be assessed by a formula but whether the formula in Australia is satisfactory or whether it can be improved. The debate now is not whether child support obligations should be enforced through the Taxation Office but whether its procedures need to be improved so as to become more efficient and effective. (Child Support Evaluation Advisory Group, 1992, p. iv)

Australia's example provides a succinct summary of the process of rendering technical described by Li (2007) and others (Jamrozik and Nocella, 1998). As a result of such processes, the way that child support could be discussed in Australia was confined. The lenses through which the child support programme could subsequently be viewed focused on effectiveness and efficiency. However, as outlined in Chapter 6, the enforcement of obligations through the Tax Office was soon removed and private collections were made mandatory. As such, while the original intent of child support as a feminist intervention was to effectively ensure payments, technical measures that impeded men's autonomy were removed (for a more detailed account of the gendered unwinding of Australia's child support programme, see Cook, 2020). Rather, in Australia reform efforts have prioritised the 'fairness' of the system – where fairness is focused on ensuring palatable payment amounts for fathers, rather than whether a fair share of resources is provided to children through effective enforcement (Cook and Skinner,

2019). 'Efficiency' within Australian child support reforms has been pivotal to promoting private agreements and collections, where parents can seemingly work things out for themselves without state 'interference' (Joint Select Committee on Certain Family Law Issues, 1994). These processes of reduced government involvement in private life took place in Australia at a time when neoliberal welfare and other government policies were coming to the fore (Wolfinger, 2014). These processes of reprivatisation mirrored those occurring internationally, whereby the social protections provided by the Keynesian welfare state were being eroded and replaced with a rhetoric of individual responsibility and the removal of government interference. The increasingly technical nature of child support internationally, and the gender relations that these reflect and reproduce, should thus be viewed through the lens of neoliberalism, which – despite rhetoric of small government – sees the expansion of governmental techniques to ensure (some) citizens' 'responsibility'.

Technical 'improvement' practices

As stated in Chapter 2, the governmental practices of 'improvement' described by Li (2007) are achieved through the processes of problematisation, antipolitics and rendering technical. Li's (2007) description of social problems that are rendered technical reveals how their technical management – through such processes as criteria, application processes, formulae and agreements – does not eliminate the political and economic processes that structure these problems. Rather, they can foreground them. Thus, the political tactic of confining social problems to narrow technical terms is often an insufficient means of constraining fundamental social challenge. For men, this has resulted in backlash, as described in Chapter 6. For mothers, their limited temporal, economic and social resources vis-à-vis those of fathers, their limited access to power and the expectation that nothing will change have combined to stifle significant challenge to state claims that child support is the most effective means of managing their post-separation financial needs.

What I examine here are the technical processes that have been incrementally applied to child support in order to better 'manage' it. In these contexts, technical measures serve to keep child support from being seen as a social problem requiring wider, social solutions. There are two mechanisms through which issues are rendered technical, as described in this chapter. These include the way that child support reality is able to be represented within technical systems, and the subsequent way that technical systems respond to this reality. As a result, this chapter provides an illustration of Li's (2007) claim that social problems can be backgrounded rather than eliminated through their technical management. But, more insidiously than merely changing the framing of a problem, technical solutions can also inflict material harms upon those they purportedly seek to assist. Across countries, the imposition of technical child support systems can actually exacerbate rather than alleviate child poverty. As Wimberly (2000, p. 733, original emphasis) wrote two decades ago with respect to US reforms, 'instead of assisting financially strapped single-mother households, the CSRA [Child Support Recovery Act] punishes men *and* women, and low-income women in particular, for making procreative choices outside the confines of the nuclear family'. This is a striking example of the power of technical reforms to reinforce the social order.

Representing technical child support reality

Within technical governance regimes, research has described how views of 'client' populations become narrowed. For example, as noted in Chapter 2, Jamrozik and Nocella (1998) describe different views of social problems, from the vantage points of social welfare service clients, front-line staff, administrators and legislators. Each of these views entails a different frame, which draw on increasingly abstract accounts. Across these levels, the focus is narrowed as data are aggregated.

Turning back to the leaky pipeline of child support outlined in Chapter 4, the sites of child support failure – for women – are almost never the sites of policy intervention. Indeed, often the sources of child support policy failure are actively excluded from policy review and reform. The administrative context in which child support data exist includes unresponsive bureaucratic or legal systems, cumbersome processes with lengthy delays, and government regimes that are expensive to operate. Research suggests that women have great difficulty evidencing and documenting their experience of the child support system, including underpayments, financial control and care-time manipulation (Cook and Natalier, 2013; 2014, 2016). These gaps reveal how administrative and social science data are unable to capture the complexity of child support payments and their transfer. Instead, technologies of governance are introduced, which often ignore the leaky pipeline issues of accessing the child support system, enacting orders, having them paid reliably and not suffering resultant undue consequences within the welfare system. These failures exist because of the different epistemic views held by policymakers, administrators, front-line staff and clients. Here, power and interests maintain those issues of attention to policymakers and administrators, while the views of clients are obscured. For example, as the US federal informant noted:

> 'Most data are kept at the state level rather than the federal level. The federal level also has a set of data, large set of data. The consequence of not having much case management data, much data on who the parents are and the case load and what their relationship is to the kids and to

each other has meant that child support for many years has been – has performed mechanically, meaning that the collection efforts – many of which are automated – happened without clear context for, or clear casework understanding of the family context. The consequence of that has been that enforcement efforts have often gone – have been futile too, because there is a lack of data or understanding.' (US, federal level)

Such accounts remove parents' lived experiences from the knowledge process. Thus, with respect to child support, as women engage with social services and respond to legal and policy procedures, their lived experiences of care and injustice are erased. In their place, women's experiences are quantified and accounted for only with respect to the interests of the system. Single mothering as lived experience is translated into a verbal account of mothering in case-worker interviews and exchanges with institutional staff. As phenomenologist van Manen (1990, p. 28) notes with respect to research interviews, but which also applies to service interviews, 'in each case the concept of interview is charged with the reality assumptions, truth criteria and the general goals of the disciplined methodology within which the interview functions'. Upon entry into a technical institutional system, 'the words we use to refer to the phenomenon have lost some of their original meaning. Words that once could reverberate with lived meaning and reveal a living word now have become lame, limp, mute, emptied and forgetful of their past power' (van Manen, 1990, p. 58). I argue that upon entry into the child support system, women's words that convey the meaning of sole mothering in a state of financial vulnerability are translated into technical signifiers that are emptied of the significance of gender and stripped of any institutional, personal or cultural power. These processes reflect what Smith (1999, p. 33) describes as textually grounded ruling relations.

The inward-looking, technical gaze of child support systems also shapes the evaluation of how child support programmes are 'working'. Such evaluations do not include or require an assessment of children's poverty. Rather, their focus is on key performance indicators (KPIs), such as call centre wait times, caseload numbers served and government expenditure on child support recovery efforts (Cancian et al, 2019). For example, in the US, there are five federal KPIs that state child support performance – and thus funding – is tied to. As one US state-level informant described, these KPIs can create perverse incentives for states to close child support cases:

'One example of the performance measures is the percentage of cases that obtains an arrears payment. Well, that arrears payment under the measures can be just one dollar, and then that case will get credit from a federal perspective. ... But that [one dollar] collection does nothing for anybody. The one that's emphasised by the state and the feds are

> the percentage of cases with a current support payment. But while that sounds good, but it is incentivised to sometimes close a case – which surely doesn't do any family any good – just because we didn't get a collection or couldn't locate somebody for a couple of years. … It's clear that some counties, some states, do game it [the KPIs] which is unfortunate because it is supposed to be incentivised to actually help a family out there, help a child, and I don't think it is.' (US, state level)

In some cases, money received by parents is included in national evaluation reports, but there is not a focus on the difficulty with which these funds were obtained, the adequacy of the funds, or their timeliness and regularity – which is key to impoverished recipient families' survival. As such, administrative procedures and their evaluations illustrate governmental tools that support and reinforce the further implementation of manageable, technical responses. Over time, the original social problems that these measures sought to address are removed and the issues are depoliticised.

Responding to technical child support reality

The problems made visible in Chapter 6 regarding child poverty, welfare state expenditure and individual responsibility may pose threats to the state's credibility, as they may reveal awkward truths that run contrary to the expressed purpose of child support, or other social benefits. As such, the technical tools introduced to manage child support may serve more to deflect attention away from underlying and enduring social problems, and instead locate the solutions to the 'new' problems as lying with either more refined technologies or the programme participants themselves. Of interest in this chapter is how the technical solutions to child support problems respond to, buttress or diffuse power and interest. Across systems, and across the points of failure identified in Chapter 4, I find that technical child support processes mirror and reinforce the status quo where the highly technical nature of child support can be seen as a means of governing gender and as a site that reveals the gender of state governance (Brush, 2003). Through technical child support systems, the social hierarchy is preserved and reinforced.

Across contexts, mothers, as the intended recipients of child support, are disproportionately subject to child support technologies while fathers, the intended payers of child support, are largely freed from surveillance and management. Given that in all contexts women have little control over when, how much and if payments are made, the disproportionate involvement of the state and the gendered distribution of risk, responsibility and autonomy are telling. The technologies of child support governance that are disproportionately applied to separated mothers are portrayed as routine, normal, necessary and effective – despite these processes having little, or indeed the opposite, effect.

A range of Anglo-Saxon countries, most notably Australia, the US, New Zealand and (prior to its complete policy reversal) the UK, have contributed to the rise of technical responses to the 'problem' of child support. These countries are positioned as leaders in child support policy and administration, held up as exemplars for other countries to follow (see, for example, Joint Select Committee on Australia's Family Law System, 2020). Technical developments in these and other contexts include calculating the costs of children and 'right-sizing' orders, incorporating the income of one or both parents in the formula, including the distribution of care-time across households, creating processes to deviate from the formula or modify existing orders, collecting child support through wage-withholding, and identifying and pursuing non-compliance.

While many countries have reformed their child support laws and policies in ways that respond to child poverty as a technical matter, what has become progressively problematic is the increasing complexity of incomes, family forms and care-time (Skinner and Hakovirta, 2020). Here, fluctuations in wages make setting, paying or relying on child support payments highly problematic. The mismatch between formula expectations and parents' realities undermines confidence in the scheme to set reasonable orders and ensure that they can be paid as stipulated. These problems are mirrored when family forms become more complex: new children are added to each household, with the formula often penalising one household and rewarding the other with increasing or decreasing required payments. These new families may then break down, resulting in further sets of order and amounts that the formulae are typically more well equipped to manage, as these changes are more long-term than monthly payment cycles. However, with care-time becoming more diverse than the previously typical 'every second weekend and half the school holidays', there is more likelihood of variation across the month, with payers or recipients expecting this to be reflected in the amount of money – purportedly to cover children's costs – that is paid or received.

The problems that child support originally sought to solve, such as child poverty, welfare expenditure and a lack of paternal responsibility, are becoming detached from the reality of child support calculations, processes and transfers. The increasing precarity and uncertainty of work globally (Standing, 2011) makes incomes more unpredictable. Paying parents' capacity to pay child support, or payee parents' need for child support, may not match the data held about their incomes by child support agencies or be reflected in child support orders. Given some countries' expectations for shared care, children's residences have become more fluid. Children move between houses, often in ways that differ over time from what is agreed in orders. Whether child support orders are amended to reflect such changes depends on the ease of doing so and the standards of evidence required. In Australia, again, it is often difficult for mothers to 'prove' that non-resident parents are not taking up their care-time as specified in parenting orders (Cook et al, 2019). Often this is because deviations to agreements begin as one-off changes or are sporadic, but over time, they result in significant redistribution of the costs of children that are not reflected in child support payments. The addition of new children also requires ongoing data collection and reporting by parents and states if they are to accurately reflect capacity to pay and need for payments. The growing rates of multi-partner fertility, found particularly in western countries, make this an increasing issue, but one to which most child support formulae have not responded.

By focusing on the child support formula as a key site of technical governance, I am not positioning it as the sole governance process – although it certainly does add rational calculation to social concepts that defy quantification. Rather, I contend that the technical processes of child support refer to a wide suite of policies, procedures and rules that shape far more of separated parents' lives than the monetary value determined by the formula. These technical governance systems also span a far wider range of laws or policies than child support, marking out child support as an inadequate solution to address the problems these systems create. Here, welfare state eligibility requirements, activity tests, childcare subsidies and access to legal aid – to name but a few – all contribute to a picture of what is socially supported behaviour and what is not. When systems make it hard, if not impossible, for single mothers to gain access, their design is telling them 'this is not for you' and 'you should not be asking for this'. For example, some countries, such as Canada, are removing requirements for women to seek child support in order to claim benefits:

> 'Two provinces have now removed the requirement for families getting welfare to get a [child] support order. They can if they wish and if they get one they can … enrol it in the enforcement service. I think what our experience has suggested is this, when a family is seeking welfare benefits from the state, they're usually in a relatively difficult if not desperate state. They need help now and in many areas, they can get help, but not right now. … If they've got kids, they've probably got a lot more worries on their mind than getting a [child] support order. Our experience before, when we had a requirement to get support orders [in order to receive benefits], I don't think it's unfair to say, that a lot of them when they were told well you have to get a support order, probably responded with, "What's the point, he's never going to pay." In fact, when they did get a support order and

> enrolled it in the programme, guess what, he did pay. Not voluntarily, not willingly.' (Canada)

In provinces that have removed the requirement to seek child support as a condition of benefit eligibility, the focus is on women's immediate needs, and child support is a secondary consideration, if anything. However, the Canadian informant's experience was that when child support seeking was mandatory, and when orders were enrolled in the state collection service, payments begrudgingly followed. As is explored in the subsequent chapter, when mothers are left to work out child support with reluctant ex-partners by themselves, payments are much less likely.

At the same time, while the state may periodically request information such as tax returns, payments or circumstantial details from payers, these can be provided or foregone, often – but not always – without penalty. Where there are penalties, such as in the US – where jail time is a common punishment for non-compliance with often unreasonably high child support orders – these punitive measures have racial dimensions (Cozzolino and Williams, 2017) that reveal the governance of other 'problematic' populations, rather than the social value of and support for single mothers. In Australia, for example, due to benefit interactions, far more punitive practices apply to women as recipients than men as non-compliant payers. Here, calculations of what should be paid are used to determine benefit payments rather than what was paid, complicating these calculations and resulting in financial penalties to recipient women when the figures that they cannot control do not match.

To remedy the failures of existing child support measures, administrative systems have become increasingly technical. As Elrod (1990, p. 104) remarked with respect to the adoption of state-wide child support guidelines in the US in 1987:

> Federal regulations added the requirement that the guidelines be numerical. The Family Support Act of 1988 not only affirmed the use of mathematical child support guidelines but also mandated that those setting child support in all states use the guidelines as a rebuttable presumption of the proper child support award.

Child support research and administration has spent considerable effort refining the technical means through which the system might produce better outcomes. For example, child support formulae have become more complex, including both parents' incomes, percentage of care-time, other caring responsibilities, and a variety of payment methods, such as direct payment of school fees. These technical refinements have added more complexity and have resulted in greater requirements being placed on states to enact and enforce them. As the cost of running a child support system increases, more labour is downloaded onto mothers. The result is often that these processes require mothers to provide more information and prove more of their private circumstances in order to be considered eligible, or to receive the maximum possible child support or social security benefits.

Payment technologies

Despite being more able to structure their child support case as they wish, such as through private agreements or alternative payment methods, the power of the state and ex-partners over single mothers typically remains. Given mothers' receipt of part-pensions, housing or family benefits, single mothers remain captured by the state's logic whereby they must pursue child support. The solution often promoted by the state is to pursue child support in ways that avoid state power, such as through private agreements, which best align with the simultaneous message that mothers should eschew such dependencies. For example, in Australia, private agreements comprise more than 50 per cent of the compulsory child support caseload. These orders do not receive state oversight and thus are not enforced by the state. But, illustrating the state's power to define and manage 'problems', the state assumes that all private child support orders are paid in full, and imputes this income in the calculation of single parents' other benefits. Thus women's autonomy and authority are given with one hand – where they can operate privately, outside of state surveillance – but simultaneously taken away with the other – whereby the state defines women's payment reality in ways that provide maximum benefit to themselves, in the form of reduced benefit outlays. At the same time, there is no scrutiny of whether fathers pay, and mothers must take on the responsibility of the state to try to coax fathers' payments. The original purpose of child support – to reduce the poverty of children living in single parent households – is erased from the technical operation of child support.

While the US and UK have, respectively, softened or eliminated the interactions between child support and welfare benefits, other mechanisms exist that clawback child support either explicitly as a percentage of the payment, or implicitly through the reduction of the recipient's other benefits (for a summary see Skinner et al, 2017b). As these authors show in their vignette study of a range of model family scenarios, child support policy did not reduce single-mother-headed family poverty in any country where the mother was a stay-at-home caregiver. In only a very small number of instances was their poverty reduced: when the mother worked part-time and received high-value child support payments (UK), or when the mother worked full-time and received moderate or high-value child support (UK and Australia). In these instances, the authors conclude that it is the value of cash benefits, child support and earnings that are important to poverty reduction, and that child support has only 'latent potential to reduce child poverty' (Skinner et al, 2017b, p. 19). This is contrary to the purported aims of child support, leading the authors to note that, 'this is contrary to much of the policy rhetoric emphasising the value of child maintenance to poverty reduction' (Skinner et al, 2017b, p. 19).

Finally, the growing number of transnational families, many of whom will become transnational separated families, obscures the number of non-resident parents who live in another country to their children and ex-partners, as these 'individuals' are not often considered as having responsibilities lying elsewhere. While international processes exist for the collection and payment of cross-border child support, these functions are often flawed and yield significantly lower compliance rates than the already poor rates experienced within countries. This is often because there are no mechanisms to find, order and compel payments. As the Hague Conference on Private International Law (2015, p. 1) noted in the Conclusions and Recommendations from its 'Global Conference on the Recovery of Child Support and Family Maintenance in Asia Pacific and Worldwide', in order to improve cross-national transfers, there is 'the need to improve national child support and family maintenance systems, and the need to strengthen regional and international co-operation to this end'.

Compliance and enforcement technologies

For all child support systems, child support non-compliance has been a perennial problem. Despite the anti-poverty benefits that child support can provide, state policies have typically failed to ensure adequate enforcement of payments. Of the 22 countries included in the OECD's (2011) analysis of Luxemburg Income Study data, compliance rates varied from as high as 91 to 100 per cent in Denmark and Sweden (prior to reform in 2016), respectively, to lows of almost 15 per cent in Ireland and just above 20 per cent in the UK and Italy. Across contexts, other studies show that compliance figures are equally poor. Research conducted in the UK using a variety of methods has consistently found that only approximately one third of eligible lone parents receive payments (Bryson et al, 2013; Skinner and Main, 2013), which is similar to the figure reported in the US (Grall, 2016). Yet studies that draw on self-reporting or administrative data are likely to underestimate the true nature of underpayment. Empirical research (Cook et al, 2015b) has demonstrated that women who leave child support payment amounts 'blank' on self-report surveys – because no payments were expected or received – are often removed as 'missing data'. Bureaucratic datasets also often inaccurately record partial or unpaid liabilities, as the onus is on individual women to report and manage non-compliance. For example, in Australia, private transfers are presumed to be 100 per cent compliant (Ministerial

Taskforce on Child Support, 2005). The results of such data 'blind spots' are that the significance of non-compliance is obscured and the case for policy action is impeded.

While there are multiple sites where the technical management of child support is failing, programme interventions of policy discussions focus on how to improve these lacking systems, rather than focusing on the bigger picture of single mothers' and children's ongoing poverty and social subjugation.

Understanding child support as a product of neoliberal individualism

While the introduction of child support policy was heralded as a 'win for femocrats' in some contexts, feminists also raised concerns about its underpinning logic of the 'eternal biological family' (Sevenhuijsen, 1986) and the expansion of models of familial, rather than public, sources of support. Across contexts, the introduction of child support often illustrates how 'states have embraced women's movements and women's policy agencies' discourses and policy agendas and adapted them to their own, often neoliberal, priorities' (Kantola and Squires, 2012, p. 385).

The introduction of child support policy in many countries coincided with the reshaping, relocating and rearticulating (Banaszak et al, 2003) of formal state powers as a function of neoliberal discourses emerging during this time period (Kantola and Squires, 2012). As has been documented extensively elsewhere (Lemke, 2001; Peck and Tickell, 2002), the neoliberal project is less an explicit political enterprise and more an assemblage of techniques of governmental control that serve to collapse the epistemological distinctions between economy and society. As a result of the blurring of the economic and the social, neoliberal policies extend economic calculation into traditionally non-economic arenas (Pollack and Rossiter, 2010). Child support is a quintessential example, as child support formulae assign a dollar value to caring labour and the opportunity costs that caregivers experience.

While there is no uniform or coherent account of neoliberalism, as it entails an often-contradictory mix of logics and practices, there are common and interconnected features observable (Peck and Tickell, 2002), particularly as they relate to social policy contexts including child support. First, commentators have identified the undermining and 'rollback' of Keynesian welfare systems (Peck and Tickell, 2002; Kantola and Squires, 2012; Luzkow, 2016). Second, in order to replace the diminished Keynesian welfare state regime, new forms of governance and regulatory regimes are 'rolled out' (Peck and Tickell, 2002). These new forms include processes of responsibilisation that compel self-surveillance, and the uptake of calculative technologies that locate otherwise subjective reasoning and experience within the logics of objectivity, neutrality and legitimacy (Miller, 2001; Kantola and Squires, 2012). Child support shares many of these features, including responsibilisation and calculative technologies being applied to more areas of family life than ever before. Women are increasingly urged to not look to the state to provide pathways to child support. Returning to the Australian example provided earlier, women should not look to the Tax Office to enforce payments. Rather, in addition to prioritising private collections, recent legislative reform in Australia made provisions for individual women to take legal action against their non-compliant ex-partners whom the state had not pursued (Australian Government, 2021). The onus on women to fulfil the duties of the state is on full display. But in other countries too, women are removed from state systems and urged to look to themselves rather than the state to secure child support. Across contexts, women are increasingly being rendered as personally responsible for seeking and procuring payments, which locates women as responsible for enacting the system and achieving the interests of the state. Should payments not be forthcoming, this failure can also be attributed to women rather than the state. While women may be 'allowed' to return to state systems, such as by paying fees in the UK, demonstrating payment non-compliance in Sweden, or by making an application in Australia, the payment issues that women experience are not cast as failures of the child support system.

The second feature of neoliberal child support policy concerned the roll out of calculative technologies. Ajzenstadt (2009, p. 70) describes how 'this mode of rationality removes the responsibility of caring for individuals' well-being from a collective, state-based risk management system to individuals, who are expected to act rationally and responsively in order to manage risk'. In relation to child support administration, these ideas locate parental behaviour within systems of rational calculation and responsibility that prioritise the promotion of self-interest. Within these logics of risk management and calculative technologies, it is no surprise that researchers examine such issues as parents' 'strategic bargaining' around overnight care-time to maximise their financial advantage (Smyth and Rodgers, 2011), worldviews that are echoed in policymaking forums (Joint Select Committee on Australia's Family Law System, 2020). Here, child support formulae have come under intense scrutiny regarding the extent to which they adequately calculate each parent's contribution. However, seemingly technical changes to child support formulae, to recognise both parents' incomes for example, hold with them significant assumptions about the gender roles of mothers and fathers that are often incompatible – or at least in tension with – assumptions that underpin child support. While liberal feminists made great advances in demanding equal rights for women, and freeing up women's access to the labour market, these advances have been critiqued by radical feminists for enlisting women within the neoliberal project. Thus, liberal aims for equal treatment obscure women's unequal opportunities (Cook and Skinner, 2020), thus rendering women responsible for ensuring their own self-sufficiency through attachment to the labour market, while remaining disproportionately burdened by their responsibility to care.

Neoliberal welfare policies internationally also increasingly expect single mothers to earn their own income, and often compel such behaviour through welfare-to-work programmes. State requirements for mothers to pursue work take up individualised, and masculinised, frames of references which exclude mothers' caregiving responsibilities and the gendered moral rationalities that these entail. At the same time, in many states, women's workforce participation influences child support eligibility and may feed directly into child support formulae calculations. As a result, welfare and child support policy may present contradictory messages about the employment responsibility of women, and single mothers in particular. In the calculative technologies of neoliberalism, the responsibility of fathers to support children – enacted by the technical 'income shares formula' that is used to determine the proportion of each parent's capacity to support children – is removed from its social and moral context. If a mother earns more than the father, in many child support formulae, the technical, rational application of the income shares formula absolves fathers of their responsibility, or at least deeply lessens it. While mothers cannot easily abdicate their caregiving responsibilities, fathers' economic responsibilities to children can be entered into a formula, which produces a detached outcome regarding capacity – but not responsibility – to pay. Some states without elaborate formulae, such as South Korea and Hong Kong, position mothers as being able to seek either child support *or* benefits. Such formulae provide contradictory messages to fathers – and mothers – about where responsibility for children's financial well-being lies. If mothers receive benefits from the state, fathers have no responsibility to children beyond what they individually choose to provide. Children's right to support from both parents is ignored.

The consequences of a technical approach

Drawing on Keynes, Luzkow (2016) posits that welfare states function best when they are conceptualised as a moral – as opposed to technical – enterprise. Child support is viewed similarly, although Eekelaar's work (1991a, 1991b) develops an argument that support for children has social, as opposed to moral, bases (for an analysis of Eekelaar's position as it applies to child support see Cook and Skinner, 2020). Irrespective of its moral and social bases, child support can be undermined by removing societal concerns from the purpose of child support, and instead managing it as a technical concern (for examples of how fathers' claims for reform deviate from the justifications that underpin child support see Cook and Skinner,

2020). Here, the introduction of a technical child support system with the aim of addressing social problems, such as the gendered distribution of work and care, may be a prime example of being unable to dismantle the master's house with the master's tools (Lorde, 2017). Indeed, as Coltrane and Hickman (1992) noted with respect to the likelihood of child support or child custody reform in the US, such reform was most possible when it was incremental, attracted little media attention (in that it was not controversial), and fit within prevailing ideology – ideology that is deeply gendered. The lesson for child support scholars is that the technical tools of the state cannot dismantle the house of patriarchal oppression that buttresses fathers' financial authority and autonomy.

Given the technical organisation of child support in many states, child support policy and function in its current technical form serves neither the state's budgetary interests nor single mothers' interests, in terms of enforcing responsibility or reducing child poverty. Nor does child support provide the individualised justice or autonomy that men's rights activists demand (Cook and Skinner, 2020). Rather than solving the underlying problems that child support seeks to address, the proliferation of technical processes has moved the problems of child support elsewhere. Child support orders that are produced as a result may not necessarily deliver significant benefits for children and can simultaneously impoverish paying fathers (Hakovirta et al, 2019). For example, in the US, child poverty still exists in high numbers. Clawing more money from also-impoverished fathers cannot solve children's poverty, but has further impoverished and even criminalised fathers (Cozzolino and Williams, 2017).

My contention is that the technical tools of child support governance described in this chapter do not serve to 'improve' child support payment outcomes, but rather serve to render child support non-payment as an inadvertent outcome of either women's failure to appropriately engage with the system, or the unforeseeable outcome of complex processes (Stone, 1989). In Stone's latter explanation, further technical refinements are required, as many countries have conducted. However, when women are at fault for not engaging with the system appropriately, across the myriad of child support systems, women are often punished and subject to increasing discipline and surveillance. The critical point is that the state works to move the failures of child support – and the social problem of single mothers' and children's poverty – elsewhere. In its most successful form, governmental processes relocate the source of failure onto those that the system was, allegedly, originally designed to serve.

As the Australian example illustrates, the problems that child support originally sought to solve, such as child poverty, welfare expenditure and a lack of paternal responsibility, have become detached from the reality of child support calculations, transfers and enforcement. Child poverty still remains a significant issue and has increased in more than half of the OECD countries with available data between 2006 and 2016 (OECD, 2019a). The poverty rates are highest for children in single parent households, and the gap between the poverty rate for children in dual- and single-parent families is highest in Australia, Canada, Ireland, Japan, South Korea, New Zealand and the US (OECD, 2019a). However, between 2001 and 2008 and 2010 and 2015–16, expenditure on income support to the working-age population decreased in many countries (OECD, 2019b). During this period, however, the emphasis in administrative child support systems with welfare state interactions has been on increasing maternal responsibility to seek income elsewhere. This is either from the market or from their ex-partner, and ideally, privately. What has changed, then, is the implicit expectation that women can expect any recompense for their socially reproductive labour. As I turn to discuss in the next chapter, any expectation that fathers will recompense mothers for the opportunity costs of care is returned to private conversations within the context of the gendered social contract.

8

The gendered offer of personal solutions

Following the residualising process described by Jamrozik and Nocella (1998) and the individualising mechanisms of masculinism outlined by Nicholas and Agius (2018), this chapter examines the dynamics of personal child support approaches. Such personal accounts exist in less well-developed systems where there are few administrative resources available to women, and within highly developed systems that have evolved to reframe child support as an individualised endeavour. Examples of these latter systems include such countries as Australia, Canada, the UK and Sweden, which have more fully realised child support as an individualised, neoliberal project. However, despite presenting private child support arrangements as the 'conclusion' of Jamrozik and Nocella's (1998) residualising process, this chapter positions the conversion of child support into a personal issue as returning to a pre-child support policy state of affairs, and the situation that exists in many less technically developed systems existing in Asia, southern Europe and South America. Rather than contending that these arrangements are the inevitable result of neoliberal processes, I draw on Nicholas and Agius's (2018) account to foreground gender as a key explanatory mechanism for how child support has unfolded across contexts. By locating individualised child support action within Risman's (2004) account of gender as a social structure, the chapter notes which social hierarchies are preserved by the re-privatisation of child support and which are eroded by the personalisation of post-separation financial management.

Nicholas and Agius (2018, p. 10) chart the logics, assumptions and effects of masculinism, which they pose as a 'broader logic … internalised and operationalised by both women and men, as well as institutions, structures, and discourses, which inheres the subordination of women and other non-dominant groups to the masculine norm'. The authors illustrate how patriarchal structures are reproduced by masculinist logics that operate at individual, interpersonal, policy and international levels. Drawing on their framework, here I analyse child support policy as illustrating these same logics. I argue that the administration of child support serves to manage contestations over the gender roles of breadwinners and caregivers, but in diverse ways that are more or less explicit. First, I argue that the many points in legal or administrative processes where women fall out of 'leaky' child support systems, or are prevented from entering them, are sites where the idea of child support is being rejected. Systems can hamper women's ability to seek and receive the appropriate amount of child support in an array of different ways, but these systems typically have one thing in common. They typically valorise men's autonomy, which occurs unchecked and in private, while limiting women's agency and commanding women's dependence, which is publicly scrutinised through the welfare system. However, women's work on behalf of the public system is left unexamined, as is men's failure to engage with these same processes.

The child support agreements and transfers that occur within private systems obscure the representation of women's reality. Following the same reasoning as was outlined in the previous chapter with respect to the gendered data gaps and omissions created through a focus on technical measurement, this chapter documents the gendered data gaps produced by returning child support payments to the private sphere. Australia, once again, provides a more extreme example, whereby all child support orders that are to be collected privately are deemed 100 per cent compliant – with no opportunity for women to correct the record. The social underpinnings of the more significant problem – single mothers' and their children's poverty – are further removed from policymakers' frame of reference as, from their perspective, the system is working as intended. In order to interrogate the logics and consequences of private child support transfers, this chapter plots the rise of these personal solutions within institutional and policy domains. It must be noted that in each of the systems examined here, it was never women calling for personalised child support as a solution to non-compliance. That, in itself, is telling.

According to Nicholas and Agius (2018), state responses to the identified problems with child support policy can be viewed through the lens of the masculinist state. According to the authors, challenges to feminism, and I would argue challenges to feminist policies such as child support, exist within two complex and masculinist foundations. First, they describe the '*rejection* of feminism as a label and political project, and second, its *co-option* in the context of neoliberal individualism' (Nicholas and Agius, 2018, p. 2, original emphasis). The rejection of feminism and backlash against child support was described in Chapter 6. The co-option of child support as a calculative technology to serve neoliberal welfare state ends was described in Chapter 7. In this chapter, I focus on the individualising processes of neoliberalism. In particular, I examine how privatised models of child support assume gender equality, but apply it to private child support interactions in ways that reference and reinforce gender inequality.

The conclusion gleaned from the previous chapters is that, in many countries, child support orders have either been decoupled from the calculation of benefit entitlements, either completely or in part, have never been implemented in meaningful ways, or were never embedded within them at all. Working backwards from this 'solution', as per Bacchi's (2009) approach, the problem that private arrangements solve is the reduction in state involvement, and thus a reduction in the cost of enforcing child support obligations. However, this is not consistent with the child poverty problem that the provision of child support money purports to resolve.

At its heart, the individualisation of child support returns women to the gendered relations of familial power that exist prior to separation, whereby mothers must draw on gendered performative strategies to demonstrate deservingness. As Risman (2004, p. 438) puts it, 'women often gain the economic benefits of patronage for themselves and their children in exchange for their subordinate status'. Within personalised child support relations, while the state may suggest that women have more agency, this likely remains limited. Mothers may need to concede on many fronts in order to be considered worthy of receiving child support by their ex-partners; a performance that women must repeat each time payments are due or renegotiated. Across academic and policy debates in favour of private arrangements, there is a significant nexus between women's purported agency and 'victim blaming'. For example, it is often suggested that if mothers gave fathers more access to their children, or worked privately to request and receive payments, fathers would be more likely to pay child support. Research and commentaries confirm this individualised approach, where parents merely need to 'get along' in order to establish functional child support agreements. However, locating the causes of policy problems in individual terms plays into the individualising processes of masculinism, which ignore the tight, gendered relational spaces that mothers must navigate to receive payments, and leave structural and institutional inequities in place. An historical reflection on the US child support system prior to the introduction of national guidelines noted: 'The degree of enforcement varied widely, too. In many counties, little was done about fathers who fell behind in their payments. Rather, the burden of collecting overdue support fell to the resident mother' (Garfinkel et al, 1998, p. 15). At this time in the US, these failures were regarded as personal concerns. What is of relevance here, however, is that while the US system has moved on, such processes remain in operation for the majority of child support systems internationally. This includes in seemingly 'developed' systems such as in Australia and the UK, where the majority of parents collect privately.

Rather than private agreements allowing parents to work collaboratively and come up with an arrangement that suits their individual circumstances and needs, as proponents of private agreements in Australia, Sweden and the UK suggest, private agreements can entrench and reinforce gender hierarchies whereby children's right to income from their father (received by their mother) is relegated to a secondary concern. At the same time, policies that make child support a non-compulsory, private matter return post-separation finances to a state of gendered control and authority. Women's contention is that seeking child support privately is not worth their already limited time and energy. As was described in the previous chapter by the Canadian informants, to restate what the Swedish informant claimed in Chapter 5, and as the German informant notes here, privately seeking child support is difficult and can result in personal and administrative harms.

> 'I was just going to say that we don't know – if the people don't come back, we don't know if it is because it's been working or if it is because they don't feel that they want to put the effort into trying again. If that just means that they say, "Oh fine, I'm not going to deal with it anymore. Just let him have it. I'll be okay." They don't pursue it anymore.' (Sweden)

> 'Most of the time they [mothers] have to fight for it [child support] in order to receive the welfare. You have to prove that you have a child to locate the parent … you have to prove what you did [to obtain support].' (Germany)

These gendered and individualised sentiments feed into masculinising processes that buttress the existing social order. Indeed, were women to seek a child support order, as the Canadian provincial and Swedish government officials contended in the previous chapter, these would likely be paid. However, in systems that privilege and promote private arrangements, or make child support optional, fathers do not need to pay, and indeed in many instances are not even asked to pay. Such sentiments were expressed across contexts. For example, in Hong Kong, the informant noted:

Interviewee:	The poverty rate is quite high among the divorced mothers in Hong Kong. It's about 40 per cent of them are below the poverty line. It's much higher than the general population. It's 14 per cent in general population.
Facilitator:	You would think that they would have a financial need to receive child support.
Interviewee:	They have need, but they prefer to rely on the government. We have a comprehensive social security allowance for low-income family. Thus mothers just rely on our social security system and not rely on their ex-spouse, because they are not reliable.

Across contexts, the unreliability of fathers' child support payments made them unattractive to mothers. Fathers' inaction and failure to meet their responsibilities to children were typically not pursued, and the state did not feel it was their business to intervene in fathers' abrogation of their responsibility to provide for their children. Only when women expended great effort – often with accompanying financial, emotional and relational costs, and even physical costs in instances of domestic violence – were payments or enforcement likely.

When the state is removed from the exchange between unreliable or reluctant ex-partners and the mothers and children who rely on their support, there is no external authority to draw on to promote and enforce payments. Mothers are left with few means of extracting payments. Natalier and Hewitt's (2014) work on child support as a gift exchange, which has subsequently been taken up by Keil and Elizabeth (2017, 2019), sets out the relational work that women must do in interactions with their ex-partners to facilitate payments. While these studies examine the personal experience of child support interactions, these gendered patterns are also visible within child support systems.

The gender of interpersonal child support interactions

Following Risman's (2004, p. 432) account whereby 'the social structure as the context of daily life creates action indirectly by shaping actors' perceptions of their interests and directly by constraining choices', this section reflects on how gendered individuals are freed or constrained from acting within the context of child support systems. The aim is to identify how gender inequities are produced and entrenched through child support processes, locating these processes within a particularly gendered domain of the social structure. The assertion is that systems that have sought to re-privatise child support relocate its negotiation back within the gendered context of social expectation and interaction.

As was outlined in Chapter 2, child support typically references traditional assumptions regarding breadwinners and caregivers, irrespective of whether national policies and practices use gender-neutral language (Hakovirta et al, 2020). Drawing on Nicholas and Agius (2018), this process illustrates the protectionist process of masculinism. Here, women as child support recipients are cast as perpetually dependent on a former male breadwinner, irrespective of whether mothers or their ex-partners want this (cf. Cook and Skinner, 2020). Women are discursively constructed by child support policy as deficient, dependent and different (Battle, 2018, 2019; Cozzolino and Williams 2018; Goodall and Cook, 2021a). Men's compulsory 'protection' of their ex-partners' financial well-being also reinforces and naturalises their distinct gender roles. Men's financial autonomy is buttressed as they provide payments on their terms. Recipient mothers, by contrast, must perform the grateful gift-recipient who uses their benevolent non-resident breadwinner's money in ways deemed socially appropriate (Natalier and Hewitt, 2010;

Natalier and Hewitt, 2014; Cozzolino and Williams, 2018; Goodall and Cook, 2021). While single mothers may seek financial autonomy following separation and may claim the authority to compel their ex-partner's child support payments, societal expectations and interactional power dynamics reduce women's opportunities for agency and return women to their subordinate position vis-à-vis their ex-partners. Often, these gendered interactions between parents reference policy settings, which then refer back – rightly or wrongly – to gendered ways of 'being' mothers or fathers, with unequal access to the authority to define how private child support payments will work.

For example, the New Zealand informant describes the gendered frames of reference existing within administrative settings that allow payers to gain credit for the payment of direct expenses, such as private school fees or medical costs. However, this system is being applied more broadly by fathers in their interactions with their ex-partners, who feel that they are entitled to direct what expenditure constitutes child support. Mothers then defer to fathers' financial authority, despite such definitions existing outside of the policy parameters:

> 'In New Zealand we've added a qualifying payment criteria in the last round of amendments and so the qualifying payment is set to child support. So, you can reduce the amount that you pay. If you've contributed for example – but it's a qualifying payment but it's two exceptional things. Let's say you've paid for private school tuition or if your child has special needs, and the father – the liable parent – is paying towards that. You can reduce, you can make exemptions to how much [child support you pay]. So there seems to be a misunderstanding though in terms of that, because some of the mothers talked about fathers saying that they're going to apply [to reduce their child support payments]. That they're sick of dealing with the mother; that now they're going to apply. They bought something small, like soccer uniforms, and they're going to try to get that deducted. … So, because they're [the mothers are] talking to their former partner, the former partners are saying something, because they don't quite understand. Sometimes they think that the father then understands.' (New Zealand)

Despite the policy not operating in the way that fathers believe it to, this does not mean that fathers are not able to achieve concessions. Through personal interactions, fathers' hierarchical social position allow them to define what does or does not constitute child support, as they are 'sick of dealing with the mother', who is deemed not sufficiently grateful or subordinate in passively receiving whatever offering the father deems to be an appropriate contribution. Their gendered hierarchical positions and perhaps women's resigned understanding that social policies do not work in their interests, means that in New Zealand, women often accept fathers' accounts of the reasons for reduced child support payments, despite this not being the policy reality. What the excerpt from New Zealand reveals, and as other researchers have also indicated (Skinner, 2013; Natalier and Hewitt, 2014), is that women must not make paying fathers 'sick of' them, and instead must make themselves – despite payments being the right of their children – worthy of support.

The gender of making oneself 'worthy' of support

While some countries have 'officially' moved to private agreements, such as Australia, New Zealand, Sweden and the UK, other countries have individualised elements of the process, by encouraging parents to work outside of formal systems. This has either been a deliberate attempt to reduce state expenditure on administering the child support system, or it has been due to the lack of spending on child support systems from the outset, such as in countries with less well-developed systems, whereby a lack of access or institutional infrastructure has meant that women are on their own to pursue child support, often irrespective of the legal and administrative arrangements that exist on paper.

> 'For middle-class families [in the US] who – where typically both parents are working, they both have stable paycheques, often have good paycheques, I think there is – there are new services that are springing up that allow for an internet platform, an app, that allows parents to mediate their relationship and account for payments and make decisions about the kids without using government services. … So, the agreement's private, or at least not in the child support programme, the collection efforts are not needed, the payments are voluntary and they're managed through such things as apps that allow for some of the emotion to drain away. I think some parents are finding that quite attractive if there is enough money to go around. It's a matter of sort of a civilised relationship.' (US, federal level)

> 'Even just the emphasis in terms of, "It's much better if you can work out an arrangement. What have you tried to do to privately work out before you do this?" It's women who are coming to apply for it so it's … it's expecting … "Are you sure there's nothing else that you can do to go and massage the relationship to make it a little bit better?" … It's reminiscent of, "What did you do to him for him to leave you or for him to abuse you." It's this, "well, what did you do or what can you do to make him better able", rather – because a lot of them talk

> about – that's why it was interesting when I was trying to – when I was saying child support is technically an entitlement. It's something you're entitled to receive and that's why the government regulates it. But women, they come from a guilty place. They're just so guilty about wanting that entitlement. So, it's not an – because they don't see it.' (New Zealand)

These excerpts reveal what is at stake for women in private child support arrangements. What is implicit is the gendered nature of 'civilised' relationships, and women's acquiescence to fathers' autonomy and authority as a fundamental part of keeping the peace. As Natalier and Hewitt (2010) have examined with respect to the Australian child support situation, child support payments are understood by parents as a form of gift relationship. This places child support squarely within the realm of private relations, outside of any government requirements or controls.

According to Zelizer (1998), it is the 'gift' recipient, rather than the giver, who is required to manage their 'worthiness' to receive the gift. The gendered characteristics that women, as worthy recipients of child support, must display are their selfless focus on the needs of their children, and due acknowledgement of the 'gifts' to children that the father provides. Women's deference to men in post-separation relationships 'allows for some of the emotion to drain away', as the US informant put it, where this seemingly universal emotion is men's anger and resentment at being told what to do by the state. Women's emotions in such seemingly 'civilised' child support relationships may including frustration, acquiescence and feelings of vulnerability and being dominated by a partner who can at any point renew custody disputes or withhold payments. These emotions are unable to be acknowledged or addressed by policymakers. Rather, a 'child-support-non-system' is seen as entirely functional and appropriate. Collection efforts 'are not needed' and payments are 'voluntary'. The fact that it would require significant funds, resilience and effort for a woman without a state agreement to pursue unpaid child support through the courts is rendered invisible. Women, through the masculinist worldview and actions of the state, are governed into being uncomplaining about their subordinate financial and social position relative to their ex-partners, as this is the natural gender order. The net effect of these changes is that women are, essentially, 'on their own' to fight patriarchal systems that prop up men's 'right' to choose if, how and when they will support their children and the gendered relational conditions placed on mothers who seek payments. While women do have agency, their ability to exercise it, given the resources required to do so and the consequences of any action, is severely constrained. In response, some systems provided space for women to avoid the child support system. Yet, in other contexts, women faced the discursive and financial consequences if they do not engage with fathers to seek child support, despite their severely restricted ability to do so.

It is worth returning to Risman (2004) in order to locate these processes within a theory of gender, as an organising social structure reveals why child support has largely failed. While countries have introduced child support regimes, often under the guise or with the aim of addressing gendered financial inequality (OECD, 2011; Edwards, 2019), these institutional reforms have failed to intervene in gendered patterns of interaction and social expectation. Decades later, child support institutions are being reconstituted by gender. Rather than allowing feminised child support policy expectations to imbue interactions, personalised modes of child support re-centre individuals' gendered selves and the gendered patterns of interaction and cultural expectations that these entail. The result is that child support – while claiming to be conducted in detached, legal, administrative and technical domains – is returned to the gendered social structure and the gender routines that exist across individual, interactional and institutional settings.

Embedding interests in interaction

While Chapter 6 set out how states' claims that they have a functional system can stand in for actually having a functional system, here the focus is on a second process that renders the child support system ineffective, and which benefits individual fathers and the state. This second process is the gendered nature of interactions on which child support business relies. This business is conducted either between parents, or between parents and the state. But, typically, such business is initiated by women trying to get the child support system to work, or by women wanting to extricate themselves from the unwanted consequences of the child support regime. In either case, however, the result is typically the same: benefits accrue to individual fathers, often at the expense of single mothers and their children.

This second process entails active attempts to design or reform the system in ways that privilege men and thus buttress the extant gender order. These gendered designs pervade the child support process, usually resulting in a 'fatal flaw' somewhere along the leaky pipeline that either sees women give up, or men absolved from having to pay. These flaws are often bureaucratic and involve complex processes and forms that take up too much of impoverished single mothers' valuable time or require too much of their emotional resources in order to engage with their ex-partners or the state. They may require women to appease their ex-partner in ways that diminish the value of payments or render them contingent on women's subordination to their ex-partners' demands. Child support systems might determine that all money paid on the back of women's efforts should be retained by the state, or that they reduce the value of her benefits – sometimes even regardless of whether child support is actually paid. When pursuing non-compliance, states may require women to take on the costs of court action, effectively rendering the process inaccessible. Here, I examine the interests served at each site of failure and how these benefits confer to the parties involved (mothers, fathers and the state). The secondary purpose of this analysis is to examine the process of structuring in child support failure, and how these processes align with social, technical and personal levels of responsibility.

Enacting child support through personal interaction

In many countries, the enactment of child support is done through interaction. Alternatively, child support can be avoided, which is often preferable if it entails actively engaging with an ex-partner. The Japanese informant noted such dynamics when they contrasted child support with public benefits available to single mothers: "The public welfare, social welfare, is very good. So, without contacting the ex-husband, they can get support from the local government. Although it's not sufficient, but for them it's better than contacting the ex-husband" (Japan). In Hong Kong, as in many countries, a multi-faceted benefit system exists depending on whether – and how much – child support is received. Women have some discretion in seeking child support or not, but they cannot seek the Comprehensive Social Security Allowance if there is no child support order in place. However, rather than following through on enforcing orders, and making fathers financially responsible for the costs of children, the state condones a workaround – but a workaround that women must enact. In Hong Kong, an insignificant amount of child support can be sought per annum. This enables the mother to qualify for the allowance, while at the same time it frees the father from sharing his income. As the informant explains:

> 'It's better to apply only for annual maintenance of one Hong Kong dollar. It's much better arrangement for the single mother because they can directly apply. They are qualified for the Comprehensive Social Security Allowance and no need to do any legal action to ask their ex-spouse for any money. The government will give them money. … The means test is based on the family income of the family, so maintenance or child support is part of the family income.' (Hong Kong)

If mothers apply for a significant sum of child support, which is subsequently not paid, they cannot apply for the allowance. Rather, women in such positions must undertake significant legal efforts to recoup their child support entitlements from their ex-partner. Again, rather than enforcing payments, there is a work-around to allow women to subsequently claim the allowance, and free fathers from having to pay:

Facilitator: If, say, the child support was quite valuable, say HK$100 a month …

Interviewee: They don't get the social security allowance.

Facilitator: But, say, the HK$100 a month was quite unreliable – some months you get it, some months you don't get it – and they want to get the more reliable government payment. Is there some process they have to do to waive or give up the child support?

Interviewee: They have to apply for the legal aid to ask the court for the paid maintenance or child support payment.

Facilitator: First?

Interviewee: After they make the legal aid, then legal aid can give them a certificate or something to prove that their ex-spouse hasn't paid them anything. Then they can apply for the social security allowance. But, if the court ordered the ex-spouse to pay, to clear up all the payment, then the single mother has to give the money back, to repay the government for what they get from the social security allowance from the money they get from the ex-spouse.

If, contrary to the way the system is seemingly intended to work, women somehow manage to recoup payments, these payments must be paid to the state. Despite women having to take action to recoup payments, they receive no benefit for their efforts. Again, the informant provides further insight into the logic of the system and the role that reducing state costs plays in setting the policy and administrative agenda:

> 'Because I think the Hong Kong government considers [that] if they take an interventionalist approach to help the single mother to make their ex-spouse to pay the child support and maintenance, it costs [too] much then. They directly give the money to the single mother and the child. The administrative fee is high for them, because it's quite difficult to make those who [are] not willing to pay the money, to pay the money.' (Hong Kong)

In Hong Kong, notions of what's 'better' for women subtly discipline them to apply for a meaningless amount of child support, strikingly revealing its nonperformative nature. Given such conditions, if women misguidedly pursue a higher amount, enforcing compliance will require a lot of work and preclude them from financial security in the form of state payments.

Some readers may suggest that the European – and predominantly Nordic – model of guaranteed payments undermines the credibility of the preceding argument, in that the state provides payments in place of child support, relieving women of the work of chasing and enforcing payments. However, interviews with Nordic child support staff revealed the same gendered disciplining effects, albeit in different guises. At the core remained the minimising of fathers' responsibility and the rendering of men's involvement voluntary. Guaranteed payments had the perverse effect of disincentivising the collection of payments, by either women or the state. While the Nordic model of guaranteed payments provides single-mother-headed families with a reliable and sufficient income, fathers are freed from any mandatory obligations. Furthermore, the level of guaranteed payments sets a normative example of how much fathers 'should' contribute. Even when fathers have far greater means, the guaranteed amount caps how much of their income they share with their children – if any.

In the logic of individualising masculinism, child support policy debates are cast in terms of fairness, which typically reference the amount of money to be paid. However, even in Nordic systems regarded as the leader in gender equality (Eydal and Friðriksdóttir, 2012; Hakovirta et al, 2020), child support gender inconsistencies are evident, and women are burdened with the responsibility of enacting the child support system. For example, continuing the excerpt presented in Chapter 5, in Sweden, women – whose responsibility is minimised in the following excerpt's reference to 'parents' – can either pursue high-value payments through the courts, initiate negotiations directly with their ex-partner to form a private agreement, or be 'content with' a lower-value payment.

> 'Parents [mothers] are not actually using the option of going to court or agreeing on a private agreement because they don't know they can do that. They don't know that the amount can be higher if they go that direction – or they have conflict that they don't want to surface. They're [mothers are] content with the lower amount [referenced to the guaranteed payment amount] because they feel more secure that way and have you a buffer … Also, the amount we provide in maintenance has been as [the] norm … It's been very – yeah. That's the amount that fathers say that they're supposed to pay and if you try to tell them that, "Well, that's the amount that the state has agreed it can afford to pay to mothers. It doesn't mean that's what you're supposed to pay in child support". They say, "No. That's the standard amount."' (Sweden)

What is also striking from this example, and seen across contexts, is men's authority to define how the system will work, what will be paid and how they will engage with it. As the informant describes, the Swedish state is seemingly rendered powerless to challenge men's expectations. While children may be entitled to more financial support from their fathers than the guaranteed payment amount, these funds are not made available to single-mother-headed families. Single mothers are also not supported by the state to ensure an equitable distribution of breadwinning income post-separation.

Converting child support back into a personal problem

As described in Chapter 5, without evidence of their experience, mothers have been unable to reframe the problems of child support away from men's technical and individual concerns. States have also been unconcerned with – and have instead contributed to – the gendered nature of child support problem identification and its solutions. The role of the state in reinforcing gender hierarchies has been taken up by family law and policy researchers from a range of perspectives and disciplinary traditions, such as Graycar and Morgan (2002) in their analysis of the hidden gender of law, Bacchi's (1999) analysis of women's interests within public policymaking and Smith's (1987) account of the gender of institutional evidence and processes. While these researchers take very different approaches and examine the issue with a range of epistemological perspectives, a common thread is that gendered processes shape what can be heard, what can be known and how knowledge claims are recognised and acted upon within institutional systems. The economically rational world of men, and their concerns and pressures, thus dominate child support research and technical policy reform. But women's concerns, particularly those that lie beyond the economic domain, are unable to be heard, spoken of, or even imagined without significant backlash. This serves to silence alternative ways of knowing, thus excluding such knowledge from future policy reform processes. Here, following the work of Ahmed (2006, 2007), the tools of silence, inaction and backlash reinforce the social order and maintain the status quo. When women have then complained about the unmet promises held by the introduction of child support systems, or the failures of child support that they have experienced as individuals, the state has typically not taken significant action – if any – to intervene.

As I explored in Chapter 5 with respect to official representations of the problems with child support, where there are no data, there are no issues. Rather, the lack of attention paid to child support serves a governmental function: maintaining extant social relations along gender and class lines. As such, silences are useful at both institutional and interactional levels. Taking these in reverse order, for individual women, there is often safety in child support silence.

Many researchers have described women's desires to not 'make waves' with their ex-partners, which can be done by seeking payments, pursuing unpaid child support or requesting changes to child support orders to recognise additional costs or fathers' increased capacity. Although child support avoidance may be a strategic means of women exercising agency to keep themselves and their family safe, maximising the chances of maintaining payments, or avoiding challenges to contact arrangements, women's use of silence as a tactic is ultimately built upon the gendered assumption that women are passive and docile. Women's silence ultimately relies upon them accepting fathers' accounts of their capacity or willingness to pay, and the consequences that will follow from women's acquiescence or resistance to this. However, more than this, the inaction of men and the state silences women. In turn, silence, silencing and inaction become political tools that are structurally imposed and mediated.

In addition to the financial inequities experienced by mothers and their children, they also often experience the shame of divorce or separation, poverty and inadequacy. Thus silence, inaction and shame operate in reinforcing ways to ensure that particular topics, such as fathers' inadequate support of children, cannot be voiced or heard. As described by interview informants and in published research, women often do not know about the child support system, or do not know what to ask for to maximise its benefits. When payments are not forthcoming, it is often best for women to step away in silence. There are no mechanisms for women to share their experiences and hold the systems that failed them to account. Their experiences are individualised and thus silenced, despite their widespread similarity within and across countries. Thus, across countries, silencing can be seen as a process with the effect of rendering child support claimants passive and accepting of child support as a 'gift' (Zelizer, 1998) that their ex-partner may or may not bestow.

If we return to the three purported aims of child support, these align with competing interests in child support law and policy as follows: children have an interest in poverty reduction; resident parents share this interest in poverty reduction, which could be achieved through the enforcement of non-resident parents' financial responsibilities to children. States have an interest in reducing poverty, as it produces opportunity costs elsewhere in the economy and society in terms of healthcare costs, lost productivity, and so on, and also share the interest that this aim could be achieved by enforcing parental responsibility. However, what interest do non-resident parents have in achieving the aims of child support? I am not suggesting here that fathers do not want to pay. What I am suggesting is that for some fathers, there is no clear 'personal' imperative that sees child support work in their interests while individualising processes, such as privatised payments, further reduce more social imperatives. Research has also examined where fathers' interests lie in child support, with several researchers asking if fathers are less likely to pay child support if they believe the amount is unfair (see, for example, Lin, 2000; Skevik, 2006; Lin and McLanahan, 2007; Hawthorne and Lennings, 2008). In particular, Hans and Coleman (2009) suggest that fathers with child support obligations may perceive themselves to have under-benefitted, leading to resentment. This aligns with instances of backlash against individualising strategies, as identified by Nicholas and Agius (2018), and also earlier discussions of fathers not 'levelling up' as a result of the child support system (Luzkow, 2016). The consequences of such individualising approaches, as can be seen in Hans and Coleman's (2009, p. 11) work, are recommendations for child support enforcement programmes to be 'sensitive and responsive to the experiences and perceptions of fathers' because they might be more successful than 'heavy handed' approaches that lead to resentment. However, while support for the 'soft touch' persuasion approaches abound (Oldham and Smyth, 2018), these programmes have not proven to be effective. Rather, they illustrate the permanence of child support non-compliance as a function of gender relations. Collecting the money is not the endgame; preserving men's autonomy to choose whether or not to pay, and thus their dominant position in gender relations, is primary. In contrast, a solution to men's resistance may be for the state to publicly advertise and champion the social benefits of child support. I have not seen such campaigns reported in the media or research, although this does not mean that they don't exist. My hypothesis, however, is that state activity to promote child support as a social good would lead to significant backlash.

Most of the backlash against child support has come from fathers' rights groups, as described in Chapter 6. However, this is puzzling given that the purported targets of the policy – non-resident fathers as resultant payers of child support – have no stake in complying with the policy, other than to avoid sanctions. As sanctions are often weak or non-existent and compliance is low, a governmental sensibility, with its attendant focus on the nature and location of the problem that child support seeks to resolve, suggests that the 'real' target of child support policy likely lies beyond non-resident fathers. Furthermore, given the nature of compliance rates, enforcement and penalty regimes beyond the atypical US, it appears that enforcing non-resident parents' financial responsibility to children is also more rhetorical than material.

In many countries, inaction or evasion on the part of the father stalls child support proceedings. The benefits of such inaction accord to fathers, who then do not have to pay, can delay payments, or can decide what they will or won't provide. For mothers, they are required to expend considerable effort and sometimes money to pursue payments. When funds, time or energy run out, women often give up. For example, a UK informant adept with cross-border cases explained how fathers in other countries could thwart their clients' efforts by doing nothing:

> 'Another one would be an Australian case actually, where it made little progress because they couldn't find the father, which is of course a common problem too, to serve the English court paperwork. There

> were several trips done by our bailiffs to find him at various addresses and in one instance they even turned up to see a man of the same name, but it wasn't the right one. … There have been three or four hearings adjourned because of this. So, she couldn't afford to instruct us any further and who knows what's happened and I think this is a typical problem. We had another New York order, sadly substantial arrears. They continued to accrue, he's paying a bit less because he's just decided what he'll pay. She's got no way of enforcing the order.' (UK)

Drawing on the example of violence against women to illustrate processes of individualism, Nicholas and Agius (2018, p. 69) note that Australian interventions have 'reduced all of the locus of change to individual men, divorced from structural contexts which can fail to address the more salient causal factors than individual attitudes, or divorce them from their context'. Similar processes are evident within child support. For child support programmes internationally, many court-based or administrative processes can be avoided if substituted with private agreements. Within these processes, individual parents are regarded as the most appropriate locus of deliberation and agreement. However, within these individualised systems, gendered logics of autonomy and authority prevail. As has been argued by Salter (2015, p. 12) with respect to individually focused programmes to address violence against women, which applies equally to individualising child support policy in the face of widespread non-compliance, 'it is reasonable to ask whether normative change can be achieved while structural inequality and social stigma are left in place'. With respect to promoting 'private agreements' in child support programmes, such as in the UK and Australia, these place a disproportionate burden of responsibility and evidence-gathering onto separated mothers (Allbeson, 2017; Cook, 2020). The disproportionate burden of responsibility is in stark contrast to the lack of responsibility and surveillance applied to fathers. Social stigma, on the other hand, reveals the governmental work that child support law and policy conduct. Mothers experience the shame of poverty, benefit receipt and single parenthood, which are a result of – but also reinforce – a lack of child support enforcement (Battle, 2019; Goodall and Cook 2021).

Individualised interaction as policy

The individualisation of authority over child support payment terms is evident across contexts. What is more troubling, however, is that in systems where the amount of child support received has financial implications for the value of benefit payments, such as in Australia, women are expected to achieve more effective results than the state and are financially penalised if they do not achieve these.

The residualising liberal welfare state trends described in previous chapters see reforms that decouple child support from state policy regimes through the privatisation of child support agreements and payments. In reformist child support systems, such as in the UK, the child support system has effectively been dissolved, and parents make agreements and transfer these privately unless both parties pay fees to re-enter the skeleton child support system. In Australia, more than half of the child support agency's caseload reportedly transfers the state-agreed amount privately between parties, outside the purview of the system and with the technical burdens and penalties outlined earlier. As such, in Australia and to a lesser extent the UK, there exists the simultaneous residualisation of child support policy back into the hands of parents, but a concurrent strengthening of the state's governance of single mothers as it pursues its own financial interests. This occurs through the mandating of child support agreements for low-income single parents, requiring payment for services, and increasing the value of transfers so as to reduce welfare state expenditure. Where payments fail to materialise, the state's response often lies at the personal level, as if parents had better relationships, or if the amount to be paid was mutually agreed, or if care-time better reflected the wishes of payers, then perhaps payments would be more likely forthcoming. These reforms have the unintended – or perhaps intended – consequence of entrenching gender inequities. These consequences are anathema to the original purpose of child support in particular, and redistributive liberal welfare states in general.

> 'There is increasingly a sense amongst a lot of Canadians who are – [unclear] in family matters, that the system's just irrelevant. You know, "Oh yeah sure there's a maintenance" – if they know about there's a maintenance enforcement programme or if they know they could go to court, "Yeah, we could but that's not for us, that's for other people. We'll muddle through. My mum will help out." You know, "You have a sister, your sister – just see the kids. Sort of like, he's a total loser why do you think I divorced him." They've gone from that sort of 30 years ago the feminist approach of 40 years ago – "He should pay because it's not fair that a woman would pick up all that" – to 'Oh well this is life. He was a loser when we were together, he's a loser now and the system's for someone else. The system's not for us. It doesn't respond."' (Canada)

In Australia, the normative position that parents will transfer payments privately has a doubly perverse effect due to the erroneous assumption that private payments are fully compliant, and the subsequent inclusion of 'fully compliant' private payments in benefit calculations. First, while there is a purported but undemonstrated claim that private transfers will improve compliance due to parents being able to manage their affairs outside of state surveillance, there is no evidence that payment rates are better than those made through the system. Second, in Australia, for well over a decade, private collections have made up more than half of the child support caseload (Ministerial Taskforce on Child Support, 2005; House of Representatives Standing Committee on Social Policy and Legal Affairs, 2015). But as is the case in many advanced welfare states that operate child support programmes, in Australia, child support receipts are included as income in the calculation of other benefits. Here, private payments are regarded as fully compliant and benefits are scaled on this basis. This assumption belies the reality of child support payments collected through the system or existing internationally. Yet, the convenient assumption that payments will be more reliable if made outside of the government's purview justifies this course of action; the result of which is that single parents may lose out on both their child support payments and a proportion of their benefits (Cook, 2013). Furthermore, no compliance action is taken against private payers, and the government expends no money on collection or enforcement programmes (Cook, 2020). The only possible losers are low-income women and their children – a fact that reveals the government's motives and respective valuation of the interests of mothers and fathers therein.

Examining the preservation or reform of systems to cast child support as a personal issue reveals the ways in which state processes serve to reinforce the gender order. Achieving the permanence of the gender order in this case relies on boundary work to mark out those who are able to define problems and solutions, and those who are subject to them, and the depoliticisation of child support problems so that they appear best addressed though personal means (Jamrozik and Nocella, 1998; Li, 2007). In preservationist systems, this means that no reforms are required. In reformist systems, this results in changes that prioritise men's autonomy and women's responsibility for managing both the state and men's expectations.

> 'Personal networks advise them, tell them keep your right but ask just for one [Hong Kong] dollar. It's the best way out if your ex-spouse don't seem to be a very reliable person. Actually, many women divorce their husband because he is totally unreliable so, according to this impression, we [women] have to get rid of this man as far as possible. The Hong Kong government is more reliable than most husbands.' (Hong Kong)

The rise of personal solutions within child support policy, including the complete decoupling of child support from the welfare state, as in the UK, and the introduction of private agreements and transfers, moves to increase individual autonomy within existing agreements. These moves are consistent with Jamrozik and Nocella's (1998) account, but also can be seen to reflect broader governance frameworks that seek to 'responsibilise' single mothers (Treloar and Funk, 2008) and reinforce the gendered hierarchies of men's control over finances and women's subordination to keep the peace and not make waves in the hopes of receiving future child support payments. The finding is that the personal management of agreements and transfers of child support makes more possible the recognition of and response to changing economic life, and can accommodate diverse family forms, but can also entrench problematic aspects of gender roles and power dynamics.

In the UK, while all parents default to private arrangements, they can re-enter the state system. However, women must pay a fee to enter the system, and both parties must pay a collection fee in addition to the child support that is paid (by fathers) and received (by mothers). Presumably, the system entry fee serves as a deterrent, to discourage parents from seeking state support when they do not need it. As was described with respect to the UK system that exists for those outside of the benefit system, one way for women to avoid needing the system is to acquiesce to the autonomy and authority of their ex-partner. However, when women do seek to step outside of their subordinate gender position and enforce their ex-partner's financial responsibility to his children, whether for financial or affective reasons, fees apply. "One of the things that came in the 2012 scheme was you that you paid £20 to get your enforcement done, which doesn't sound a lot of money but if you've got no money in the first place, why should that person have to pay for that?" (UK). Again, stripping back the rhetoric of what child support policy does and how it works exposes questions of gender, power and responsibility that lie at the heart of child support and which remain unspoken, unchallenged and thus reinforced. Requiring women to pay an entry fee poses another barrier to the effective functioning of child support in the UK. It serves only to deliberately exclude the most financially vulnerable who cannot afford to pay, likely because they are not receiving vital child support income from their ex-partner.

While these individual gender relations and their effects are not new, what has not previously been explicated at an international level is the state's role in establishing, reinforcing and entrenching women's subordinate position. This is especially disappointing in establishing child support systems that are claimed to have been the fruits of feminist intervention. Incremental reform in Sweden, the UK, Australia, the US and elsewhere has seen a move to retract the interventionist state in ways that return mechanisms to a pre-child support state of affairs – one where women are beholden to whatever money their more wealthy and powerful ex-partner chooses to provide. While a more developed welfare system to support single mothers exists in some countries, such as in some of the Nordic states (Hakovirta and Eydal,

2020), in other countries such as Australia, single parents are punished for the failures of the state to provide support for collecting child support.

Given the limits of a technical approach to managing the social issues underpinning child support, I argue that some countries – including the UK and Australia in particular – have further residualised child support into a personal concern. I argue that the conversion of child support into a personal issue is, in some respects, a return to a pre-child support policy state of affairs. It is telling here that in Australia, where payments are still connected to benefit systems, the compulsory elements of child support policy are still applied to recipient women, rather than the fathers deemed to be avoiding their responsibilities, as was one of the original justifications for the system. It is ironic that research using vignettes to explore the poverty reduction effects of child support in the UK, USA, Australia and New Zealand (Skinner et al, 2017b) showed that the UK's 'lack of a system' was most able to move single parents out of poverty, as the original systems intended. What I am interested in here is that Australia, Sweden and the UK, in particular, have been eager to move child support back to a personal responsibility.

In response to persistent child support non-compliance, child support policy development in a number of countries has moved away from the state enforcement of payments and has instead promoted parents' private negotiation and transfer of payments as a way to increase compliance. There is a spectrum of private systems. At one end there are countries that provide parents with agency to decide agreements as they wish (within the context of enduring gendered power relations), enforced by the state. Norway provides an example of this extreme type, which represents more than 50 per cent of their caseload, according to the informant.

> 'Well, in Norway, we try to encourage parent to agree privately on the child support. A private agreement is made very easily. It's just basically they just write it on a piece of paper what they want and both sign it. As long as they have done that in writing, it can also be collected through the collection agency.' (Norway)

At the other end of the spectrum are countries that compel the terms of the child support agreement but locate the collection of payments within the private capacity of receiving parents. Australia provides an example of this extreme, where private collections comprise more than 50 per cent of the caseload (Ministerial Taskforce on Child Support, 2005). Unlike Norway, the amounts are determined with reference to the child support formula, but payments (irrespective of whether they are received) are recorded as being 100 per cent compliant and Family Tax Benefits are reduced by 50 cents for every dollar of 'expected' child support as a result (Department of

Human Services, 2019). In between these extremes exist countries that use private agreements or collections in ways that buttress the interests identified in Chapters 6. Confusingly to mainstream understandings of the Nordic family policy type (Hakovirta and Eydal, 2020; Hakovirta et al, 2020, 2021), Sweden provides an example of a 'middle' country, but one that lies much closer to Australia than Norway, as child support is to be collected privately in all but the most difficult cases (Fernqvist and Sépulchre, 2021), making the reality of receiving child support less likely.

Also problematising family policy types when it comes to child support is the UK, where fathers' resistance to state-mandated payments resulted in the abolition of the CSA (Skinner, 2013). However, the move towards private agreements and a 'soft' approach to the enforcement of orders is by no means consistent across the English-speaking world. At the other extreme, the US has most doggedly pursued child support, jailing serially non-compliant fathers (Cozzolino, 2018), likely in part because payments received go towards offsetting welfare state expenditure, and may not be received in full, or at all, by lone-parent families (OECD, 2011; Skinner et al, 2017b). However, these extreme cases of judicial sentences for non-compliance apply most often to poor Black men with children from multiple ex-partners who rely on state benefits, resulting in the distribution of prison terms for non-compliance along racial lines. What is consistent across contexts in which individual, parental responsibility for children is foregrounded is the lax framing of fathers' responsibility to children and the extent to which this framing has translated into effective compliance policies. Countries that do not sit at the extremes of child support law and policy configurations still provide avenues through which child support justice can be seen to be done, without providing the means for justice to actually be done, and for fathers to actually be compelled to pay, or pay an appropriate amount.

An absence of data on the private troubles of child support

When states promote, default to or acquiesce to private arrangements and transfers, they lose not only the ability to manage and compel payments, but they also lose oversight of what occurs in these agreements – if they are agreed on and implemented at all. In a context of increasing state surveillance and oversight of private affairs, it is counter-normative that states are seeking less involvement in and oversight of child support, despite the significant impact that it can potentially have on state budgets and the welfare of populations. This points to other factors at play than states wanting to increase the efficiency and effectiveness of child support systems, as was outlined in Chapter 6. The promotion of private child support arrangements across reformist and preservationist regimes illustrates not only the state's minimisation of the costs and obligations of running a child support regime, but also the obscuring of problems that might lead states to have to take more action.

Private transfers shape how states 'see' or rather 'fail to see' child support problems. These problems, however, are known – but may remain inadvertently, or wilfully, unknown by politicians, lawmakers and bureaucrats.

> 'I don't think we have a whole lot of data on that [private agreements and payments]. I mean, we see some cases where people have made a private agreement and then they sort of maybe fall out. If it doesn't work out, then then come to us. Sometimes they ask us to stipulate that they don't want the collection agency to collect. They want to do the collection privately. That also happens. So, there are some cases that sort of are in and out of the system. Those are really the only ones that we see. There are the ones that have sort of a functioning private agreement. I guess we don't see them. They don't contact us. I'm sure there are some that have no agreement at all and don't contact us as well. But I don't have a lot of data on that myself.' (Norway)

> 'In [South] Korea, the government has no way to monitor how the child support system is working because first of all they don't really collect or distribute [the money]. The only way they can know about it is actually the Child Support Agency is doing this; they call the mothers and ask them monthly. This isn't really actual.' (South Korea)

Facilitator: Do you have a sense of what compliance rates are in Malaysia? Or there's no data, so it's not collected?

Interviewee: No, there's no data. It's not collected. … Also, we have the welfare department whereby the issue … for people as well … asking – and asked them about data on single mothers, they say, 'Okay, we don't really have the data. We don't really collect it.' She [a bureaucrat from the welfare department] said that it's private and confidential.

Prior to the introduction of federal child support guidelines and state involvement in the US, knowledge of private agreements was patchy, at best. In the lead-up to developing their national system, a child support module was added to the US Census (Garfinkel et al, 1998). Responses reported that only 60 per cent of mothers who may have been eligible had a court-based order, and that of these, only half were paid in full. Of the remainder, half of these orders were partially paid, whereas the others were not paid at all (Garfinkel et al, 1998). A decade and a half later, the situation was the same, with national statistics reporting that only half of custodial parents had a child support agreement in 2015 (Grall, 2018). These issues are evident internationally.

9

Conclusion

This book has sought to examine the nature, process and effects of child support law and policy in order to illustrate the norms that are expressed and reinforced therein. The assumption underpinning the analysis is that internationally child support systems reflect and reinforce social hierarchies, in this case on the basis of gender and class. As the analysis outlined in the preceding chapters revealed, for low-income women across countries, child support is organised in ways that buttress the interests of men and the masculine interests of the state. In this context, the analysis sought to understand child support as gendered governance practice and, in doing so, expose the mechanisms through which child support is used to manage and discipline single mothers, thus rendering child support largely ineffective when fathers do not pay voluntarily and willingly. While the contours of child support vary from country to country, there are several features – inaccessibility, inactivity and irresponsibility – that remain remarkably consistent.

Most significantly, child support rarely does what it says it does, rendering it an inactive and inefficient means of redistributing money to children or allowing them to share in both of their parents' resources. Child support systems also typically contain design features that render them inaccessible. Judicial and administrative systems require mothers to have at least some combination of knowledge of the system, time to spend completing documentation or attending appointments and hearings, geographic access to offices, and sufficient evidence of their and their ex-partners' circumstances. Herd and Moynihan (2018) describe such administrative burdens as limiting access to justice along existing social hierarchies. This book provides a high-level account of how gender and class, in particular, shape programme participants' burdens and impose barriers to accessing and enacting the child support system. While I have provided the first analysis of the role of burdens in child support system functioning (Cook, 2021b), far more research – academic and government – is required in each country to understand how programme participants make their way through, are prevented from entering or fall out of the child support system. Given low-income women's already subordinate positions, existing child support systems should work harder to ensure women's inclusion rather than assuming that women's lack of engagement is voluntarily chosen. However, even if women are able to enter the child support system, without men's voluntary engagement, the time, effort and information they provide is often ineffective. As Chapter 5 illustrated, there are far too many sites where women's agency is curtailed or constrained and women can be prevented from entering or can fall out of the child support system. But as Chapters 7 and 8 set out, as child support systems become more technical, or remain within or are returned to the private domain, women falling out of the system is both the problem with child support, in that money does not flow, and stands in for the problem with child support, in that the problem can be reframed as laying in women's lack of administrative or relational effort rather than a lack of payments. Irrespective of administrative and legal structures, child support money is very often not passed from non-resident fathers to resident mothers, as OECD (2011) figures indicate. Across countries, child support works best – or often only works – when fathers pay willingly. Taken another way, the child support system works best when the child support system is not needed. But across countries, when the child support system is needed, it seldom works well.

Child support across contexts is underpinned by gendered logics that work to limit women's access and any return on their efforts. These are the processes that translate women's action into system inaction, operating at individual, interactional and institutional levels. Women's agency is constrained by norms that prescribe what good separated mothers 'should' do – not make waves, keep the peace, don't rely on their ex-partners. Given the impossibility of separated mothers' financial self-reliance, welfare systems – particularly in western liberal regimes – often require mothers to re-engage with their ex-partners. Women are then placed in an unwinnable situation: to make waves or to forego financial transfers. The state is blind to the gendered identities and interactions that mothers and fathers bring to child support expectations and behaviours. These norms, of men's financial autonomy and women's deference to men's autonomy and authority, make men's mandatory financial support for the eternal, yet physically separated, biological family untenable. Yet at the same time, when the state plays an active role in compelling women's child support seeking, the state demands that women behave in counter-normative ways. It is no wonder that separated fathers are often outraged, and mothers often give up. Here, women's agency may take the form of resisting the system's, or their ex-partner's, demands. However, in response to unpaid child support, state solutions that provide mothers with payments irrespective of whether payments are made do not solve the underpinning problems. Guaranteed payments provide much needed money to mothers and children, but do little to intervene in – and even reinforce – fathers' non-compliance. While the system is claimed to work, it does not work as originally intended.

Given system inaccessibility and inaction, there is a lack of responsibility for the failure of the system. Where there is a focus on responsibility, the gaze of the state often falls on the most vulnerable party. Where responsibility is embedded within systems, it often appears as *women's* responsibility to enter, initiate and enact a dysfunctional child support system. Women are held responsible to enact this ineffective system in the context of ex-partner hostility or apathy and institutional ambivalence. Fathers' and the state's failure to take responsibility, or be held responsible, rewards – and obscures – their irresponsibility.

In the overwhelming majority of cases, women hold no responsibility for making child support payments, yet across systems they are held responsible for making payments happen. If they are prevented from entering the system, women have not enacted *their* responsibility. If they fall out of the system, women have abrogated *their* responsibility. If they remain in the system but payments do not flow, women have failed *their* responsibility as good mothers. However, good mothering in the context of child support is judged on fathers' terms: sharing custody, facilitating contact, spending payments on items that denote good fathering. Indeed, when asked about widespread tax return non-filing in Australia and the opportunities for child support to be used as a tool for economic abuse, Australia's Minister for Human Services, Senator Anne Ruston, recently claimed that 'it is important that both parents work together to ensure that they are providing correct, up-to-date information and lodging their tax returns in a timely manner' (Hitch 2021, n.p.). While low-income women's tax returns are mandatory in order to receive benefit payments, women are discursively conjoined to their ex-partners and share responsibility for fathers' often deliberate non-compliance. What Senator Ruston's remarks reflect is a wider, and international, focus on women's responsibility for entering, enacting and enforcing the child support system. What this framing achieves is the obscuring of men's responsibility. Instead, women are held responsible for the payment behaviour of fathers, the enactment of the child support system, and the 'success' of the policies of the state. The reason that women are held responsible is because their conduct as mothers, ex-partners, benefit recipients and citizens is gendered and thus organised in ways that buttress the extant gender order.

Child support systems worldwide work on implicit, and sometimes explicit, assumptions regarding the appropriate roles of mothers and fathers, post-separation. To operationalise these norms, states construct child support systems in ways that reflect these gendered norms, curtailing or deferring to the autonomy of mothers and fathers, respectively. These cultural expectations play out at the levels of interaction and interaction, as identified by Risman (2004), underpinned by the gendered identities that mothers and fathers bring to their personal child support interactions, as administrators and in policy development. I suggest that child support is often contested on symbolic grounds, where fathers' responsibility becomes a matter for public debate (for examples, see Battle 2018, 2019; Edin 2018). When fathers' individual autonomy and authority are proposed to be curtailed, institutional avenues – in the form of weak child support systems – are available to reinstate fathers' freedoms, should they wish to take them up. As women are positioned as responsible for their ex-partner's irresponsibility, where (non)recipients are dissatisfied with their child support arrangements, the solutions lie solely in interaction. Women can lobby their ex-partners, or they can lobby administrators. But these avenues are likely not to lead to success, as they fail to intervene in the unequal power relations that exist and the gender of both interaction and the gender of institutions that women experience (Risman, 2004). Individually, men are free to choose whether to comply with child support or not. It is an invitation, but it is not one that requires men to carefully consider the consequences of acting one way or the other. Indeed, returning to the OECD's (2011) purported aims, child support serves to increase fathers' responsibility. However, statements of increasing responsibility are nonperformative with respect to enacting child support payments. Fathers' responsibility within child support is not necessarily to provide payments, but to choose how post-separation families should be symbolically structured. Through interaction, women can take their personal, individual complaints up either with their ex-partners, or with institutions, but doing so entails emotional, administrative and perhaps even physical burdens and still little likelihood of financial returns.

Together, these features are mutually reinforcing. Gendered logics regarding mothers' appropriate post-separation behaviour (Natalier and Hewitt, 2014; Goodall and Cook, 2021) shape how they can, or should, interact. Love or fear trumps money as a motivator for women while cunning or force prove useful to unwilling men, often irrespective of technologies of control and surveillance applied by the state. Weak or gendered institutions provide an unresolvable contradiction where mothers cannot win unless fathers willingly engage, or the state steps in to pay on fathers' behalf. The contradiction that mothers face is that, relationally, it is often not appropriate for mothers to seek money from ex-partners. Institutionally, however, mothers are regarded as not acting appropriately by not seeking money from ex-partners. Resolving this contradiction requires mothers to balance whether there are greater risks in seeking child support or breaching government requirements. But when women enter the system – by force, on principle, or out of financial need – they often find that it fails to provide them with any material benefit. On the contrary, the system may instead do them harm.

Reimagining child support

The question to be asked of existing child support law and policy, from a feminist perspective, is whose responsibility it is to enact the system and facilitate payments? Many of the reforms introduced, across countries, in recent years have placed more responsibility on the shoulders of women, while alleviating the administrative demands placed on men. Here, research needs to examine where responsibility for child support lies in existing systems – with individual country analyses delving more deeply than the bird's eye view provided here. How is the child support system enacted, by who and at what level? Systems that render women responsible for enacting the child support system through personal interactions with their ex-partner stand in for having no system at all. Where is the state's responsibility for transferring payments, as set out in the UNCRC?

Given that technical child support systems, typically introduced to alleviate single mother and child poverty, have ratcheted up the administrative demands placed on mothers while failing to ensure that similar requirements to pay child support are applied to fathers, what does this mean for the purportedly redistributive and feminist ideals that child support once held? Compulsory child support programmes often seek to develop welfare recipient mothers into more 'responsible' citizens (Treloar and Funk, 2008) by reducing their burden on the welfare budget. At the same time, a relative lack of state involvement in the collection, transfer and enforcement of payments relegates the public problem of single-parent and child poverty into a private trouble, reinforcing gender hierarchies in their wake. Across contexts, mechanisms such as silence, inaction and resistance undermine the progressive and feminist aims of child support in ways that reinforce the gender order in interaction and in institutions, internationally. These mechanisms achieve two purposes. First, they pose barriers to accessing or reforming the child support system at individual and institutional levels. Second, they reframe the way that child support is and can be discussed. In doing so, processes of silence and inaction narrow the focus of child support reform and practice in ways that buttress the extant gender order and increase separated fathers' symbolic and material power vis-à-vis their ex-partners. Here, acts and omissions reveal the gender of interaction and of institutions, and how reform, or lack of, serve to reinforce the interest of the dominant social structure. The remaining challenge is to examine how these problems can be overcome to re-imagine child support as an equitable system that that works for all parties: mothers, fathers and their children.

To paraphrase and appropriate Connell's (2019, p. 168) characterisation of the 'good university', good child support systems already exist – in many fragments. What is good about child support is the attempt to recognise the costs of care work conducted overwhelmingly by mothers, and the opportunity costs that result from this care work that reduce women's earning capacity and income security. Child support, at its simplest, attempts to redistribute money from earning fathers to caring mothers, but in ways that require more unpaid labour from mothers. As this book has shown, unless fathers actively engage – or are easily included in government programmes of wage withholding, for example – women's efforts to secure additional income to support their care work may be dangerous, unreliable or unrewarded. These problems exist because in many systems child support is individualised through state laws and policies, and through the UNCRC. Until parenting relations – both pre- and post-separation – can be de-gendered to distribute the opportunity and material costs of raising care more equitably, child support will remain entrenched in issues of inaccessibility, inaction and irresponsibility. Increasing technical measures to monitor or compel parents' behaviour, or requiring parents to 'work it out themselves' will not intervene in the underlying social conditions that cause single mothers' and their children's financial vulnerability, which permeate institutional, interactional and individual responses. Only valuing care work on equal terms with paid work will intervene in the gendered social structures that maintain women's subordination. Child support as a technical response cannot achieve this end.

While time and effort could be spent here, and by child support advocates and activists worldwide, to propose and pursue amendments to existing systems to harness the 'good fragments' of existing child support systems, such amendments will be built on the gendered status quo. Rather, I contend that feminist solutions to the technical and gendered problems with child support cannot be tweaked or reassembled in ways that overcome their structural causes. As child support problems reflect and reinforce the problems inherent in the gendered social order, interventions need to be similarly aimed at the social and structural level, rather than the technical or personal. By resolving women's subordinate social and economic status, such as through equal pay and employment opportunities and the equal sharing of caring labour, the need for child support would be diminished. Child support systems could be disbanded, as states would construct policies and programmes to support men and women to be financially independent and also engage meaningfully in their children's care. Children's right to support from both parents would be willingly provided in financial and relational terms. In a feminist world, domestic violence would be eradicated, as power differentials between parties would be eliminated as women would command respect in public and private spheres. As a result, there would be no need for provisions to secure resources from violent ex-partners while maintaining physical distance between perpetrators, mothers and children. However, these structural revolutions are a long way off. Further, to only pursue structural solutions ignores the fact that child support systems currently exist, and currently exist in ways that entrench rather than ameliorate women's social and economic disadvantages. As such, a two-tiered approach is necessary, to identify how existing systems can be reformed to minimise their harms, and how longer-term gender equity – and finally equality – can be achieved.

Drawing on principles identified by Ahmed (2017) in her killjoy manifesto, the work of building a feminist system begins with recognising inequalities in the status quo. This book has attempted to document this status, primarily along the lines of class and gender. The next step is to identify how – and where – things could be different. Ethnicity, indigeneity, race, religion and sexual identity are equally likely social hierarchies that are preserved and permeated by child support law and policy. Far more research is required to explicate the experiences of both indigenous populations and migrants living in countries with 'developed' systems (cf. Keil and Elizabeth, 2017, 2019), minority populations (cf. Cozzolino and Williams, 2017; Cozzolino, 2018), sexual minorities (cf. Gahan 2018, 2019) and women living in non-westernised contexts (cf. Armstrong, 1992; Goonesekere, 2006; Khunou, 2006; Cuesta and Meyer, 2014, 2018; Nor et al, 2018, 2020; Chung and Kim, 2019; Ahmad et al, 2020). The exclusion of race, indigeneity, ethnicity, sexuality and religious identity from the vast majority of contemporary child support research is a particular blindspot; one that was not extensively considered in this work, yet it needs to be addressed in the next generation of child support research.

While this book has set out broad trends that exist across contexts, what is needed to reform systems is detailed knowledge of the sites of inequity within each child support jurisdiction and its particular social context, to identify the intersectional structures and relations through which women's subordination is achieved and reinforced. While child support research is replete with studies conducted by administrators, economists and psychologists, more work is needed on the lifeworlds of women – not only at the level of mothers' identities or in their interactions with ex-partners, but on how women' concerns and experiences are expressed and taken up within child support institutions. More work is required to flesh out women's troubled experiences of child support processes and practices across the world in more depth than was possible in this multi-context study.

Detailed, context-specific research is needed to problematise the assumptions on which the conduct of child support exists and to render visible the erroneous responsibilisation of women therein. Many excellent scholars have been undertaking this work, but more ongoing research needs to be done to identify the commonalities in women's experiences, to identify these as structural, systemic and entrenched. Only deeply uncomfortable, troubling and decisive research will lead to similarly structural and systemic change. Naming and calling states out on gendered processes is an act of defiance and an exercise of women's agency and empowerment. Research that calls out the inequities in existing systems shifts the power dynamic between parties, and also allows taken for granted practices – such as private collections, falling out of child support systems and women's responsibility for the behaviour of fathers, the system and the state – to be unsettled and upended. However, the first step in this process is to make such issues visible.

Returning to Jamrozik and Nocella's (1998) account of the competing lenses and worldviews of policymakers, programme administrators, front-line staff and recipients, research is needed to join these views together, to identify how policymakers' assumptions about the nature of the problems with child support diverge from the experiences of (half of) its policy targets. However, the job for feminists is to ensure that policy problems are not reframed by vocal but minority men's rights activist groups that have been so influential in child support policy reform to date. As Risman (2004, p. 445) suggests, when studying inequality, such as in this case the entrenchment of women's social and economic subordination through child support, the most important question to ask is, 'what mechanisms are currently constructing inequality and how can these be transformed to create a more just world?' To hold policymakers to account, research needs to assess current or proposed law and policy settings against the purpose of child support. In previous chapters, reducing child poverty was seen to trump other purported aims of reducing welfare expenditure or increasingly parental responsibility, which were shown to be red herrings when it comes to what child support payments are meant to achieve. So, when assessing the impact or experience of child support policy or law, I would suggest evaluating the extent to which it facilitates the transfer of child support payments, particularly from able, but unwilling, payers. If the proposed solutions do not facilitate payments, then likely the problem that they seek to resolve has little relevance to women's desires and expectations for child support policy and its conduct.

Reimagining child support as a more gender-equitable policy throws up big questions about the nature of state and family relationships. Similarly, as Ahmed (2017, p. 256) states, 'feminist principles are articulated in unfeminist worlds', rendering them subject to claims that they are unable to be implemented, fanciful or naive. Such criticisms are attempts to maintain the status quo. The difficult path to achieving a feminist vision should not prevent an investigation of how we might get there. If nothing else, this book has identified possibilities for feminist child support reform that can be taken up and further interrogated. While feminist solutions remain elusive within the context of the 'unfeminist' worlds in which child support exists, it does not mean that solutions should not be proposed or pursued.

Luzkow's (2016) avenues for reform of the Keynesian welfare state identify two possibilities that can be adapted to re-imagine child support through a feminist lens. First, child support could be further institutionalised to embed it even more thoroughly within the welfare state, however, such configurations would need to avoid punitive child support–benefit interactions or unfairly placing responsibility on the benefit-recipient parent rather than the child support payer. A thoughtful and gender-sensitive integration of child support within the welfare state could lead to a redistribution of the risks and responsibilities of child-raising across society and away from their current individualised focus on mothers and fathers. What this might look like is more akin to the Nordic state's guaranteed child support – whereby fathers' responsibility to children is unfortunately eschewed, but mothers have an easier path to financial security and well-being. However, providing unconditional support and spreading the risk and responsibilities across the population requires communal trust, which is eroded by increasing technical requirements at an individual level. Second, the alternate path for child support is to decouple child support from welfare altogether and re-individualise payments so as to free women up from the oppressive structures of the state, such as exists in many of the court-based systems examined in this book. However, this locates women back within the gendered hierarchies of personal interactions and cultural and familial expectations. Within Nordic, liberal or traditional child support systems, this analysis has found that there are no easy answers and no clear pathways to provide women and their children financial or relational justice. For example, an analysis of thirteen countries that reflected these three policy systems found that the countries comprising each type had as much difference between them as they did in common when it came to child support obligations in shared-care cases (Hakovirta et al, 2021). As such, the path to simple and effective policy reform is fraught with both complexity and cultural considerations. Douglas and Nagesh (2019), however, discuss the pros and cons of guaranteed and individualised child support systems in the context of domestic violence. They conclude that irrespective of the system design, self-agency of parents should be paramount. At present, however, child support systems, irrespective of whether they are guaranteed or individualised, agency-administered or court-based, disproportionately promote the agency of fathers, while diminishing the agency of mothers.

Regardless of particular design features, child support systems work to maintain gender hierarchies. Child support enacted through law or policy illustrates the power of the patriarchy to shape identities, interactions and institutions in ways that confer benefits to men while making women responsible for their systemic disadvantage. A new path for child support reform based on feminist principles of equality, autonomy and dignity will ultimately see the end of the child support system. The project of systemic and social transformation that is required to overcome the gender inequities built in to child support systems obviously still lies ahead. But, to intervene in child support inequity is to intervene in the enactment of the patriarchy. Clearly this is not going to be easy, and it will be resisted at every turn. But the prospect of resistance does not mean that this project should not be vigorously pursued. On the contrary, the pursuit of equality, autonomy and dignity should be made a personal, organisational, national and international priority.

References

Ahmad, B., Azahari, R. Hj., Ab Rahman, A. and Abdul Wahab, M. (2020) 'Assessing the rate of child maintenance (financial support) from a Shariah perspective: The case of Malaysia', *Al-Jami'ah: Journal of Islamic Studies*, 58(2), pp. 293–322.

Ahmed, S. (2006) 'The nonperformativity of antiracism', *Meridians*, 7(1), pp. 104–26.

Ahmed, S. (2007) '"You end up doing the document rather than doing the doing": Diversity, race equality and the politics of documentation', *Ethnic and Racial Studies*, 30(4), pp. 590–609.

Ahmed, S. (2017) *Living a Feminist Life*. Durham, NC: Duke University Press.

Ajzenstadt, M. (2009) 'Moral panic and neo-liberalism: The case of single mothers on welfare in Israel', *British Journal of Criminology*, 49(1), pp. 68–87.

Alexander, L. (1995) 'Australia's Child Support Scheme', *Family Matters*, 42, pp. 6–11.

Allbeson, J. (2017) *Children Deserve More: Challenging Child Maintenance Avoidance*. London: Gingerbread.

Armstrong, A. (1992) 'Maintenance payments for child support in southern Africa: Using law to promote family planning', *Studies in Family Planning*, 23(4), pp. 217–28.

Atkin, W.R. (1994) 'Child support in New Zealand runs into strife', *Houston Law Review*, 31, pp. 631–42.

Australian Government (2021). *Child Support Guide*. Available online: https://guides.dss.gov.au/child-support-guide/5/4/7.

Australian Law Reform Commission (2012) *Family Violence and Commonwealth Laws – Improving Legal Frameworks*, Report No. 117. Canberra: Australian Government.

Australian National Audit Office (2015) *Management of Smart Centres' Centrelink Telephone Services*. Australia: Commonwealth of Australia. Available at: https://www.anao.gov.au/sites/default/files/ANAO_Report_2014-2015_37.pdf.

Bacchi, C.L. (1999) *Women, Policy and Politics: The Construction of Policy Problems*. London: SAGE Publications.

Bacchi, C.L. (2009) *Analysing Policy: What's the Problem Represented to Be?* London: Pearson.

Bacchi, C.L. (2012) 'Why study problematizations? Making politics visible', *Open Journal of Political Science*, 2(1), pp. 1–8.

Banaszak, L.A., Beckwith, K. and Rucht, D. (2003) 'When power relocates: Interactive changes in women's movements and states', in Banaszak, L.A., Beckwith, K. and Rucht, D. (eds.) *Women, Gender, and Politics: A Reader*, pp. 1–29. Cambridge: Cambridge University Press.

Battle, B.P. (2018) 'Deservingness, deadbeat dads, and responsible fatherhood: Child support policy and rhetorical conceptualizations of poverty, welfare, and the family', *Symbolic Interaction*, 41(4), pp. 443–64.

Battle, B.P. (2019) '"They look at you like you're nothing": Stigma and shame in the child support system', *Symbolic Interaction*, 42(4), pp. 640–68.

Beaumont, P., Hess, B., Walker, L. and Spancken, S. (2014) *The Recovery of Maintenance in the EU and Worldwide*. Oxford: Hart Publishing.

Bertoia, C. and Drakich, J. (1993) 'The fathers' rights movement: Contradictions in rhetoric and practice', *Journal of Family Issues*, 14(4), pp. 592–615.

Bourdieu, P. (2001) *Masculine Domination*. Stanford, CA: Stanford University Press.

Boyd, S.B. (2004) 'Demonizing mothers: Fathers' rights discourses in child custody law reform processes', *Journal of the Motherhood Initiative for Research and Community Involvement*, 6(1), pp. 52–74.

Boyd, S.B., Chunn, D.E., Kelly, F. and Wiegers, W. (2015) *Autonomous Motherhood? A Socio-legal Study of Choice and Constraint*. Toronto: University of Toronto Press.

Bradshaw, J. (1996) 'Lone parents and employment: A comparison of Belgium with 19 other countries', in Haegendoren, M. (ed.) *Femmes Pauvres/Arme Vrouwen*, pp. 105–31. Diepenbeek, Belgium: Point d'appui Women's Studies.

Bradshaw, J. and Finch, N. (2002) *A Comparison of Child Benefit Packages in 22 Countries*. Norwich: Department of Work and Pensions.

Bradshaw, J., Skinner, C., Stimson, C. and Williams, J. (1999) *Absent Fathers?* London: Routledge.

Brady, M. and Cook, K. (2015) 'The impact of welfare to work on parents and their children', *Evidence Base: A Journal of Evidence Reviews in Key Policy Areas*, 3, n.p. Available online: https://journal.anzsog.edu.au/publications

Brittan, A. (1989) *Masculinity and Power*. London: Basil Blackwell.

Brush, L.D. (2003) *Gender and Governance*. Lanham, MD: Rowman Altamira.

Bryson, C., Skipp, A., Allbeson, C., Poole, E., Ireland, E. and Marsh, V. (2013) *Kids Aren't Free: The Child Maintenance Arrangements of Single Parents on Benefit in 2012*. London: Nuffield Foundation.

Cancian, M., Meyer, D.R. and Wood, R. (2019) *Final Impact Findings from the Child Support Noncustodial Parent Employment Demonstration (CSPED)*. Available at: https://ideas.repec.org/p/mpr/mprres/93c8996bb09444a29 2e2598d2d315aa3.html.

Carlson, M.H. (2009) 'United States perspective on the new Hague Convention on the International Recovery of Child Support and Other Forms of Family Maintenance', *Family Law Quarterly*, 43(1), pp. 21–35.

Case, A.C., Lin, I.-F. and Mclanahan, S.S. (2003) 'Explaining trends in child support: Economic, demographic, and policy effects', *Demography*, 40(1), pp. 171–89.

Cavaghan, R. (2013) 'Gender mainstreaming in the DGR as a knowledge process: Epistemic barriers to eradicating gender bias', *Critical Policy Studies*, 7(4), pp. 407–21.

Chambers, D.L. (1982) 'The coming curtailment of compulsory child support', *Michigan Law Review*, 80, pp. 1614–34.

Child Support Evaluation Advisory Group (1992) *Child Support in Australia: Final Report of the Evaluation of the Child Support Scheme*. Canberra: Commonwealth of Australia.

Chung, Y. and Kim, Y. (2019) 'How cultural and policy contexts interact with child support policy: A case study of child support receipt in Korea and the United States', *Children and Youth Services Review*, 96, pp. 237–49.

Clark Blickenstaff, J. (2005) 'Women and science careers: Leaky pipeline or gender filter?', *Gender and Education*, 17(4), pp. 369–86.

Clarke, J. (2005) 'New Labour's citizens: Activated, empowered, responsibilized, abandoned?', *Critical Social Policy*, 25(4), pp. 447–63.

Collins, C., Landivar, L.C., Ruppanner, L. and Scarborough, W.J. (2021) 'COVID-19 and the gender gap in work hours', *Gender, Work & Organization*, 28(S1), pp. 101–12.

Coltrane, S. and Hickman, N. (1992) 'The rhetoric of rights and needs: Moral discourse in the reform of child custody and child support laws', *Social Problems*, 39(4), pp. 400–20.

Commonwealth Ombudsman (2012) *Annual Report, 2011–2012*. Canberra: Commonwealth of Australia.

Commonwealth Ombudsman (2014) *Submission by the Commonwealth Ombudsman, Submission 55*. Canberra: House of Representatives Standing Committee on Social Policy and Legal Affairs.

Connell, R. (2007) *Southern Theory: Social Science and the Global Dynamics of Knowledge*. Cambridge: Polity Press.

Connell, R. (2019) *The Good University: What Universities Actually Do and Why It's Time for Radical Change*. Melbourne: Monash University Publishing.

Cook, K. (2013) 'Child support compliance and tax return non-filing: A feminist analysis', *Australian Review of Public Affairs*, 11(2), pp. 43–64.

Cook, K. (2020) 'The devaluing and disciplining of single mothers in Australian child support policy', in Pascoe, C. and Bueskens, P. (eds.) *Australian Mothering: Historical and Sociological Perspectives*, pp. 381–402. Cham: Palgrave Macmillan.

Cook, K. (2021a) 'State tactics of welfare benefit minimisation: The power of governing documents', *Critical Social Policy*. https://doi.org/10.1177/02610183211003474.

Cook, K. (2021b) 'Gender, malice, obligation and the state: Separated mothers' experiences of administrative burdens with Australia's child support program', *Australian Journal of Public Administration*. https://doi.org/10.1111/1467-8500.12522.

Cook, K. and Natalier, K. (2013) 'The gendered framing of Australia's child support reforms', *International Journal of Law, Policy and the Family*, 27(1), pp. 28–50.

Cook, K. and Natalier, K. (2014) 'Selective hearing: The gendered construction and reception of inquiry evidence', *Critical Social Policy*, 34(4), pp. 515–37.

Cook, K. and Natalier, K. (2016) 'Gender and evidence in family law reform: A case study of quantification and anecdote in framing and legitimising the 'problems' with child support in Australia', *Feminist Legal Studies*, 24(2), pp. 147–67.

Cook, K. and Skinner, C. (2019) 'Gender equality in child support policy: Fathers' rhetoric of "fairness" in a parliamentary inquiry', *Social Politics*, 26(1), pp. 164–87.

Cook, K. and Skinner, C. (2020) 'Technical fixes as challenges to state legitimacy: Australian separated fathers' suggestions for child support policy reform', *Social Politics*, 28(2), pp. 501–20.

Cook, K., McKenzie, H. and Natalier, K. (2015a) 'Mothers' experiences of child support: Qualitative research and opportunities for policy insight', *Journal of Family Studies*, 21(1), pp. 57–71.

Cook, K., Given, L., Keam, G. and Young, L. (2019) 'Technological opportunities for procedural justice in welfare administration: A review of available apps', *Critical Social Policy*, 40(4), pp. 627–48.

Cook, K., McKenzie, H., Natalier, K. and Young, L. (2015b) 'Institutional processes and the production of gender inequalities: The case of Australian child support research and administration', *Critical Social Policy*, 35(4), pp. 512–34.

Corden, A. (1999) *Making Child Maintenance Regimes Work*. London: Family Policy Studies Centre.

Costello, P. (2005) *Budget Speech, 2005–06*. Canberra: Commonwealth of Australia.

Cozzolino, E. (2018) 'Public assistance, relationship context, and jail for child support debt', *Socius*, 4. https://doi.org/10.1177/2378023118757124.

Cozzolino, E. and Williams, C.L. (2017) 'Child support queens and disappointing dads: Gender and child support compliance', *Social Currents*, 4(3), pp. 228–45.

Craig, L. (2020) 'COVID-19 has laid bare how much we value women's work, and how little we pay for it', *The Conversation*, 21 April. Available at: https://theconversation.com/covid-19-has-laid-bare-how-much-we-value-womens-work-and-how-little-we-pay-for-it-136042 2020].

Crenshaw, K.W. (1991) 'Mapping the margins: Intersectionality, identity politics, and violence against women of color', *Stanford Law Review*, 43(6), pp. 1241–99.

Crowley, J.E. (2003) *The Politics of Child Support in America*. Cambridge: Cambridge University Press.

Cuesta, L. and Meyer, D.R. (2014) 'The role of child support in the economic wellbeing of custodial-mother families in less developed countries: The case of Colombia', *International Journal of Law, Policy and the Family*, 28(1), pp. 60–76.

Cuesta, L. and Meyer, D.R. (2018) 'Child poverty and child support policy: A comparative analysis of Colombia and the United States', *Children and Youth Services Review*, 93, pp. 143–53.

Cuesta, L., Hakovirta, M. and Jokela, M. (2018) 'The antipoverty effectiveness of child support: Empirical evidence for Latin American countries', *Social Policy and Administration*, 52(6), pp. 1–19.

Dados, N. and Connell, R. (2012) 'The Global South', *Contexts*, 11(1), pp. 12–13.

DeKeseredy, W.S., Dragiewicz, M. and Schwartz, M.D. (2017) *Abusive Endings: Separation and Divorce Violence against Women*. Berkeley: University of California Press.

de Vaus, D., Gray, M., Qu, L. and Stanton, D. (2017) 'The economic consequences of divorce in six OECD countries', *Australian Journal of Social Issues*, 52(2), pp. 180–99.

Department of Human Services (2018) *2017–18 Annual Report*. Canberra: Commonwealth of Australia. Available at: https://www.servicesaustralia.gov.au/sites/default/files/2018/10/8802-1810-annual-report-web-2017-2018.pdf.

Department of Human Services (2019) *Child Support and Pour Family Tax Benefit, Part A*. Canberra: Australian Government. Available at: https://www.servicesaustralia.gov.au/individuals/topics/child-support-and-your-family-tax-benefit-part/29646.

Department of Social Services (2020) *Guides to Social Policy Law: Child Support Guide*. Australian Government. Available at: https://guides.dss.gov.au/child-support-guide.

Dinçer, F. (2010) 'The light and dark romantic features of Irving, Hawthorne and Poe', *The Journal of International Social Research*, 3(10), pp. 218–24.

Douglas, H. and Nagesh, R. (2019) 'Domestic and family violence, child support and "the exemption"', *Journal of Family Studies*, 27(4), pp. 1–16.

Dudová, R. (2006) 'Old obligations in the modern world: The father as provider before and after divorce', *Sociologický Časopis/Czech Sociological Review*, 42(3), pp. 573–90.

Edin, K. (1995) 'Single mothers and child support: The possibilities and limits of child support policy', *Children and Youth Services Review*, 17(1), pp. 203–30.

Edin, K. (2018) 'Child support in the age of complex families', *Issues in Science and Technology*, 34(2), pp. 38–45.

Edin, K. and Lein, L. (1997) 'Work, welfare, and single mothers' economic survival strategies', *American Sociological Review*, 62(2), pp. 253–66.

Edwards, M. (2019) 'The Child Support Scheme: What innovative collaboration can achieve', in Luetjens, J., Mintrom, M. and Hart, P.t. (eds.) *Successful Public Policy: Lessons from Australia and New Zealand*, pp. 139–63. Canberra: ANU Press.

Edwards, M., Howard, C. and Miller, R. (2001) *Social Policy, Public Policy: From Problem to Practice*. Crows Nest: Allen & Unwin.

Edwards, R. and Duncan, S. (1996) 'Rational economic man or lone mothers in context? The uptake of paid work', in Bortolaia Silva, E. (ed.) *Good Enough Mothering? Feminist Perspectives on Lone Motherhood*, pp. 114–29. London: Routledge.

Eekelaar, J. (1991a) 'Are parents morally obliged to care for their children?', *Oxford Journal of Legal Studies*, 11(3), pp. 340–53.

Eekelaar, J. (1991b) 'Parental responsibility: State of nature or nature of the state?', *Journal of Social Welfare & Family Law*, 13(1), pp. 37–50.

Elrod, L. H. (1990) 'The federalization of child support guidelines', *Journal of the American Academy of Matrimonial Lawyers*, 6(1), pp. 103–30.

Eydal, G. B. and Friðriksdóttir, H. (2012) 'Child maintenance policies in Iceland: Caring mothers and breadwinning fathers', *European Journal of Social Security*, 14(4), pp. 267–85.

Fehlberg, B. and Maclean, M. (2009) 'Child support policy in Australia and the United Kingdom: Changing priorities but a similar tough deal for children?', *International Journal of Law, Policy and the Family*, 23(1), pp. 1–24.

Fehlberg, B., Millward, C. and Campo, M. (2010) 'Mothers who are liable to pay child support', *Family Matters*, 86, pp. 62–71.

Fernqvist, S. and Sépulchre, M. (2021). 'Guaranteed or conditional child maintenance? Examining the 2016 reform in Sweden', *Critical Social Policy*. https://doi.org/10.1177/02610183211036563.

Fletcher, M. (2016) 'New Zealand's Child Support Amendment Act 2013: Some likely short-term effects of the new liability assessment formula', *Australian Journal of Family Law*, 30(1), pp. 28–50.

Fletcher, M., Maré, D.C. and Maloney, T. (2020) 'The economic consequences of marital separation for parents in New Zealand: Insights from a large administrative dataset', *International Journal of Law, Policy and the Family*, 34(3), pp. 289–313.

Fogarty, K. and Augoustinos, M. (2008) 'Feckless fathers and monopolizing mothers: Motive, identity, and fundamental truths in the Australian Public Inquiry into Child Custody', *British Journal of Social Psychology*, 47(3), pp. 535–56.

Foucault, M. (1980) 'Two lectures', in Gordon, C. (ed.) *Power/Knowledge: Selected Interviews and Other Writings, 1972–1977*, pp. 78–108. Brighton: Harvester.

Friedman, G. (2014) 'Workers without employers: Shadow corporations and the rise of the gig economy', *Review of Keynesian Economics*, 2(2), pp. 171–88.

Frohmann, B. (1992) 'The power of images: A discourse of the cognitive viewpoint', *Journal of Documentation*, 48(4) pp. 365–86.

Garfinkel, I., McLanahan, S.S., Meyer, D.R. and Seltzer, J.A. (1998) *Fathers Under Fire: The Revolution in Child Support Enforcement*. New York: Russell Sage Foundation.

Goodall, Z. and Cook, K. (2020) 'The forms and functions of child support stigma', *Social Currents*, 8(2), pp. 145–62. https://doi.org/10.1177/2329496520968211.

Goonesekere, S. (2006) 'Family support and maintenance: Emerging issues in some developing countries with mixed jurisdictions', *Family Court Review* 44(3), pp. 361–75.

Gorlick, C. and Brethour, G. (1998) *Welfare-to-Work Programs in Canada: An Overview*. Ontario: Canadian Council on Social Development.

Graham, H. (1983) 'Do her answers fit his questions? Women and the survey method', in Gamarnikow, E., Morgan, D., Purvis, J. and Taylorson, D. (eds.) *The Public and the Private*, pp. 132–47. London: Heinemann.

Grall, T. (2016) *Custodial Mothers and Fathers and Their Child Support: 2013*. Washington, DC: United States Census Bureau.

Grall, T. (2018) *Custodial Mothers and Fathers and Their Child Support: 2015*. Washington, DC: United States Census Bureau.

Graycar, R. and Morgan, J. (2002) *The Hidden Gender of Law*. Alexandria: Federation Press.

Hadjian, A. (2013) 'The children of Shari'a', *The Los Angeles Lawyer Magazine*, April 2013, pp. 32–9.

Hague Conference on Private International Law (2015) *Global Conference on the Recovery of Child Support and Family Maintenance in Asia Pacific and Worldwide: National and Regional Systems and the Hague 2007 Convention and Protocol*. Hong Kong: Hague Conference on Private International Law.

Hahn, H., Kuehn, D. and Hassani, H. (2019) *Relief from Government-Owed Child Support Debt and Its Effects on Parents and Children*. Washington, DC: Urban Institute. Available at: https://www.urban.org/sites/default/files/publication/100812/relief_from_government-owed_child_support_debt_and_its_effects_on_parents_and_children_2.pdf.

Hakovirta, M. (2011) 'Child maintenance and child poverty: A comparative analysis', *Journal of Poverty and Social Justice*, 19(3), pp. 249–62.

Hakovirta, M. and Eydal, B.G. (2020) 'Shared care and child maintenance policies in Nordic countries', *International Journal of Law, Policy and the Family*, 34(1), pp. 43–59.

Hakovirta, M., Cook, K. and Sinclair, S. (2020) 'Gender equality prior to and following separation: Nordic and liberal policy inconsistencies', *Social Politics*. https://doi.org/10.1093/sp/jxaa010.

Hakovirta, M., Meyer, D.R. and Skinner, C. (2019a) 'Does paying child support impoverish fathers in the United States, Finland, and the United Kingdom?', *Children and Youth Services Review*, 106. https://doi.org/10.1016/j.childyouth.2019.104485.

Hakovirta, M., Meyer, D.R. and Skinner, C. (2021) 'Child support in shared care cases: Do child support policies in thirteen countries reflect family policy models?', *Social Policy and Society*. https://doi.org/10.1017/S1474746421000300

Hakovirta, M., Skinner, C., Hiilamo, H. and Jokela, M. (2019b) 'Child poverty, child maintenance and interactions with social assistance benefits among lone parent families', *Journal of Social Policy*, 49(1), pp. 19–39.

Hancock, L. (1998) 'Reforming the child support agenda: Who benefits?', *Just Policy: A Journal of Australian Social Policy*, 12, pp. 20–31.

Hanewall, C. and Lopoo, L.M. (2008) 'Child support enforcement and child poverty: a long-term perspective based on findings from the United States', *International Journal of Public Administration*, 31(2), pp. 195–210.

Hans, J.D. and Coleman, M. (2009) 'The experiences of remarried stepfathers who pay child support', *Personal Relationships*, 16(4), pp. 597–618.

Hansen, D.D. (1999) 'The American invention of child support: Dependency and punishment in early American child support law', *Yale Law Journal*, 108, pp. 1123–53.

Hansen, H.T., Lundberg, K. and Syltevik, L.J. (2018) 'Digitalization, street-level bureaucracy and welfare users' experiences', *Social Policy and Administration*, 52(1), pp. 67–90.

Hanson, P. (2016) *First Speech*. Canberra: Parliament of Australia.

Harris, D.A. (2015) '"You just have to look at it as a gift": Low-income single mothers' experiences of the child support system', *Journal of Poverty*, 19(1), pp. 88–108.

Hawthorne, B. and Lennings, C.J. (2008) 'The marginalization of nonresident fathers: Their postdivorce roles', *Journal of Divorce & Remarriage*, 49, pp. 191–209.

Hellum, A. (2000) 'Human rights and gender relations in postcolonial Africa: Options and limits for the subjects of legal pluralism', *Law and Social Inquiry*, 25(2), pp. 635–55.

Henman, P. and Mitchell, K. (2001) 'Estimating the cost of contact for non-resident parents: A budget standards approach', *Journal of Social Policy*, 30(3), pp. 495–520.

Henman, P., Percival, R., Harding, A. and Gray, M. (2007) *Costs of Children: Research Commissioned by the Ministerial Taskforce on Child Support*, FaHCSIA Occasional Paper No. 18. Canberra: Commonwealth of Australia.

Herd, P. and Moynihan, D.P. (2018) *Administrative Burden: Policymaking by Other Means*. New York: Russell Sage Foundation.

Hitch, G. (2021) 'Rex Patrick calls for punitive measures for child support payers and payees not lodging tax returns'. *ABC News* (Australia), 1 April. Available online: https://www.abc.net.au/news/2021-04-01/calls-punish-child-support-payers-payees-not-lodging-tax-returns/100041416.

Hodges, L., Meyer, D.R. and Cancian, M. (2020) 'What Happens when the amount of child support due is a burden? Revisiting the relationship between child support orders and child support payments', *Social Service Review*, 94(2), pp. 238–84.

House of Representatives Standing Committee on Family and Community Affairs (2003) *Every Picture Tells a Story: Inquiry into Child Custody Arrangements in the Event of Family Separation*. Canberra: Commonwealth of Australia.

House of Representatives Standing Committee on Social Policy and Legal Affairs (2015) *From Conflict to Cooperation: Inquiry into the Child Support Program*. Canberra: Commonwealth of Australia.

Hunter, N.D. (1983) 'Child support law and policy: The systematic imposition of costs on women', *Harvard Women's Law Journal*, 6, pp. 1–27.

Jamrozik, A. and Nocella, L.D. (1998) *The Sociology of Social Problems: Theoretical Perspectives and Methods of Intervention*. Melbourne: Cambridge University Press.

Jeans, C. (2014) 'Children's rights in policy and poverty: An analysis of Iceland, Norway & the UK', *Tímarit Félagsráðgjafa*, 8, pp. 12–19.

Joint Select Committee on Australia's Family Law System (2020) *Improvements in Family Law Proceedings – Interim Report*. Canberra: Commonwealth of Australia.

Joint Select Committee on Certain Family Law Issues (1994) *Child Support Scheme: An Examination of the Operation and Effectiveness of the Scheme*. Canberra: Australian Government.

Kantola, J. and Squires, J. (2012) 'From state feminism to market feminism?', *International Political Science Review*, 33(4), pp. 382–400.

Kaye, M. and Tolmie, J. (1998) 'Discoursing dads: The rhetorical devices of fathers' rights groups', *Melbourne University Law Review*, 22(1), pp. 162–94.

Keil, M. and Elizabeth, V. (2017) 'Gendered and cultural moral rationalities: Pacific mothers' pursuit of child support money', *Women's Studies Journal*, 31(1), pp. 34–47.

Keil, M. and Elizabeth, V. (2019) "It's not like I ever use the money for me to go out and live the café lifestyle': Pacific mothers talk about child support money', *Journal of Family Studies*. https://doi.org/10.1080/13229400.2019.1689153.

Khunou, G. (2006) 'Fathers don't stand a chance: Experiences of custody, access and maintenance', in Richter, L. and Morrell, R. (eds.) *Baba: Men and Fatherhood in South Africa*, pp. 265–77. Cape Town: HSRC Press.

Krause, M. (2016) 'Comparative research: Beyond linear-causal explanation', in Deville, J., Guggenheim, M. and Hrdličková, Z. (eds.) *Practising Comparison: Logics, Relations, Collaborations*, pp. 45–67. Manchester: Mattering Press.

Law, J. and Urry, J. (2004) 'Enacting the social', *Economy and Society*, 33(3), pp. 390–410.

Lemke, T. (2001) "The birth of bio-politics': Michel Foucault's lecture at the Collège de France on neo-liberal governmentality', *Economy and Society*, 30(2), pp. 190–207.

Lens, V. (2002) 'Welfare reform, personal narratives and the media: How welfare recipients and journalists frame the welfare debate', *Journal of Poverty*, 6(2), pp. 1–20.

Lerman, R.I. (2010) 'Capabilities and contributions of unwed fathers', *The Future of Children*, 20(2), pp. 63–85.

Li, T.M. (2007) *The Will to Improve: Governmentality, Development, and the Practice of Politics*. Durham, NC: Duke University Press.

Liegghio, M. and Caragata, L. (2016) '"Why are you talking to me like I'm stupid?": The micro-aggressions committed within the social welfare system against lone mothers', *Affilia*, 31(1), pp. 7–23.

Lin, I.F. (2000) 'Perceived fairness and compliance with child support obligations', *Journal of Marriage and Family*, 62(2), pp. 388–98.

Lin, I.F. and McLanahan, S.S. (2007) 'Parental beliefs about nonresident fathers' obligations and rights', *Journal of Marriage and Family*, 69(2), pp. 382–98.

Lorde, A. (2017) *Your Silence Will Not Protect You*. London: Silver Press.

Luzkow, J.L. (2016) *The Great Forgetting: The Past, Present and Future of Social Democracy and the Welfare State*. Manchester: Manchester University Press.

MacKinnon, C.A. (1989) *Toward a Feminist Theory of the State*. Cambridge, MA: Harvard University Press.

Marshall, T.H. (1950) *Citizenship and Social Class, and Other Essays*. Cambridge: Cambridge University Press

Masoumi, A. (2019) 'The politics of "doing exactly nothing": Feminist legal change and bureaucratic administration of refugee protection', *Feminist Legal Studies*, 27(3), pp. 243–61.

McConnell, A. (2018) 'Rethinking wicked problems as political problems and policy problems', *Policy and Politics*, 46(1), pp. 165–80.

McCosker, A. and Milne, E. (2014) 'Coding labour', *Cultural Studies Review*, 20(1), pp. 4–29.

McKenzie, H. (2012) 'Accepting the unacceptable: Patriarchal hegemony and child support arrangements'. PhD dissertation, Deakin University, Melbourne, Australia.

McKenzie, H. and Cook, K. (2015) ' "It should be a big responsibility": Low income payee mothers' evaluations of their child support arrangements', *Australian Journal of Family Law*, 29, pp. 135–65.

Meyer, D., Cancian, M. and Chen, Y. (2015) 'Why are child support orders becoming less likely after divorce?', *Social Service Review*, 89, pp. 301–34.

Miller, P. (2001) 'Governing by numbers: Why calculative practices matter', *Social Research*, 68(2), pp. 379–96.

Mills, C.W. (1959) *The Sociological Imagination*. New York: Oxford University Press.

Millward, C. and Fehlberg, B. (2013) 'Recognising the costs of contact: Infrastructure costs, 'regular care' and Australia's new child support formula', *Australian Journal of Family Law*, 27(1), pp. 1–25.

Ministerial Taskforce on Child Support (2005) *In the Best Interests of Children – Reforming the Child Support Scheme – Report of the Ministerial Taskforce on Child Support*. Canberra: Australian Government Department of Families, Housing, Community Services and Indigenous Affairs.

Mokgoro, Y. (2003) 'Constitutional claims for gender equality in South Africa: A judicial response', *Albany Law Review*, 67, pp. 565–73.

Morgan, P.M. (1995) *Farewell to the Family? Public Policy and Family Breakdown in Britain and the USA*. London: IEA Health and Welfare Unit.

Municio, I. (2013) *Matriarchal Families and Interchangeable Fathers: How Discourses on Parenting Allocate Positions to Women and Men in Post-divorce Families*. Södertörn: Södertörn University.

Natalier, K. (2012) 'Descriptions of loss and resilience among fathers paying child support', *Journal of Family Studies*, 18(2/3), pp. 246–55.

Natalier, K. (2017) 'Micro-aggressions, single mothers and interactions with government workers: The case of Australia's child support bureaucracy', *Journal of Sociology*, 53(3), pp. 622–36.

Natalier, K. (2018) 'State facilitated economic abuse: A structural analysis of men deliberately withholding child support', *Feminist Legal Studies*, 26(2), pp. 121–40.

Natalier, K. and Hewitt, B. (2010) ' "It's not just about the money": Non-resident fathers' perspectives on paying child support', *Sociology*, 44(3), pp. 489–505.

Natalier, K. and Hewitt, B. (2014) 'Separated parents reproducing and undoing gender through defining legitimate uses of child support', *Gender and Society*, 28(6), pp. 904–25.

Natalier, K., Cook, K. and McKenzie, H. (2018) 'Single mothers' post-separation provisioning: Child support and the governance of gender', *Sociology*, 53(3), pp. 554–70.

Natalier, K., Cook, K. and Pitman, T. (2016) 'Payee mothers' interactions with the Department of Human Services–Child Support', *Family Matters*, 97, pp. 30–40.

Nicholas, L. and Agius, C. (2018) *The Persistence of Global Masculinism*. Cham: Palgrave Macmillan.

Nor, Z.M., Mohamad, N.Z. and Vellymalay, S.K.N. (2019) 'When poverty knocks on the door: Sharing the story of low income single mothers in Kelantan', *International Journal of Engineering Science*, 12(2), pp. 50–56.

Nor, Z.M., Hasana, I.S.A., Omarb, B., Vellymalaya, S.K.N. and Omar, A. (2018) 'Financial wellbeing of single mothers in Penang: The sole breadwinner', *Management and Accounting Review*, 17(1), pp. 35–44.

Nor, Z.M., Saidin, Z.H., Razdi, R.M., Hassan, M.H., Kahn, B.Z.A. and Safun, H.A.J. (2020) 'Conceptualizing sustainable livelihood for single parent households', *Albukhary Social Business Journal*, 1(1), pp. 7–12.

OECD (2011) *Doing Better for Families*. Paris: OECD.

OECD (2019a) *OECD Family Database*. Paris: OECD. Available at: http://www.oecd.org/els/family/database.htm.

OECD (2019b) *Public Social Spending Is High in Many OECD Countries*. Paris: OECD. Available at: https://www.oecd.org/social/soc/OECD2019-Social-Expenditure-Update.pdf.

OECD (2019c) *Society at a Glance 2019*. Paris: OECD. Available at: https://www.oecd-ilibrary.org/content/publication/soc_glance-2019-en.

OECD (2020) *Gender Wage Gap*. Paris: OECD. Available at: https://data.oecd.org/earnwage/gender-wage-gap.htm.

Oldham, T. and Smyth, B. (2018) 'Child support compliance in the USA and Australia: To persuade or punish?', *Family Law Quarterly*, 52(2), pp. 325–48.

Patrick, R., Cook, K. and McKenzie, H. (2008) 'Domestic violence and the exemption from seeking child support: Providing safety or legitimizing ongoing poverty and fear', *Social Policy and Administration*, 42(7), pp. 749–67.

Patrick, R., Cook, K. and Taket, A. (2007) 'Multiple barriers to obtaining child support: Experiences of women leaving violent partners', *Just Policy*, 45, pp. 30–37.

Pearson, J., Griswold, E.A. and Thoennes, N. (2001) 'Balancing safety and self-sufficiency: Lessons on serving victims of domestic violence for child support and public assistance agencies', *Violence Against Women*, 7(2), pp. 176–92.

Peck, J. and Tickell, A. (2002) 'Neoliberalizing space', *Antipode*, 34(3), pp. 380–404.

Pell, A. N. (1996) 'Fixing the leaky pipeline: women scientists in academia', *Journal of Animal Science*, 74(11), pp. 2843–8.

Pollack, S. and Rossiter, A. (2010) 'Neoliberalism and the entrepreneurial subject: Implications for feminism and social work', *Canadian Social Work Review*, 27(2), pp. 155–69.

Postman, N. (1993) *Technopoly: The Surrender of Technology to Culture*. New York: Vintage Books.

Qu, L., Weston, R., Moloney, L., Kaspiew, R. and Dunstan, J. (2014) *Post-separation Parenting, Property and Relationship Dynamics after Five Years*. Canberra: Australian Institute of Family Studies.

Risman, B.J. (2004) 'Gender as a social structure: Theory wrestling with activism', *Gender and Society*, 18(4), pp. 429–50.

Rissanen, A. and Aaltonen, M. (2019) 'What influences the size of child maintenance payments? A register-based study of maintenance payments in Finland', *International Journal of Social Welfare*, 28(2), pp. 128–37.

Rush, M. (2015) *Between Two Worlds of Father Politics*. Manchester: Manchester University Press.

Salter, M. (2015) ' "Real men don't hit women": Constructing masculinity in the prevention of violence against women', *Australian & New Zealand Journal of Criminology*, 49(4), pp. 463–79.

Seccombe, K., James, D. and Walters, K.B. (1998) ' "They think you ain't much of nothing": The social construction of the welfare mother', *Journal of Marriage and Family*, 60(4), pp. 849–65.

Services Australia (2020) *Basic Formula*. Australia: Australian Government. Available at: https://www.servicesaustralia.gov.au/individuals/services/child-support/child-support-assessment/how-we-work-out-your-assessment/basic-formula.

Sevenhuijsen, S. (1986) 'Fatherhood and the political theory of rights theoretical perspectives of feminism', *International Journal of the Sociology of Law*, 14(3–4), pp. 329–40.

Simmonds, A. (2016) 'Gay lotharios and innocent eves: Child maintenance, masculinities and the action for breach of promise of marriage in colonial Australia', *Law in Context*, 34(1), pp. 58–75.

Singh, R. (2017) ' "Please check the appropriate box": Documents and the governance of domestic violence', *Law & Social Inquiry*, 42(2), pp. 509–42.

Skevik, A. (2006) 'Fairness in child support assessments: The views of non-resident fathers in Norway', *International Journal of Law, Policy and the Family*, 20, pp. 181–200.

Skinner, C. (2012) 'Child maintenance in the United Kingdom', *European Journal of Social Security*, 14(4), pp. 231–51.

Skinner, C. (2013) 'Child maintenance reforms: Understanding fathers' expressive agency and the power of reciprocity', *International Journal of Law, Policy and the Family*, 27(2), pp. 242–65.

Skinner, C. and Hakovirta, M. (2020) 'Separated families and child support policies in times of social change: A comparative analysis', in Nieuwenhuis, R. and van Lancker, W. (eds.) *Palgrave Handbook of Family Policy*, pp. 267–301. London: Palgrave.

Skinner, C. and Main, G. (2013) 'The contribution of child maintenance payments to the income packages of lone mothers', *Journal of Poverty and Social Justice*, 21(1), pp. 47–60.

Skinner, C., Bradshaw, J. and Davidson, J. (2007) *Child Support Policy: An International Perspective*. Leeds: Corporate Document Services.

Skinner, C., Cook, K. and Sinclair, S. (2017a) 'The potential of child support to reduce lone mother poverty: Comparing population survey data in Australia and the UK', *Journal of Poverty and Social Justice*, 25(1), pp. 79–94.

Skinner, C., Hakovirta, M. and Davidson, J. (2012) 'A comparative analysis of child maintenance schemes in five countries', *European Journal of Social Security*, 14(4), pp. 330–47.

Skinner, C., Meyer, D.R., Cook, K. and Fletcher, M. (2017b) 'Child maintenance and social security interactions: The poverty reduction effects in model lone parent families across four countries', *Journal of Social Policy*, 46(3), pp. 495–516.

Smart, C. (1989) *Feminism and the Power of Law*. London: Routledge.

Smith, D.E. (1987) *The Everyday World as Problematic: A Feminist Sociology*. Toronto: University of Toronto Press.

Smith, D.E. (1999) *Writing the Social: Critique, Theory, and Investigations*. Toronto: University of Toronto Press.

Smith, D.E. (2001) 'Texts and the ontology of organizations and institutions', *Studies in Cultures, Organizations and Societies*, 7(2), pp. 159–98.

Smyth, B. and Henman, P. (2010) 'The distributional and financial impacts of the new Australian Child Support Scheme: A "before and day-after reform" comparison of assessed liability', *Journal of Family Studies*, 16(1), pp. 5–32.

Smyth, B. and Rodgers, B. (2011) 'Strategic bargaining over child support and parenting time: A critical review of the literature', *Australian Journal of Family Law*, 25, pp. 210–35.

Son, V., Smyth, B. and Rodgers, B. (2014) 'The impact of child support changes on the financial living standards of separated families in Australia', *Australian Journal of Family Law*, 28(2), pp. 193–232.

Standing, G. (2011) *The Precariat: The New Dangerous Class*. London: Bloomsbury.

Stewart, E. (2019) 'When child support isn't paid, families struggle in more ways than one', *ABC News* (Australia), 2 December. Available at: https://www.abc.net.au/news/2019-12-02/child-support-payments-parents-report-reveals-failures/11750710.

Stone, D.A. (1989) 'Causal stories and the formation of policy agendas', *Political Science Quarterly*, 104(2), pp. 281–300.

Summerfield, T., Young, L., Harman, J. and Flatau, P. (2010) 'Child support and welfare to work reforms: The economic consequences for single-parent families', *Family Matters*, 84, pp. 68–78.

Tam, B.Y., Findlay, L.C. and Kohen, D.E. (2017) 'Indigenous families: Who do you call family?', *Journal of Family Studies*, 23(3), pp. 243–59.

Tarrant, A., Way, L. and Ladlow, L. (2020) *Negotiating 'Earning' and 'Caring' through the COVID-19 Crisis: Change and Continuities in the Parenting and Employment Trajectories of Young Fathers*, Following Young Fathers Further Briefing Paper No. 1. Brayford Pool: University of Lincoln.

Titmuss, R.M. (1950) *Problems of Social Policy*. London: H.M.S.O.

Treloar, R. and Funk, L. (2008) 'Mothers' health, responsibilization and choice in family care work after separation/divorce', *Canadian Journal of Public Health*, 99(2), pp. 33–7.

United Nations (1989) *Convention on the Rights of the Child*. New York: United Nations.

Uviller, R.K. (1978) 'Fathers' rights and feminism: The maternal presumption revisited', *Harvard Women's Law Journal*, 1, pp. 107–30.

van Manen, M. (1990) *Researching Lived Experience Human Science for an Action Sensitive Pedagogy*. New York: SUNY Press.

Victoria Legal Aid (2020) *Child Support and the Law*. Melbourne: Victoria Legal Aid.

Vnuk, M. (2010) 'Merged or omitted? What we know (or don't) about separated mothers who pay or should pay child support in Australia', *Journal of Family Studies*, 16(1), pp. 62–76.

Vogel, L.K. (2020a) 'Barriers to meeting formal child support obligations: Noncustodial father perspectives', *Children and Youth Services Review*, 110. https://doi.org/10.1016/j.childyouth.2020.104764.

Vogel, L.K. (2020b) 'Help me help you: Identifying and addressing barriers to child support compliance', *Children and Youth Services Review*, 110. https://doi.org/10.1016/j.childyouth.2020.104763.

Walby, S. (1993) 'Backlash in historical context', in Kennedy, M., Lubelska, C. and Walsh, V. (eds.) *Making Connections: Women's Studies, Women's Movements, Women's Lives*, pp. 76–86. London: Taylor & Francis.

Walker, L. (2015) *Maintenance and Child Support in Private International Law*. London: Bloomsbury.

Waller, M.R. and Plotnick, R. (2001) 'Effective child support policy for low-income families: Evidence from street level research', *Journal of Policy Analysis and Management*, 20(1), pp. 89–110.

Waring, M. (1999) *Counting for Nothing: What Men Value and What Women Are Worth*. Toronto: University of Toronto Press.

Wimberly, C. (2000) 'Deadbeat dads, welfare moms, and Uncle Sam: How the Child Support Recovery Act punishes single-mother families', *Stanford Law Review*, 53(3), pp. 729–66.

Wolfinger, E. (2014) 'Australia's welfare discourse and news: Presenting single mothers', *Global Media Journal – Australian Edition*, 8(2), pp. 1–16.

Woods, M. (1999) *The Behaviour and Expenditures of Non-resident Parents during Contact Visits*, Research Paper No. 75. Canberra: Department of Family and Community Services.

Workplace Gender Equality Agency (2020) *Gendered Impacts of COVID-19.* Available at: https://www.wgea.gov.au/topics/gendered-impact-of-covid-19#_edn1.

Wyss, B. (2001) 'Gender and cash child support in Jamaica ', *Review of Radical Political Economics*, 33, pp. 415–39.

Yanow, D. (2000) *Conducting Interpretive Policy Analysis.* Thousand Oaks, CA: SAGE Publications.

Zelizer, V.A. (1994) *Pricing the Priceless Child: The Changing Social Value of Children.* Princeton, NJ: Princeton University Press.

Zelizer, V.A. (1996) 'Payments and social ties', *Sociological Forum*, 11(3), pp. 481–4.

Zelizer, V.A. (1998) 'How do we know whether a monetary transaction is a gift, an entitlement, or compensation?', in Ben-Ner, A. and Putterman, L. (eds.) *Economics, Values, and Organization*, pp. 329–34. Cambridge: Cambridge University Press.

Index

A

abuse 84, 85, 110
active labour market programmes 4, 87–8
administrative approach 102
administrative practices 16
administrative systems 14, 36, 59, 67, 77, 120, 151
administrative technologies 23, 87
advocates 2, 12, 32, 34, 156
Africa 37, 38, 59, 61–2, 68, 71
agency 12, 13, 15–16, 141, 157, 159
  limiting 129, 130, 133, 135, 152
Agius, C. 23, 24, 104, 128, 132
  on individualism 129, 142, 143
Ahmed, S. 13, 105, 140, 156, 158
  and nonperformatives 24, 79, 104
Ajzenstadt, M. 124
America 21, 37, 38, 84–5
  South 37, 53, 58–9, 62, 108–9
  see also Canada; US
antilaw 24
antipolitics 24–5, 104, 114
Armstrong, A. 41
Asia 37, 38, 61, 62, 63, 102–3, 149
  see also Hong Kong; Japan; Malaysia
Atkin, W.R. 57
Australia 52, 63, 86, 94, 105–8, 113, 118, 120
  administrative approach 102
  and bureaucratic agencies 37
  and care-time 45, 119
  and child support reforms 87
  and compliance 10, 122
  and domestic violence 21–2, 85
  Family Tax Benefits 4, 7, 10
  and male breadwinning role 6
  and men's rights 90
  and non-compliance 124
  and paternity 59, 60
  and personal responsibility 147
  and poverty 9, 40, 107
  and private agreements 121, 144–5, 147
  and private collection model 47, 129
  and tax return non filing 153
  welfare benefits 20, 46, 57, 65, 72
Austria 6, 37
autonomy
  and reformist systems 145
  women's 133
  see also men's autonomy

B

Bacchi, C.L. 15, 19–20, 23, 75, 100, 130
  on administrative approach 102
  on policy 11–12, 24, 25, 140
backlash 47, 90, 92, 94–6, 105, 114, 129, 140
  and fathers' rights groups 142
Belgium 37
benefits 80, 91, 92, 101, 102–3, 129–30
  and child support 102–3, 109–10, 111, 119–20, 125, 137–8, 143, 145, 147
  UK and US 121
  unemployment 98
  see also welfare benefits
Black men, jailing of for child support non-compliance 60, 148
boundary work 15, 23, 145
Bourdieu, P. 24
Boyd et al 54, 57
Bradshaw et al 28
breadwinner 4, 6, 19, 39, 42, 44, 91, 92, 102
Brittan, A. 23
Brush, Lisa 8, 11, 19, 23, 24, 77
  on power 21, 97
bureaucratic agencies 37

C

calculative technologies 124, 125
Canada 57, 66, 69, 84–5, 98, 119–20
  court-based system 37
  irrelevance of child support system 144
care 42, 43, 62, 97, 102, 111, 155–6
  sharing 7
  subsidies for 119
care-time 35, 41–2, 45, 118
Caribbean 38
caring labour 102
Carlson, M.H. 59
Case et al 40
causal stories 12, 15, 24, 25–6, 80, 96–7, 104
Cavaghan, R. 87
Central Europe 7, 37–8
childcare *see* care
child poverty 29, 30, 40, 78, 96, 99, 101, 112
  due to escalations in divorces and separations 80
  and invisibility 43
  in the OECD 126–7
  reduced by 21 per cent by child support in Australia 9

and Skevik 36
and technical child support systems 115
children's rights 36, 60–1
child support, definition 5–9
Child Support Agency (CSA)/UK 47
child support orders 35, 53, 68, 84, 121, 126, 131
amendments to 118–19, 140
and Australia 129
and benefits 129–30, 137
and care-time 45–6
and divorce 50
and fathers 69, 78, 93, 98
and non-compliance 37, 120
choice, personal 65–6, 67, 84, 115, 132
to be a stay-at-home mother 88
and class 8
and parents 38, 48
class 8, 27–8, 47, 75, 76–7, 93, 140
see also middle classes
clawback, child support 7, 57, 102, 103, 112–13, 121
coercive control 84
Coleman, M. 141–2
Coltrane, S. 126
comparative approach, to child support 11, 32, 34
compliance 7, 9, 10, 47, 87, 107
cross-border 122
and guaranteed payments 38
and power 97
and private agreements 147
and Sweden 6, 52
and UK 122
see also non-compliance
Comprehensive Social Security Allowance 137–8
Connell, R. 13, 155
costs, of claiming child support 61–5
court-based systems 35–6, 37, 102
COVID-19 43
furloughs 42
Cozzolino, Elizabeth 45, 60
cross-border child support 122, 142–3
Crowley, J.E. 4, 93, 94, 95
Cuesta, L. 40

D

data collection 86, 119
DeKeseredy et al 84
Denmark 6, 37, 122
deservingness 21, 28, 39, 130
dignity 13, 28, 159
Dinçer, F. 13
disciplinary power 21
divorce 50, 53, 54, 80, 99, 101–2, 108
laws 36
no-fault 91, 102
shame of 141
domestic violence 21, 65–7, 84–5, 156, 159
Douglas, H. 159

E

earnings 44–5, 94
see also income
Edwards, Meredith 106
Eekelaar, J. 125
efficiency 113, 114, 148
Elizabeth, V. 57, 132
Elrod, L.H. 120
emotions 5, 13, 28, 62, 63, 134, 135
and harm 18, 84, 110
and women's well-being 73
employment 41, 42, 80, 125, 156
employment income 79, 88
enforcement 68–73, 130, 142, 143
Europe 6, 7, 37–8, 60–1, 62, 71, 122, 131
see also Malta; Nordic Countries
evidentiary requirements 21, 62
Expenditure Index 86

F

fairness 113, 139
families 91
extended 39
lone parent 80
single-mother-headed 36, 42, 58, 102, 103, 104, 121, 140
family forms 35, 42, 118, 146
family law 30
Family Tax Benefits (Australia) 4, 7, 10, 147
fatherhood policies 11
fathers 11, 29, 78, 93–4, 95–6, 98, 117
aggrieved 5
autonomy 9, 57, 58, 60, 61, 135, 154
breadwinning role 6
and caring roles 42
and children 103, 131–2, 148
downplayed as actors 10
failure to engage 16, 17, 65, 109, 111, 155–6
freed from child support debts 21
freed from mandatory obligations 139
inaction of 108, 142–3
and income shares formula 125
in Malta 141
with multiple child support orders 45–6
in Nordic countries 4
and power 155
reducing child support payments 133–4
resentment 141–2
and responsibility 41, 68, 69, 81, 88, 99–100, 102, 121, 153, 154
and trust 39–40
Fehlberg, B. 86
female caregiver role 42, 43

feminism 23, 79, 129
feminist policy 28
feminists 123, 124, 158
Fernqvist, S. 66, 101
financial control 115, 146
financial inequality 136, 141
Findlay, L.C. 57
Finland 4, 6, 45
Flexibility, Efficiency, and Modernization in Child Support Programs (US) 20
Foucault, M. 20
France 37

G

Garfinkel et al 2, 93, 130
gender
  of institutions 154, 155
  interactions 154, 155
  as a social structure 11, 12, 128, 132–6
  and the state 19–20
gender contract 6, 35, 44, 79, 91–2
gendered governance practice 13, 33, 40, 87
gendered pay gap 42
gender equality 4, 6, 44, 88, 111, 129
gender hierarchies 28, 94, 130, 140, 155, 159
gender inequality 32, 46, 129
gender-neutral terminology 7–8
gender privilege 34
gender roles 38, 41–3, 44, 45, 88, 96, 146
Germany 37, 60–1, 62, 131
gift relations 5, 28, 132, 135, 141
Gill et al 83
'Global Conference on the Recovery of Child Support and Family Maintenance in Asia Pacific and Worldwide' 122
Global South 34, 37
good fathers 5, 153
good mothers 5, 29, 31, 152, 153
Goonesekere, S. 41, 62
governance, and power 20–9
Graycar, R. 12, 16, 140
guaranteed maintenance 71, 81, 100, 159
guaranteed payments 7, 10, 37–8, 138–9, 152, 159

H

Hadjian, A. 64
Hague Conference on Private International Law 122
Hakovirta et al 45
Hans, J.D. 141–2
Hansen, D.D. 60
Hanson, Pauline 22
harms 18, 84, 96, 110
Hellum, A. 58, 59
Herd, P. 151
Hewitt, B. 28, 132, 135
Hickman, N. 126
hidden gender of law 16, 140
high-income men 107
high-value orders 98
Hong Kong 63–4, 65, 72, 83, 131, 137–8, 145

I

Iceland 4
illegitimate children 57
imprisonment 20, 21, 41, 45, 60, 69, 120, 148
improvement practices 23–4, 104, 114–23
inaction 10, 89, 90, 109, 152, 155, 156
  and causal stories 104
  of fathers 65, 108, 131–2, 141, 142
  and governance 17
  ignored 24
  and masculine interests 105
  and status quo 140
inadvertence 25
incarceration 20, 21, 41, 45, 60, 69, 120, 148
income 35, 44–5, 79, 88, 97, 107, 118
income shares formula 6, 7, 44, 125
individualisation 47, 65, 130, 143
individualism 93, 129, 142, 143
inequality 41, 129.143, 136, 158
inequity 19, 46, 157, 159
institutional level 11, 12, 15, 152, 155
interpersonal level 3, 15, 16–17, 29
interpretive policy studies 30
intersectionality 8, 15, 19, 75, 157
invisibility 24, 30–1, 87, 90, 99, 101, 103, 135
  and Brush 19
  of fathers' failure to engage 88
  and non-compliance 29
  and poverty 43
  of private agreements 78–9, 82
  and status quo 89
  of women's financial needs 109
Ireland 122
Israel 66, 71, 84, 99, 109–10
Italy 122

J

Jamaica 38
Jamrozik, A. 15, 16, 24, 27, 28, 80, 104
  on class 76–7
  conversion of social problems into technical and private problems 12, 26, 112
  different views of social problems 115
  evaluating organisational performance 32
  two types of citizens 78
Japan 50, 53, 64, 99, 137
Joint Select Committee on Certain Family Law Issues 106

K

keeping the peace 28, 135
Keil, M. 57, 132
Keynes, John Maynard 91
key performance indicators (KPIs) 116–17
Kohen, D.E. 57
Korea, South 37, 61, 63, 102–3, 149

L

Latin America 38
  see also South America
Law J. 16
Li, T.M. 12, 16, 23–4, 32, 112, 113
  on improvement 104, 114
liberal welfare states 3–4, 32, 37, 39, 46, 56
  and backlash 47
  and male-bread winner model 19
  poverty 9
lone parents
  benefits 92
  increasing number of 80
  low rates of employment 80
low-income parents 88
low-income single mothers 107
Luxemburg Income Study 122
Luzkow, J.L. 39–40, 91, 125, 158

M

MacKinnon, Catherine 11, 77
maintenance, guaranteed 71, 81, 100, 159
maintenance support payments 10
  see also guaranteed maintenance
Malaysia 62, 64–5, 70, 149
male breadwinner 4, 6, 19, 39, 42, 44, 91, 92, 102
Malta 54, 70, 82–3, 108
marginalisation of women 87
marital status 57
marriage 59
masculine autonomy 23
masculine interests 18, 89–90, 105, 107
masculinism 23, 90, 128, 130, 132, 139
masculinist worldview 15, 18, 107, 110
McCosker, A. 87
McKenzie, H. 63
mediation 82–3
men's autonomy 23, 57, 81, 112, 129, 142, 154
  and children's rights 61
  financial 40, 97, 106, 110, 132, 152
  and paternity 60
  prioritised over mother's rights 58
  women acquiesce to 135
  women subordinate to 67
men's rights 88, 90, 94, 95, 110, 142, 158
Meyer, D.R. 40
middle classes 41, 95, 101, 134
  and Luzkow 39, 91
  in US 98, 134
Middle East 51, 66, 71, 84, 99, 109–10
Millward, C. 86
Milne, E. 87
moral principles 3, 39, 97, 125
Morgan, J. 12, 16, 140
mothers
  acquiescence 135
  good 5, 29, 31, 152, 153
  never-married 54, 58
  onus on to seek payments 154
  responsibility of 125, 143, 146, 155
  and silence 141
  single 91, 92, 97, 98, 106, 107, 146
  subject to child support technologies 117–18
Moynihan, D.P. 151

N

Nagesh, R. 159
Natalier, K. 28, 132, 135
National Child Support Enforcement Agency (US) 93
neoliberalism 94, 114, 123–5, 129
New Zealand 7, 37, 57, 72–3, 102, 103, 118
  and private agreements 134–5
  and reduced child support payments 133–4
Nicholas, L. 23, 24, 104, 128, 132
  on individualism 129, 142, 143
Nigeria 61–2, 68, 71
Nocella, L.D. 15, 16, 24, 27, 28, 80, 104
  on class 76–7
  conversion of social problems into technical and private problems 12, 26, 112
  different views of social problems 115
  evaluating organisational performance 32
  two types of citizens 78
no-fault divorce 36, 80, 91, 102
non-compliance 10, 37, 69–71, 82, 118, 120, 122–3
  in Australia 107, 124
  and court costs 137
  and guaranteed maintenance 81
  and guaranteed payments 152
  invisibility of 29
  jailing of poor Black men 60, 148
  and private agreements 147
  and sanctions/penalties 20, 21
  as social problem 97
  in Sweden 100
  in US 41
  women held responsible 73
non-payment 63, 67, 103
nonperformatives 24, 78, 79

nonperformativity 104–11
Nordic countries 4, 11, 44, 94
 provide guaranteed payments 7, 37–8, 71, 138–9, 159
 see also Norway; Sweden
North America 84–5
 see also Canada; US
Norway 6, 37, 50–1, 102
 and guaranteed payments 71, 81
 and private agreements 67, 147, 149
nuclear family 57, 91

O

OECD 5–6, 126–7
opportunity costs 79, 102, 141, 155

P

Pacific 38
parents
 Jamaican 38
 and private agreements 48
 single 2, 80, 91, 93
paternal responsibility 99–100
 see also fathers: and responsibility
paternity 58, 59–61, 62
patriarchy 59, 87, 126, 128, 135, 159
pay gap, gendered 42
payments, enforcing 68–73
payment terms, failure to agree 67–8
peace, keeping the 28, 135
Pell, A.N. 51
permanence 96–103, 110
personal choice *see* choice, personal
Personal Responsibility and Work Opportunity Reconciliation Act 1996 (PRWORA)/US 4, 93, 95
Peru 53, 58–9, 62, 108–9
policymaking
 reinforces traditional power structures 97
 Swedish 81
 women excluded 85, 111
Poor Laws 56–7
Portugal 54–5, 64–5, 69, 99
poverty 18, 26–7, 29, 30, 40, 78, 97, 99, 112
 in Australia 107
 due to escalations in divorces and separations 80
 due to not claiming child support 46–7
 and invisibility 43
 in liberal welfare states 9
 in the OECD 126–7
 reduction 97, 101, 121–2, 141
 and single mothers 96
 and Skevik 36
 in Sweden 100
 in the UK 147
power 14–15, 19, 97, 98, 105, 146
 of fathers 155
 and governance 20–9
power relations 15, 154, 156
preservationist systems 145, 149
private agreements 47–8, 78–9, 82, 134–5, 143, 144
 in Australia 106, 121, 129
 and compliance 147–50
 and gender hierarchies 130–1
 in Norway 50, 67
 in Sweden 71–2, 148
private collection model, Australia 47, 129
private payments 2, 10, 47, 79, 81, 144–5
private sphere 77–8, 78–9, 156
private system 67–8, 129, 147
privilege, gender 34
problematisation 24, 114
problem representation approach 15
promiscuity 95
public sphere 77, 78–9, 156

R

reality, child support 9, 87–8, 114, 115–21
redistribution 26, 43, 91, 100, 119, 159
reformist systems 145, 149
re-partnering 95
reporting systems 86
residualisation 16–17, 24
resistance 27, 94, 141, 142, 148, 155, 159
responsibilisation 88, 123, 124, 146, 157
responsibility 73, 101, 114, 131–2, 147, 152–3
 burden of by mothers 125, 143, 146, 155
 and guaranteed payments 139
 and reformist systems 145
 see also fathers: and responsibility
rights
 children's 36, 60–1
 men's 88, 90, 94, 95, 110, 142, 158
right-sizing orders 112, 118
risk 117, 154
 physical 73, 81
 of violence 47, 65, 66, 67
 to women 18, 110
Risman, B.J. 2, 28, 32, 130, 132, 153
 on gendered social structure 11, 12, 128, 136
 on inequality 158
romanticism 13
Rush, M. 11
Ruston, Anne 153

S

Salter, M. 143
sanctions 20, 21, 142
Sépulchre, M. 66, 101
Sevenhuijsen, S. 92
shame 141, 143
shared care 7, 118–19
Shariah law 64

silence 104, 105, 111, 140, 141, 155
single-mother-headed families 36, 42, 58, 91, 102, 103, 104, 121, 140
single mothers 91, 92, 97, 98, 106, 107, 146
  and poverty 80, 96
single parent households 127
single parents
  17.2 per cent of children live with 2
  benefits 80, 91
  welfare payments 93
Skevik, A. 10, 36
Skinner et al 36–7, 47–8, 122
Smith, D.E. 16, 28, 86, 116, 140
social hierarchies 1, 60, 117, 128, 151, 157
social norms 5, 8, 10, 14, 29, 38, 96
social problems 12, 25, 26, 31, 76–7, 104, 115
  child support non-compliance 97
  increasingly number of lone-parent families 79–80
  rendered technical 23–4, 43, 112, 114
social reproduction 11
social security allowance 121, 137–8
soft power 21
South America 37, 53, 58–9, 62, 108–9
Southeast Asia 62
South Korea 37, 61, 63, 102–3, 149
the state
  and child support enforcement 72–3
  and gender 19–20, 140
  and poverty 141
  and private agreements 148–9
  reinforces women's subordinate position 146–7
  and responsibility 152–3
  role of 38, 56–7
state benefits 36, 42, 67, 102, 109–10, 148
  see also benefits
state inaction 12, 109
state welfare expenditure 101, 102
status quo 82, 105, 117, 140, 156, 157, 158
  and invisibility 89
stay-at-home mother 88, 121
stigma 143
Stone, D.A. 15, 23, 27, 73, 80, 126
  and causal stories 12, 24, 25–6, 96–7
stories 12, 15, 24, 25–6, 80, 96–7, 104
support, worthy of 134–6
surveillance 25, 77, 121, 123, 145, 148, 154
  and fathers 117, 143
  and middle-class men 41
  on women 25, 126
Sweden 37, 66–7, 86, 94, 139–40
  and compliance 6, 52, 122
  and guaranteed payments 9–10, 81
  and non-compliance 100–1
  and personal responsibility 147
  and private agreements 71–2, 131, 148
Switzerland 6
symbolic policy analysis 12, 14, 15, 17–18, 19, 22, 24, 31, 33
  and active labour programmes 88
  definition 3
  and fathers' responsibility 153

T

Tam, B.Y. 57
technical data collection 86
technical problems 27, 43
technical processes 114–15, 119, 126
Temporary Aid to Needy Families 4
time poverty 73
transnational families 122
trust 39, 93, 96, 159

U

UK
  benefits and child support 121
  Child Support Agency (CSA) 47
  child support a personal problem 17
  and compliance 122
  COVID-19 furloughs 42
  cross-border child support 142–3
  and enforcement 72
  and non-compliance 70–1
  and poverty 147
  and private agreements 144, 148
  and private payments 79
  and Skinner et al 37
  and system entry fee 146
UNCRC (United Nations Convention on the Rights of the Child) 37, 60
unemployment benefit 98
Universal Basic Income (UBI) 43
Urry, J. 16
US
  administrative approach 102
  and benefits and child support 121
  and child poverty 126
  child support guidelines 120
  and clawback 102
  and data 115–16
  and domestic violence 66
  and enforcement 40, 130
  and fathers 11, 45–6, 148
  and high-value orders 98
  key performance indicators 116–17
  national funding provided to individual states 7
  nation-wide state-based child support system 92–4
  and non-compliance 20, 41
  and paternity 58, 59–60
  and private agreements 134, 149–50
  PRWORA 4, 93, 95

and technical developments 118
Temporary Aid to Needy Families 4
welfare benefits 55–6, 57
and Wimberly 115

V

van Manen, M. 116
victim blaming 25, 130
violence 47, 82–3, 110–11, 143, 156
domestic 21, 65–7, 84–5, 159
vulnerability 73, 97, 116, 135, 156

W

wages 27, 42, 44, 62, 79, 118
see also income
wage-withholding 106, 108, 118
Walby, S. 94
welfare benefits 30, 37, 46, 55–6, 72, 102–3, 111
Australia 20, 57, 65
US 55–6, 57, 121
welfare conditionality 3, 91, 92
welfare expenditure 99, 102
welfare payments, single-parent 93
welfare state 32, 36, 91–2, 158–9
welfare-to-work 88, 111, 125
wicked problems 97
Williams, C.L. 45
Wimberly, C. 115
women
and autonomy 133
and barriers to claiming child support 52–67
and earnings 94
excluded 85
falling out of the system 52
and financial dependence on the state 57
invisibility of 109
and marginalisation of 87
not claiming child support 46–7
punished 126
and responsibilities 73, 88, 124, 125, 153
risk to 18, 110
silencing 111
the state reinforces subordinate position of 146–7
surveillance on 25, 126
well-being of 73
Woods, M. 86
workfare 88
work tests 92
Wyss, B. 38

Z

Zelizer, V.A. 135